SOUTHERN APPALACHIA AND THE SOUTH: A REGION WITHIN A REGION

Journal

of the

Appalachian Studies Association

Edited by
John C. Inscoe

1991
Volume Three

The Appalachian Consortium was a non-profit educational organization composed of institutions and agencies located in Southern Appalachia. From 1973 to 2004, its members published pioneering works in Appalachian studies documenting the history and cultural heritage of the region. The Appalachian Consortium Press was the first publisher devoted solely to the region and many of the works it published remain seminal in the field to this day.

With funding from the Andrew W. Mellon Foundation and the National Endowment for the Humanities through the Humanities Open Book Program, Appalachian State University has published new paperback and open access digital editions of works from the Appalachian Consortium Press.

www.collections.library.appstate.edu/appconsortiumbooks

This work is licensed under a Creative Commons BY-NC-ND license. To view a copy of the license, visit http://creativecommons.org/licenses.

Original copyright © 1991 by the Appalachian Consortium Press.

ISBN (pbk.: alk. Paper): 978-1-4696-3696-2
ISBN (ebook): 978-1-4696-3698-6

Distributed by the University of North Carolina Press
www.uncpress.org

Journal of the Appalachian Studies Association

Volume 3 1991

Southern Appalachia and the South:
A Region Within a Region

TABLE OF CONTENTS

Introduction — 1
John C. Inscoe

A Regionalism Within Regionalisms:
Three Frameworks for Appalachian Studies — 4
John Alexander Williams

Southern Appalachia and the South:
A Region Within a Section — 18
Richard B. Drake

Hegemony, Alienation and Identity Reformulation:
Further Thoughts on a Comparative
Approach to Appalachian Studies — 28
Richard Blaustein

The Appalachian Frontier and
the Southern Frontier: A Comparative Perspective — 36
H. Tyler Blethen and Curtis W. Wood

The Enduring Legacy of the "Southern Rebellion":
West Virginia's Well-Being — 48
David B. White

Forgotten Sisters: Mountain Women in the South — 61
Milton Ready

Historical and Theoretical Perspectives
on Appalachia's Economic Dependency — 68
Paul Salstrom

The New Deal for Tenant Farmers:
Government Planning and Indigenous Community
Development on the Cumberland Plateau _____ 82
    Benita J. Howell

Lawrence Augustus Oxley:
The Beginnings of Social Work
Among Blacks in North Carolina Counties _____ 98
    John L. Bell

Religious Freethinkers in the Southern Highlands _____ 110
    Henry J. Weaver

Two-Party Politics in Appalachia? _____ 123
    David Sutton

Political Culture in Jesse Stuart's Appalachia and the South:
From Agrarian to Industrial Development _____ 134
    Glen Edward Taul

A Cure for the Malaise of the
Dislocated Southerner:
The Writing of Jesse Stuart _____ 146
    Edgar H. Thompson

James Jones' Appalachian Soldier
in His World War II Trilogy _____ 152
    Loyal Jones

Southern Gothic and Appalachian Gothic:
A Comparative Look at
Flannery O'Connor and Cormac McCarthy _____ 166
    Louis H. Palmer III

The Roots of Appalachian English:
Scotch-Irish or British Southern? _____ 177
    Michael Montgomery

"Shall We Teach 'Em or Learn 'Em?"
Attitudes Toward Language in
Appalachian Children's Literature _____ 192
    Roberta T. Herrin

1990
Appalachian Studies Association Officers

Doyle Bickers	President
Wilburn Hayden	Vice-President
John Inscoe	Conference Program Chair
George Reynolds	Youth Conference Chair
Sallie Miller Weaver	Newsletter Editor/Secretary
Alice Brown	Treasurer
Gerald Roberts	Archivist

Steering Committee

Doyle Bickers, Chair
Barry Buxton
Rebecca Hancock
Roberta Herrin
Ken Sullivan
Howard Dorgan
Parks Lanier

Program Committee

John Inscoe, Chair
Garry Barker
H. Tyler Blethen
Susan Keefe
Bill Martin
Jeannie Reed
Maureen Reid
Durwood Dunn

Introduction

John C. Inscoe

Southerners, Jonathan Daniels once observed, are "a mythical people, created half out of dream and half out of slander, who live in a still legendary land" (Tindall 1980, 161-62). If this description is applicable to the South in general, how much more applicable it is to Southern Appalachia. In many ways, the burdens borne by the South, whether experienced historically, economically, or socially, or interpreted literarily, are burdens shared, often in more acute form, by its highlanders. Perhaps because of these burdens, both mythic and real, southern Appalachians also have shared with the rest of the South a degree of regional self-consciousness more intense and more deeply rooted than that in almost any other area of the country.

Just as the nature of being southern and the qualities that make the South the South have been long debated by scholars and journalists, by natives and outside observers, so Appalachia has been subjected, at least from the late nineteenth century on, to equal scrutiny by both insiders and outsiders seeking to identify and explain its distinctiveness as a region. There is perhaps no better example of how vital that scrutiny remains and how varied and sophisticated it has become than the annual conference of the Appalachian Studies Association.

In his study of American cultural regions, Raymond Gastil observed that as long as residents of a region "see success as achievable only outside their region, there will be no great regional cultures.... On the other hand, as long as those who remain in the 'boondocks' see their task as the glorification of whatever characteristics their regions happen to possess, they will build little that is enduring" (Gastil 1976, 16-7). Both reactions are evident among southerners, but again, they're even more pronounced in southern highlanders, simply because they seem to have been shackled with an even greater inferiority complex. As Wilma Dykeman has noted, such self-perceptions have made it hard for Appalachians "to be neither defensive nor offensive about the region where we live" (Dykeman 1984, 14).

No less than four papers presented at the 1990 Appalachian Studies Conference at Unicoi State Park in Georgia (two of which are included in this volume) cited Chapel Hill sociologist John Shelton Reed's obviously often quoted 1982 observation that "Appalachia has always served as the South's 'South'" (Reed 1986, 42). This is indeed a succinct way of expressing at least the negative implications of Appalachians' perceived status not only within the nation, but within their own broader region as well. Elsewhere Reed has confronted the whole dilemma of distinguishing between subregions within regions. "Does one—or rather when does one—speak of Sicilians, for example, rather than Italians, or Jamaicans rather than West Indians?" he asks (Reed 1982, 14). Indeed, when does one speak of Southern Appalachians rather than southerners? How do the identities, experiences, and interests of these two groups intersect, overlap, diverge, or contradict each other? These were the questions confronting participants at last year's Appalachian Studies Conference at Unicoi. The papers in this volume are for the most part reflections of the wide variety of ways in which those issues have been and can be addressed. The theoretical and practical implications of regional identity, of marginality, of ethnic commonalities, and of comparative perspectives are laid out in broad and often provocative terms in the first several essays, after which the same questions are applied to more specific aspects of the Appalachian and/or southern experience, such as gender and race; historical turning points from frontier settlement to the Civil War, the Great Depression and World War II; political trends and religious expression; and both individuals and groups coping with dual regional identities and the means by which that duality has been expressed, either literarily or linguistically.

The 1990 conference was the association's largest yet, in terms of both program participants and attendance. Because of the wealth of material presented at the Unicoi conference, both in quality and quantity, the essays here are but a small sampling of the approaches taken in dealing with these issues. Most of the papers not included in this volume are available through the ASA archives at Berea College, Berea, Kentucky, and no doubt many of them will appear in print elsewhere.

The success of that conference was due to a number of factors, but none more so than the dynamic leadership of the association's president, Doyle Bickers. His energy, enthusiasm, and dedication to the Appalachian Studies Association, combined with a managerial style all his own, inspired all of us who had the privilege—and the pleasure—of working with him last year. The program committee, particularly Tyler Blethen, Susan Keefe, Jeannie Reed, and Durwood Dunn, deserves far more credit that it usually receives for the myriad of ways, large and small, it contributed to pulling together yet another in what is becoming a tradition of rich and varied conference programs. George Reynolds almost single-handedly organized a fresh and innovative Youth Conference, thus perpetuating what Rebecca Hancock has made an increasingly significant facet of the association's efforts. Bill Martin at the Appalachian Consortium and Linda Turner at Unicoi State Park worked steadily and efficiently behind the scenes to coordinate what managed to be a smoothly run and crisis-free weekend. I am grateful for the support and cooperation I enjoyed on my own campus, particularly from my department head, Lester Stephens, and from Sheree Dendy, who generously gave of her own time and considerable talent in coordinating the program planning at our end. Finally, Pat Arnow and the staff at East Tennessee State University's Center for Appalachian Studies and Services are fast becoming the unsung heroes of the association for their vital contributions in time and talent in editing and printing this journal.

Works Cited

Dykeman, Wilma. 1984. *Explorations*. Newport, Tennessee: Wakestone Books.

Gastil, Raymond D. 1976. *Cultural Regions of the United States*. Seattle: University of Washington Press.

Reed, John Shelton. 1982. *One South: An Ethnic Approach to Regional Culture*. Baton Rouge: Louisiana State University Press.

Reed, John Shelton. 1986. *Southern Folk, Plain and Fancy: Native White Social Types*. Athens: University of Georgia Press.

Tindall, George B. 1980. "The Resurgence of Southern Identity." *The American South: Portrait of a Culture*. Ed. Louis B. Rubin, Jr. Baton Rouge: Louisiana State University Press.

John Inscoe is Assistant Professor of History at the University of Georgia and Editor of the *Georgia Historical Quarterly*. He was the 1990 program chair of the Appalachian Studies Association Conference and guest editor of the *Journal of Appalachian Studies Association*.

A Regionalism Within Regionalisms: Three Frameworks for Appalachian Studies

John Alexander Williams

In the papers of Frederick Jackson Turner at the Huntington Library in California, is an outline for a history of the industrialization of southern Appalachia between 1880 and 1930. The outline proposes research on the social and political impacts of industrialization in the region, the problem of absentee ownership, and labor history. Its author was John Barnhart, a doctoral student of Turner's at Harvard, who was then beginning his career as an assistant professor of history at West Virginia University (Barnhart 1932). Barnhart's outline of proposed research amounts to a prospectus for much of what now comprises the scholarly field of Appalachian Studies, but nothing came of his project except a single article, which neither he nor any other scholar followed up on (Barnhart 1931, 581-94). He went on to teach and to write about midwestern history at Indiana University. It was not until the 1960s and 1970s that professional historians began to carry out the research program that Barnhart had outlined a generation before.

I regard both Barnhart's outline and its timing to be equally significant. The outline itself tells us something about the history of American regionalism. Turner was the foremost academic contributor to this movement, which embraced a loose constellation of scholars, reformers, and artists who believed that regional patterns provided the key to the proper understanding and ordering of American history, society, and culture. Regionalist scholars, especially historians like Turner, were less theorists than practitioners; they did not elaborate much of a systematic theory of regionalism. Barnhart's outline, however, is evidence that regionalist historians worked from a model, although the model was more often implicit rather than explicit in their research. The regionalist model began with the environment and focused on those institutions and issues which were derived from the exploitation of spatially-distributed resources. Turner's student and self-described "disciple," Herbert E. Bolton, put it succinctly: "European expansion and the building of American societies . . . has been determined largely by geographical forces. Caribbean development has been much the same whether Spanish, French, Dutch, Danish or English . . . The type of prairie society does not change essentially across the forty-ninth parallel" (1926). Barnhart's outline—constructed at the time when Turner, Bolton, and other scholars were laying the foundation for regional research in the South, Midwest, West, and Spanish Borderlands (Bolton's name for what we would now call the Sun Belt)—shows that Appalachia could have fit equally well within the regionalist scheme. But Appalachian Studies did not develop until a generation later. Thus, Barnhart's outline tells us that we must look to factors other than the development of regionalist ideas to explain the lag.

To explain the lag, we must move from the history of ideas to the sociology of knowledge. As applied to American regionalism, the history of ideas tells us how regional concepts developed and spread through the domains of the humanities, social sciences, public administration, literature, and the arts during the first half of the twentieth century. The sociology of knowledge seeks to explain intellectual history not only in terms of the articulation of, and structural relationships among, concepts, but also in terms of social relationships among the proponents of related ideas and of the organizational frameworks within which they worked. This approach asks not only why American regionalism, developed during the first decades of the century, flourished during the 1920s and 1930s, and declined after 1945. It also seeks to identify patterns of uneven development which cannot be explained by the content of the ideas involved — such as why Borderlands studies developed during this period but Appalachian Studies did not — and it probes for organizational patterns, such as the impact of regionalist scholars in the humanities and social sciences in founding scholarly institutions and conventions which survived long after the regionalist paradigm had ceased to exert intellectual appeal.

Regional inquiries customarily begin with a series of definitions. Howard Odum and Harry Estill Moore came up with some forty definitions of region in their book *American Regionalism* (1938, 3-21). The recent bibliography compiled by Clarence Mondale and Michael Steiner identifies 1,652 items, many of which offer definitions of their own or confirm someone else's (1988). Sorting through so many definitions is a daunting task, yet it is possible to make some fairly simple general statements about the subject. Most arguments about the definition of region turn on whether we conceive of a region as a thing or a concept, with most humanities scholars coming down on the side of region as a thing, social scientists on the side of region as concept. Geographers have come down on both sides of this issue, but, increasingly, their work today integrates the two arguments by emphasizing the importance of perceptual regions: regions whose origins are in mental constructs, but whose representations assume a life of their own and thus a form of objective reality. Regionalism may be defined as the ideological form of the regional concept — the belief in the primary importance of region as the organizing principle for the work to be done: cultural study, economic planning, political reform, architectural design — whatever it is that the definer wants to accomplish.

Regionalism originated in the search for a natural social order. A belief in the existence of natural regions and in their importance as the foundation of progressive economic planning drove the activities of John Wesley Powell and other pioneer regionalists of the late nineteenth and early twentieth centuries and guided them to their most enduring achievements: Powell's Irrigation Survey of 1890 and the resulting creation of the Bureau of Reclamation in 1906, the Regional Planning Association and the interstate compacts of the 1920s, and of course the Tennessee Valley Authority. A broad overview of regionalism's political achievements leaves two overriding impressions: the swiftness with which the regionalist project collapsed in the years following World War II, and the extent to which regionalist creations such as TVA or the New York-New Jersey Port Authority stand accused today of betraying many of the ideals which animated their founders. It would seem that regionalism as a doctrine was more successful in inspiring the creation of institutions than in guiding them after those institutions matured.

Academic regionalists of the early twentieth century did not bend their efforts to the construction of dams or the reshaping of cities, but they too, were reformers in their way, and like watershed and metropolitan regionalists, they founded institutions which outlived their ideology. For in such fields as history, geography, folklore, and sociology, regionalism provided a key impetus to a process which Robert McCaughey has called the "academic enclosure" of disciplines (1984). Among historians, regionalism provided the opportunity and excuse for the enclosure of state and local history, an enterprise whose institutions and concerns were considerably older than academic history departments.

By "academic enclosure" McCaughey means both "the more general process by which the primary responsibility for the pursuit of learning in America has been transferred from the American intellectual community at large to the universities" and the specific processes by which a given intellectual discipline is transformed into an academic enterprise, with the attendant institutionalization of resources for teaching and research in the discipline and for the regulation of individual academic careers. He deliberately chooses the historic English word "enclosure" for this process, with its connotation of "converting pieces of common land into private property" and with reference to his own field of international studies, reminds us of Adam Smith's dictum that "the advantage of enclosure is greater for pasture than for corn" (McCaughey 1984, xiv-xv).

From this standpoint, the significant development in early twentieth century regionalist historiography is the way in which history professors laid claim to the resources—libraries, archives, journals, and tax subventions—which earlier generations of amateur scholars and collectors had founded, and then bent those resources to the promotion of academic research, publications, and to the advancement of academic careers. Bolton's career in Texas and later in California provides a perfect example. Rather than lament the low esteem in which Texas history was held in academic circles, Bolton and his friend Eugene C. Barker worked to give the field a regional framework, renaming the state historical journal "Southwestern" and securing state funds to build up research resources with materials from Mexican archives. While Bolton was unsuccessful in persuading the state historical societies of other southwestern states to pool their resources with those of Texas, he flooded their journals with articles by his graduate students, persuaded ancestor clubs to fund dissertation fellowships, and built a program of regional research around the magnificent collection which the University of California had acquired from the estate of the amateur historian and publisher Hubert Howe Bancroft. While most of his students fanned out across the Borderlands to the region's universities, other Bolton students staffed state historical societies and archives. Leroy R. Hafen, for example, went directly from his studies in Berkeley to become the Historical Society of Colorado's first professional employee; in 1924, arriving in Denver with his family, he first bought a car, then drove out to the campuses at Boulder and Colorado Springs to link up with other "Bolton men from Berkeley" (Hafen 1969, 3). On a comparable scale other Turner students initiated the academic study of state and regional history in the universities of Alabama, Tennessee, Colorado, Oklahoma, North Dakota, Nebraska, Oregon, Washington, and West Virginia and staffed midwestern state historical societies such as those of Minnesota and Wisconsin. Turner himself had led the enclosure movement at the State Historical Society of Wisconsin and in 1904 mobilized other midwestern historical society leaders into a committee within the American Historical Association. The blue-blooded historical societies of the Atlantic seaboard states and those of certain midwestern cities kept aloof from this movement, as did a number of state-funded archives and history officials, chiefly in southern states.

As with any process of change, there were winners and losers. The state historical societies had threatened to form a rival organization to the AHA in 1890, and a new threat began building early in the new century. The Illinois state historian warned Turner in 1910 of "a growing body of insurgents who will in the course of time make themselves felt" (Alvord 27 June 1910). When the rebellion against the AHA leadership finally broke out in 1916, it was led by southern state historical agency heads and the amateur scholar Frederic Bancroft. Turner sided firmly with the AHA's Ivy League leadership and broke off relations with a former student, Charles Ambler of West Virginia University, who he believed had aided and abetted the revolt (Ambler 1915 and 1916).

This pattern explains why so much regionalist history, supposedly conceived in a search for natural regions, actually conformed to existing state lines in framing research designs. To a student shopping for a dissertation topic, Turner advised taking "*state politics* in a decade . . . the economic and social transformations would serve as foundations for political history and its interpretations . . . the *general* topic of state political history can be used to cast light on the attitude and influence of a section upon general American tendencies" (Turner 1920). When another student, Thomas P. Abernethy, followed this advice, he gave the resulting book a regionalist title—*From Frontier to Plantation in Tennessee*—only to be disheartened when readers responded to it as "Tennessee history pure and simple" (Turner 1926; 1920; Abernethy 1932). "[W]hen one tries to deal with the sections statistically," Turner pointed out to a geographer in 1928, "he is practically forced by the groupings in the Census either to use its Divisions (New England, Middle Atlantic, South Atlantic, etc.) or to attempt to a rearrangement by *counties* or *precincts*, which involves work that some future group of investigators may undertake for the whole of our history but which is too big a job for one man" (Turner 1928).

The persistence of the states in regional contexts was a problem not only for historians, of course. When Governor Franklin D. Roosevelt of New York addressed a "Round Table on Regionalism" held at the University of Virginia in 1931, he bluntly informed the assembled experts that "I do not know what regionalism means. I do have fairly clear ideas in respect to the relative spheres of governments of states on the one hand and Federal government on the other hand . . ." (Roosevelt 1931). In 1944, when interest in regionalism was beginning to wane, the Chapel

Hill sociologist Howard Odum summed up the problem in a letter to Norman Cousins: "The ideal regional delineation of the United States would be one in which state lines could be ignored and cultural and natural likenesses could be clustered together with as near perfect homogeneity as possible. In America, however, the states we have with us always" (Odum 1944).

There are two obstacles to the growth of Appalachian Studies in this context. One was the fact that Appalachia, unlike the South or the West or New England, could not be defined in terms of boundaries drawn along existing state lines or studied by means of aggregate data or archives collected on this basis. West Virginia was the sole exception, and the founding of the West Virginia and Regional History Collection at Morgantown by Ambler, along with Barnhart's aborted prospectus, testify to the importance of the state framework to the regionalist project. The second obstacle was that many of the earliest proponents of Appalachian regionalism were outside of academia and were neither interested in grafting their ideas onto emerging models of academic professionalism or in a position to do so. Conceptually, the formulations of Appalachian regional identity advanced by Appalachian activists such as Olive Dame Campbell were no less sophisticated than Bolton's Borderlands, but neither the goals nor the resources of such persons matched those of the academic regionalists. Thus, while the 1920s and 1930s were also an era of institution-building for Appalachian specialists—the Council of Southern Mountains, John C. Campbell Folk School, Highlander Folk School, and Southern Highlands Handicraft Guild all date from these years—their efforts paralleled but did not converge with academic regionalists. For example, Lucy Morgan of the Penland Weavers and Potters in North Carolina was in touch with Odum during this period but her purpose—finding support for a "mountain cabin exhibit" for the upcoming Chicago Worlds Fair—did not fit in with the purposes of academic enterprise (Morgan 1932).

Consequently, while every strain of regionalism, including metropolitan regionalism and southern and southwestern literary regionalism, was represented at the Charlottesville meeting and at an earlier "Conference on Regional Phenomena" that Odum organized for the Social Science Research Council, no one with specific interests in Appalachia was there. Similarly, when, in the twilight of regionalism in 1949, the leading academic specialists gathered at Madison to discuss the field which had been so richly plowed in the two previous decades, Appalachia was not even mentioned (Jensen 1951). This was too bad, since the Rockefeller Foundation, which had funded many of the regionalist enterprises in other parts of the country, would in the next few years liquidate its program for "regional studies of the North American continent" and disburse a final round of grants which would ensure prosperity to many of the key institutions and projects that the regionalist scholars had begun.[1] We cannot say that Appalachian Studies came away from this banquet merely empty handed; Appalachia had not been invited.

In fields such as regional planning, where regionalist experts had attempted to enclose or supersede enterprises based within state government and/or politics, state officials led a determined and successful counterattack during the 1940s, beginning with the Pick-Sloan Act, which squelched the threat of a TVA-style regional agency in the Missouri Valley. Thus, when federal officials returned to regionalism during the 1960s, the agency which resulted—the Appalachian Regional Commission—was constructed so that its powers were strictly subordinated to the statehouses involved. But this is another story. I mention it here only because of the contrast with academic regionalism's generally successful mobilization of resources which had earlier been the preserve of state-based elites.

When state and local history revived again during the 1960s and 1970s, under the rubric of regional studies, Appalachia was at long last ready to dine. I will not attempt here to recount the emergence of Appalachian Studies as an academic field, with the requisite conferences and symposia, journals, centers, programs, and other hallmarks of academic enclosure. Most of the people attending the Appalachian Studies Conference are probably better equipped than I to tell this story, although I will say that I hope that when it is told, due concern will be taken to solicit the views of Appalachianists who were and remained outside the academic fold during this period.

I do want to say something about regional studies generally, however. In contrast to regionalism, regional studies entailed no implied or explicit attempt to create grand syntheses. It was a movement of discrete and usually unconnected projects, and to the extent that the movement developed theoretical concerns at all, these derived from the "new" social history and the community-action orientation of scholars influenced by the civil rights movement and the New Left.[2]

Regional studies flourished during this period for several reasons, I believe. There was, first of all, the impetus toward a new social history, whose research strategies necessarily required research at the local, regional, or other subnational level. During the 1930s, regionalism had flourished in part as an alternative to nationalism; a comparable impulse promoted regional studies in the guise of social studies during the Vietnam War. But there was also the impetus given by two patriotic celebrations, the Civil War Centennial and the American Revolution Bicentennial, an impetus born less of enthusiasm for flag waving as of an abundance of state and federal funds which could be directed to regional research. The emergence of the National Endowment for the Humanities (NEH) played an important role in this florescence as well. From 1974 on, NEH appealed specifically for proposals in regional studies, and this drive intensified during the Carter administration when the distributionist potential inherent in a regional-studies grant program assuaged agency concern over academic elitism. What the Carter people did not realize, however, and here I speak as the administrator of the regional studies program in the years between 1980 and 1983, was that an academic elite had already captured much of the program's budget for studies in social science or social history.

NEH was not the only impetus for regional studies, however. In the 1940s a new generation of academically-trained state archivists and state historical society professionals broke away from the American Historical Association to form the Society of American Archivists and the America Association for State and Local History. The American Revolution Bicentennial gave a tremendous boost to historic preservation on the local level. The rapid expansion of the Smithsonian Institution, and the museum field generally, created both opportunities and models for yet another approach to regional studies. The maturing of these trends during the 1970s, fostered by federal and state humanities grant funds, promoted a new level of professionalism and sophistication in non-academic programming (which academics moved swiftly to enclose under the rubric of "public history").

One measure of the contrasting impact of regionalism and regional studies is suggested by Carl Abbott's recent survey of course offerings and professional specializations among historians in the regional fields. His findings suggest that academic course offerings and text books are still largely a product of the regionalist era and that the predominant regional fields are still the state-based regional constructs—the South, the West, the Southwest—the teaching and research specializations created by Turner, Bolton, Walter Prescott Webb, U.B. Phillips, and their students. Abbott found much smaller configurations of resources devoted to the Pacific Northwest, the Great Plains, and New England, but Appalachia showed up in his survey only in the "other" category, along with the Ozarks, the Tennessee Valley, French Louisiana and the Sun Belt (Abbott 1990, 4-8). A survey of social history journals, however, shows that Appalachian Studies benefited from the expanded scope of regional studies projects during the 1970s and 1980s. Henry J. Weaver, a research assistant at Appalachian State University's Center for Appalachian Studies, surveyed all articles published in five journals between their founding and their fall issues of 1989. He found that 2,230 of the 5,466 articles published in the *Journal of Social History*, *Journal of*

Interdisciplinary History, Signs, Women's Studies Quarterly, and *International Journal of Women's Studies* were place-specific, that is focused on some locality, state, or region of sub-national scope. Of these, 151 dealt with a New England place, 69 with an Appalachian. If we limit the count only to Southern Appalachia, the number falls to 28. If we eliminate the feminist journals and count only articles in *Social History* and *Interdisciplinary History*, Southern Appalachia's share of place-specific articles remains roughly proportionate: 2 percent of the overall total, roughly half as many articles as those on New England. This may seem a modest gain, but when we consider that many of these article writers—Dwight Billings, Gordon McKinney, John Hevener, Archie Green, Ron Eller, David Corbin, Ron Lewis—were also among those who brought John Barnhart's prospectus to life with a rich array of monographs during the last decade, it seems reasonable to conclude that—whatever may have been the balance of corn and pasture for eighteenth century English agriculture—the academic enclosure of Appalachian Studies has produced plenty of both. And the monographs keep coming—Thomas P. Slaughter, *The Whiskey Rebellion* (1986), Altina Waller, *Feud* (1988), and John C. Inscoe, *Mountain Masters* (1989)—to name only a few of the social history monographs which have appeared in the last few years.

Anyone familiar with Appalachian history knows that the region is easier to define as a periphery of someplace else—as "frontier," "back country," "backyard," or "colony." Appalachia is one of the oldest geographic terms in North American history and it still means some place or other "out there." But a new historiographical movement, which I shall call "neo-regionalism," has emerged in recent years which actually defines Appalachia not as periphery but core. The core of what? *That* is the question which connects my topic with the general theme of the 1990 conference. Neo-regionalism makes Appalachia the heartland of an expanded Upper or Upland South that in its grandest formulation extends across the continent from Philadelphia to California.

Neo-regionalists, like their Turnerian counterparts in the first half of the century, attempt syntheses and erect theoretical frameworks which connect regionally-distributed phenomena to national or even global concerns. But neo-regionalists do not confine their research to resource-based institutions such as plantation agriculture, ranching, or mining, and they extend their gaze far beyond those state and local political institutions and cadres which focus upon state capitals. They frame cultural studies in terms of anthropological definitions of culture and search out geographic patterns that reflect actual human behavior. The result is an emerging regionally-defined, ethnoculturally focused synthesis that is potentially quite breathtaking in scope.

Three magisterial works of synthesis—one completed, two still under way—introduced us to the neo-regionalist project in the late 1980s: Donald W. Meinig, *Atlantic America* (1986) and David Hackett Fischer, *Albion's Seed* (1989), both of which are presented as the first volumes in multi-volume analyses of the roots of American culture, and *The Encyclopedia of Southern Culture* (1989). The *Encyclopedia* is not a synthesis as such, but it serves the same function in an era of pluralist scholarship. All three works promise to have a great impact on the understanding of southern history, not the least of which effect erects Appalachia as a region of the South, but not contained by it. Fischer explicitly, and the *Encyclopedia* by implication, raises Appalachia to a position of parity with the plantation South. It becomes an equivalent region, intermingled with the traditional South at its edges but something quite distinct at its core.

Meinig doesn't mention Appalachia, but in many ways his book is the most promising, if he applies to inland regions the same scope and sophistication he brings to his treatment of the Atlantic littorals which formed the initial theatres of New World history. Most importantly, while Fischer and the encyclopedists are guided by the same nation- and state-based boundaries that frame our polities and our course offerings, Meinig approaches America from the cartographic vantage points of the ocean currents and winds which guided Columbus, and the island stepping-stones, estuaries, and river corridors which guided the European approaches to North America. This approach, for one thing, clarifies the history of New World slavery in ways that all historians can profit from. As surely as Hurricane Hugo did last Fall, he lays bare the historical and cultural patterns linking the West Indies to the Carolina coast, and renders intelligible the cultural patterning which allowed Spanish Florida, French Louisiana, and Barbadian South Carolina at once to stand apart and become an integral part of the plantation-derived southern culture that borders Appalachia on the east and south.

Fischer makes Appalachia central to his thesis: that American culture in both its historic and modern regional patternings originates in four regional cultures of Britain. Appalachia's hearth he defines as "North British," as much English and Scots as the traditional Scotch-Irish, and its North American domain spreads out from the immigrant port-of-entry in Pennsylvania to the original focus in the colonial backcountry and from there across a broad arc of the upper South through the Ozarks, across north Texas, southeast Oklahoma, and east New Mexico to the southwest, where it peters out in the dusty streets of Bakersfield (Fischer 1989).

Albion's Seed runs to 946 pages and even the helpful precis, which Fischer provides to conference discussants too busy to read the book, is 65 pages long. Thus, a brief summary of the work risks caricaturing it.

(The same holds true for the *Encyclopedia*, but no one expects it to be summarized.) Fischer attributes to regional variation everything interesting in American cultural history from New England baked beans to the St. Andrew's cross on the Confederate battle flag. Revisionists and dissertation writers are going to have a field day picking holes in this thesis. But in its breadth and ambition, the book cannot help but inspire respect.

Here I want to emphasize one aspect of the book which will appall some Appalachian specialists and delight others: its failure to define Appalachia with anything resembling precision. Throughout the book, Fischer uses the term Appalachia, southern highlands, and backcountry interchangeably. The same is true of many entries in the *Encyclopedia*, where Appalachia appears interchangeably with the Upper South.[3] Is this casual approach to regional boundaries a breakthrough or a defect? I think we can expect an abundant discourse on this subject as *Albion's Seed* becomes more widely known.

Meanwhile, there are two recent monographs which offer support to Fischer's thesis: Rodger Cunningham, *Apples on the Flood* (1987) and James N. Gregory, *American Exodus: The Dust Bowl Migration and Okie Culture in California* (1989). Cunningham engages in ethnocultural regionalizing on a scale equal to Meinig and Fischer, although with considerably less attention to specifics. He avoids the Celticism of Grady McWhiney but, nevertheless, locates the origin of Appalachian culture in a pre-Anglophone, Atlantic-oriented Britain whose Welsh, Scottish, and Irish remnants in the eighteenth century foreshadow both in their cultural patterns and economic activities the pre-industrial society of nineteenth-century Appalachia. The region's domain in America is the Upland South, the arc of hilly land extending westward from the Appalachian mountain system proper through the lower Ohio Valley into the Ozarks and north Texas. He even gives this region a name, Suala, borrowed from the reports of the De Soto expedition and, thus, a fitting substitute for the more limiting Appalachia which derives from the Spanish march through the Blue Ridge (Cunningham 1987, 78-101).

Gregory's book seconds this linkage of southeastern and southwestern uplands. He sees the mass movement of "Okies" from the Ozarks and nearby districts to California as the western prong of a two-part movement. The other prong carried migrants from the Appalachian region northward, to the hillbilly enclaves of the urban-industrial Midwest. Like the movement of black Texans or Louisianians to Los Angeles, or black Mississippians to Chicago, or black Carolinians to New York, the Okie and hillbilly exoduses were of a piece (Gregory 1989, xvii-xviii; 258, n. 6). Gregory reinforces this thesis in his choice of institutional foci for his study of Okie culture: Protestant fundamentalism, country music, "plain folk Americanism," the problems of labor organizing among people whose culture resists bureaucratic mobilization. In other words, he chooses topical staples from the interdisciplinary Appalachian Studies cupboard.

Yet another form of neo-regionalism is flourishing under the rubric of "environmental history." Practitioners in this new field have initially focused upon issues of environmental policy and ecological beliefs and have generally accepted the regional frameworks—South, West, and New England—institutionalized during the regionalist era. But in their concern with "understanding how humans have been affected by [and have affected] their natural environment through time," environmental historians are also hearing calls to focus more directly on particular places at particular times and thus to undertake local and regional studies. It seems likely that Appalachia will be one of these places, and that the neo-regionalist interest in understanding cultural forces will shape future research into the successive transformations of Appalachian environments (Worster 1990, 1089).

If I may repeat my caveat about the dangers of summary becoming caricature, it seems clear that the neo-regionalist framework considerably broadens the scope of Appalachian Studies, but at what price? Certainly anyone who accepts the geographic framework offered by Fischer, Cunningham, and Gregory has to think long and hard about what to call it. Appalachia seems rather a misnomer for a region whose outliers extend around the compass from Bakersfield to Detroit to Philadelphia. On the other hand, if we slip back to the familiar geographic usage of core and periphery, the traditional, if slippery, boundaries of Appalachia—if we include the Carolina Piedmont and the Ridge-and-Valley province of Virginia, West Virginia, and Tennessee—fit rather neatly as the core of this more broadly defined region. In either case, the neo-regionalists have given us lots to think about, lots to write and talk about, plenty of ground to enclose, plenty of corn to grind.

Notes

[1] The history and operations of the foundation's regional program may be followed in the foundation's records in the Rockefeller Archives Center, Tarrytown, New York, especially Series 200 of Record Group 1.1, boxes 274-76

[2] Unless otherwise cited, my discussion of regional studies in these pages are less the result of formal study than of personal observation from the vantage point of my position as an administrator in the National Endowment for the

Humanities during the period 1979-1986 (which was preceded by a two-year term on the council of the Humanities Foundation of West Virginia).

³Eg. *Albion's Seed*, 635, 638-42, 650-51, 652, 655, 664-68, 677, 691-93, 699, 701, 714, 716-17, 729-31, 735-36, 749, 759-63, 765-69, 778, 781; *Encyclopedia*, 243, 374, 414-15, 534-39, 546, 548-49, 550-54, 988.

Works Cited

Abbott, Carl. 1990. "Tracing the Trends in U.S. Regional History." *Perspectives: American Historical Association Newsletter* 28 (2): 4-8.

Abernethy to Turner. 10 March 1932. Frederick Jackson Turner Papers, Henry E. Huntington Library.

Alvord to Turner. 27 June 1910. Turner Papers, Box 12.

Ambler-Turner Correspondence. August 1915. Turner Papers, Box 25.

———. January 1916. Turner Papers, Box 26.

Barnhart, John D. March 1931. "Recent Industrial Growth and Politics in the Southern Appalachian Region." *Mississippi Valley Historical Review* 17: 581-94.

Bolton to Turner. 15 September 1926. Turner Papers, Box 35A.

Cunningham, Rodger. 1987. *Apples on the Flood*. Knoxville: University of Tennessee Press.

Fischer, David Hackett. 1989. *Albion's Seed*. New York: Oxford University Press.

Gregory, James N. 1989. *American Exodus: The Dust Bowl Migration and Okie Culture in California*. New York: Oxford University Press.

Hafen, Leroy R. 1969. "My First Months as Colorado's State Historian." *Colorado Magazine* 46 (3): 3.

Inscoe, John C. 1989. *Mountain Masters*. Knoxville: University of Tennessee Press.

Jensen, Merrill, ed. 1951. *Regionalism in America*. Madison: University of Wisconsin Press.

McCaughey, Robert A. 1984. *International Studies and Academic Enterprise. A Chapter in the Enclosure of American Learning*. New York: Columbia University Press.

Meinig, Donald W. 1986. *Atlantic America*. New Haven: Yale University Press.

Morgan to Odum. 25 May 1932. Howard W. Odum Papers, Southern Historical Collection, University of North Carolina, Chapel Hill, Box 12, Folder 255.

Mondale, Clarence and Michael Steiner. 1988. *Regions and Regionalism in the United States: A Source Book for the Humanities and Social Sciences*. New York: Garland Publishers, Inc.

Odum to Cousins. 14 July 1944. Odum Papers, Box 26, Folder 559.

Odum, Howard and Harry Estill Moore. 1938. *American Regionalism*. New York: Henry Holt & Co.

Odum to Morgan. 3 June 1932. Odum Papers, Box 14, Folder 283.

Roosevelt, Franklin D. 6 July 1931. "Address by Gov. Franklin D. Roosevelt of New York on STATE PLANNING." Mimeograph copy in Odum Papers, Box 12, Folder 255.

Slaughter, Thomas P. 1986. *The Whiskey Rebellion*. New York: Oxford University Press.

Turner to Whittaker. 23 April 1920. Turner Papers.

Turner to Abernethy. 16 July 1920. Turner Papers, Box 30.

Turner to Abernethy. 12 March 1926. Turner Papers, Box 35.

Turner to Paullin. 20 November 1928. Turner Papers.

Waller, Altina 1988. *Feud*. Chapel Hill: University of North Carolina Press.

Wilson, Charles Reagan and William Ferris, eds. 1989. *The Encyclopedia of Southern Culture*. Chapel Hill: University of North Carolina Press.

Worster, Donald. 1990. "Transformations of the Earth: Toward an Agroecological Perspective in History," in "A Round Table: Environmental History." *Journal of American History*, 76 (4): 1089.

John Alexander Williams is Director of the Center for Appalachian Studies at Appalachian State University, Boone, North Carolina.

Southern Appalachia and the South: A Region Within a Section

Richard B. Drake

A key question for Appalachian history prior to the Civil War is, "How did the Appalachian South relate to the larger South?" Thus far, quite different answers have been given to this question. Some important historians have taken the position that the two were closely related. Champions of southern nationalism from Jefferson Davis to E. Merton Coulter and Francis B. Simkins[1] have presented their studies as if rather total southern unity were a given fact. Also, two recent studies have taken this position. Most impressive is John Inscoe, *Mountain Masters* (1989), a study of slavery, slaveholders, and secession in western North Carolina. Inscoe builds an impressive argument that the connections between the people in the mountains of North Carolina and the people in the rest of the South were very close. When secession came, the region for the most part, (he says) supported the Confederacy. The other study, Grady McWhiney, *Cracker Culture* (1988), makes the argument that the South and the mountain South were both essentially Celtic, as opposed to the Anglo-Saxon North. In fact, it is McWhiney's view that the mountain South was more "Celtic" than the rest of the South, thus presumably the most "Southern" part of the "South."

On the other hand, there have been important historians who held that Appalachia was not an integral part of the South. This position was taken first by abolitionists before and during the Civil War who saw Southern Appalachia as an ally against "Slaveocrats." Berea College's founders clearly took this view, as have pro-Union apologists such as William G. Brownlow (1862), and important Afro-American historians such as Carter G. Woodson (1916). Later historians, such as Allan

Nevins (1950), have shared this view.² But, perhaps the most significant of the recent historians who share this perspective are Carl Degler (1974), who saw a consistent "Other South" since the early nineteenth century, and Stephen Hahn (1983), who found the roots of Georgia populism in the long standing differences between downstate planners and mountain yeoman farmers.

My argument belongs in this second perspective, and will follow two lines of enquiry thus far not carefully explored. First, I will look at the thinking of Howard W. Odum as he defined the terms, "sectionalism" and "regionalism," to see how his thinking applies both to southern history and Appalachian history. Then I will explore two varieties of the agricultural experience which emerged in the Old South.

Usually writers who have evaluated the relationship between the South and the Appalachian South have followed one or more of the following lines of enquiry: 1) the conflicting responses to the institution of slavery within the Appalachian South and the Old South, and the persisting antislavery sentiment in Appalachia;³ 2) the substantially different political agendas, especially as reflected in separatist sentiment in trans-Allegheny Virginia and in East Tennessee;⁴ or 3) the opposition to the Confederate cause in large parts of the Appalachian South.

Promising as these lines of enquiry are, I will confine myself here to 1) Odum's analysis of Sectionalism and Regionalism; and 2) two separate agricultural traditions of the Old South.

Howard W. Odum's Analysis:

Howard Odum fifty years ago developed the concept of "regionalism," which he carefully distinguished from "sectionalism." The South's Civil War experience and Frederick Jackson Turner's 1928 book, *The Sections in American History*, led Odum to conclude that "sectionalism," though understandable in a nation as large and diverse as the United States, was potentially divisive and created parochializing, even separatist loyalties. Regionalism, on the other hand, Odum saw as essentially positive and in no way subversive of national interests. Regionalism as Odum saw it, sought its own economic development, and was concerned with its own traditions and the lives of its own people. But it always sought these ends within the larger and more important national loyalty (1936, 245-61).

Historian George B. Tindall suggests that in Odum's time the South never realized the "regionalism" that he desired (1976, 100-15). No specific organization seeking the South's well being and development within the nation ever emerged. Indeed, single interest agencies emerged: the Southern Regional Council, which was concerned about the South's race relations; the Southern Governor's Conference, which was concerned with governmental cooperation; the Southern Historical Association which wished to strengthen the region's historical scholarship, etc. But, Tindall says, no larger spokesman agency for the South's total interest ever emerged. Of course, the Southern Confederacy had attempted this, but with its sectionalism it surely was contrary to the general national interest.

In my view, Appalachia has developed the sense of region in the way Tindall suggests that Odum used the term. Various agencies have developed in Appalachia that have pretty much become "regional spokesmen". Two government-supported regional development efforts have emerged within the region—the Tennessee Valley Authority and the Appalachian Regional Commission. Yet neither has become a true regional agency for Appalachia, except as they relate to Odum's expectation that a regional focus is ideal for planning purposes. The TVA has drawn its principal leadership from professionals and politicians outside the region. Furthermore, TVA's concern has been narrowed toward becoming a utility company for a region not as large as the whole of Appalachia. The TVA's policies sometimes have worked against the interests of other significant areas within Appalachia. The Appalachian Regional Commission has not drawn its leadership from the area itself. Its directors and staff, except at first, have not been Appalachians. It, for the most part, has been an "outside" uplift agency with an "outside" agenda.[5]

In 1913, however, a broad regional spokesman/program agency developed with the Council of the Southern Mountains. Begun as an annual meeting of missionaries, and called initially the Conference of Southern Mountain Workers, the CSM developed as a broad umbrella agency attracting any and all who had an interest in Appalachia. After the CSM was "captured" by aggressive, reform-oriented change agents in the 1970s, the Appalachian Studies Conference emerged to provide a broad platform for those interested in the region, thus providing a place where a regional agenda can be developed.

Regionalism, in terms that Odum could understand, has been achieved to a remarkable degree in Appalachia, perhaps more fully than in any other area within the United States. To be fair to Odum, however, he never considered "the South" as a single region. Again and again, he made the point that the South was many regions. He identified twenty-seven "Southern Regions," five of which were in the Appalachian South as usually defined.[6]

Odum never gave a precise definition of "region," except to indicate that it had heavy geographic and cultural components. He was almost mystical in his insistence that regionalism was the best mechanism under which to work out the demands of local liberty, economic development, and national order. Listen to his words:

"The earlier assumption that regionalism was only a glorified localism now appears completely outdated. Regionalism is the key to attaining balanced democracy and the redistribution of wealth . . ."(Odum 1936, 156-59).

In the mid-1930s, even as President Roosevelt saw the South as a problem-prone area in a nation that was one-third ill-housed and ill-fed, Odum noted that "the rest of the nation is tired of being told that it must do missionary work in the South. The South is certainly no more enthusiastic. The middle ground of cooperative effort must be found through the regional way" (249).

Odum was born less than twenty years after the Civil War ended and in his native Georgia was filled with stories of the Lost Cause as he grew up. As a Southerner he came to be critical of the sectionalism that had led to secession. He said:

> There are fundamental distinctions between sectionalism . . . and the developing cultural and administrative regionalism of the United States of the 1930s . . . . Regionalism envisions the nation first, making the national culture and welfare the final arbiter . . . while the section thinks of the nation in terms of itself. (253-54)

Four other points Odum found differentiated sectionalism from regionalism: 1) "sectionalism emphasizes political boundaries and state boundaries" while "regionalism connotes component . . . parts of the larger national picture;" 2) "sectionalism may be likened unto cultural inbreeding in which only home stocks are advocated . . . whereas regionalism is line breeding, in which regional cultures contributed the base but not the whole;" 3) "regionalism by its very nature . . . implies more of the designed and planned society," whereas "sectionalism would abound in conflict" among interests; and 4) as a southerner he noted that "one of the most critical aspects of sectionalism is. . . .its counterpoint in potential. . . .as inevitable coercive federalism" (257-59).

Odum did not see the South in the 1930s as a section. Rather, the South was by then a set of regions. But, historically, the South had been a section, as New England had been, and a tragic confrontation had been the result.

More research and thought needs to go into probing the question, "but had an Appalachian regionalism developed in the pre-Civil War period?" The Tindall-inspired line of enquiry followed above notes that the "true regionalism" of Appalachia applies to twentieth-century Appalachia. Though there was a clear "backwoods" awareness in the nineteenth century, this "backwoods" awareness may not be related closely enough to a "regional" awareness for Odum to have recognized it.

The Two Agricultural Systems of the South:

Now for the second line of enquiry: the development of separate agricultural systems in the antebellum South.

One of the important new ways of life to emerge in early modern Europe was the approach to farming by the "English Country Gentleman." As the feudal manor disintegrated, the new leaders of agriculture developed methods quite in harmony with the rising mercantile economy and the emerging national monarchies. This "scientific agriculture of scale" pioneered new and more efficient methods, practices and technologies. Those in control of this approach to agriculture in England pressured Parliament, especially after the Settlement of 1688, to release the former common lands to them in a series of enclosure acts. Their argument was to provide "a more efficient and productive agriculture of scale," a prejudice that persists today in modern agricultural policies.

The country gentleman approach to agriculture was mercantile. He operated as an agricultural industrialist, an "agribusinessman" if you please, concerned with markets, prices, and profits. And as more and more land came under his control through inheritance, purchase, speculation, and through enclosure by Parlimentary act (or was it corruption?), this class of agriculturalists and its way of life rose to great significance. In England, this class was most prominent in the eighteenth century. In the New World, too, this group, or rather the group in America that attempted to recreate the country gentleman way of life, became powerful as well.

In America, the country gentleman ideal was approximated most closely in the Old South. The plantation way of life took this ideal as its model. The American plantation was essentially a mercantile enterprise seeking to produce crops for a market. To provide labor for its enterprise at the cheapest level possible, Negro chattel slavery was the answer arrived at. This European-derived agriculture had much persistence and attractiveness in the New World during the eighteenth and early nineteenth centuries.

There was, however, another rural way of life born during the decay of the Medieval world which emerged with some strength and attractiveness in Europe, but which developed immense significance and appeal in America. It had its largest role in the late eighteenth century, but during the course of the nineteenth and twentieth centuries it has played a defining role. I speak of the "Yeoman" way of life.

Yeomanry was a very different approach to both farming and the land from that of the mercantile country gentleman. Yeomanry had its roots in medieval peasant culture. Land in medieval times had been the principal source of wealth. It appeared, in fact, to be the basis of life itself. The peasant who had his place defined only in relation to the land he farmed, of course desired freedom from that bondage. But what good was freedom without land? Thus, the ideal emerged: land was the basis of well-being. It was place and home, that part of "Nature" that allowed one to survive. Land was, therefore, not a commodity to be bought and sold, but rather it was that which gave meaning and security to life.[12]

Yeomanry in England had another meaning too. In fact the earliest use of the term had a military meaning. The "sturdy yeoman" or "yeaman" was an infantry/archer used by Edward I, Edward III, and Henry II, in Scotland and France. The yeomen unhorsed the knights and nobility in the military revolution of the fourteenth and fifteenth centuries. As the poem, "The Yeoman of Kent" suggests:

> At Cressy and Pointers of old
> His ancestors were bowmen bold;
> Were good yew bows and sinew strong
> Drew arrows of a cloth - yard long;
> For England's glory, strew'd the plain
> With barons, counts and princes slain. (Campbell 1942, 6)

The yeoman was not a permanent soldier like the knight. Like Cincinnatus of old, once the war was over the yeoman returned to his agricultural pursuits. He was drafted by a royal levy, and once the danger was passed he returned to his acres. Government was something remote in normal times, but was something to be protected in times of crisis. So, to the yeoman who bitterly resented the weight of peacetime taxes and dues from local and national authorities, the best government was the least government.

Yeomanry, though born in Europe, developed particularly strongly in the New World. Europe found little place for the yeoman, for land there was taken over by enclosure and purchase by the Country Gentleman in England, or the Junker class of Germany. Once religious compromise and a political "settlement" was reached in Germany in 1648 and in England in 1688, the chances of acquiring land in Europe became more and more remote. Those aspiring to yeomanry were driven by the tens of thousands to Britain's North American colonies in the late seventeenth and early eighteenth centuries in quest of land. Most of the 500 thousand or so Scotch-Irish and Germans who migrated to North America between 1688 and 1775 were aspiring yeomen who found their chances for acquiring land much greater in America than in Europe.

The yeoman/farmer, backwoods/pioneer was an ideal settler. As England built her colonies, her first settlements were along the coasts where communication could be kept more easily with the mother country. But a backwoods developed quickly, beginning an elongated struggle with the American Indians. In this struggle, the pioneer/settler, an independent, self-sufficient yeoman, was a major weapon in the ultimate Euro-American triumph. More significant even than weaponry, the settler defeated the Indian as he moved relentlessly into and across the Indian's land, preempting it farm by farm.

The yeoman was particularly well suited to this task of continental conquest. His unit of cooperation was his own family and the informal neighborhood. The cost to establish him in the "wilderness" was minimal, for the yeoman desired only the land, which could be graciously granted. And he aspired only to support himself on that land in a self-sufficient way. In a time of the technology of the musket, the military tradition of self-defense was an integral and effective part of the ideal. The myths sung at Crecy fit nicely with the tradition of the Minute Men or the Heroes of King's Mountain, and of Sergeant York.

When the American Revolution was fought and the Republic created, it seemed to some as though a yeoman's utopia had been established. Thomas Jefferson, the nation's principal spokesman for that period, voiced this hope when he wrote in 1785:

> Those who labor the earth are the chosen people of God, if ever he had a chosen people . . . Corruption of morals . . . is the mark of those, who, not looking up to heaven, to their own soiled and industry, as does the husbandman [yeoman] . . . depend for it on casualties and caprice of customers. Dependence begets subservience and venality, suffocates the germ of virtue, and prepares fit tools for the design of ambition . . . [W]hile we have land to labor then, let us never wish to see our citizens occupied at a work-bench, or twirling distaff. (Foner 1944, 161-62)

The yeoman made the ideal citizen, it appeared. He made no demands upon government, and was willing to protect it in military crisis. And in return all the yeoman asked was to be let alone on his acres to make his own way in a self-sufficient manner. His land would provide for his needs.

This type of yeoman/agriculture represents no early stage on its way to a "more mature" mercantile style of agriculture. Unlike Frederick Jackson Turner's analysis of the stages of the Midwest Frontier, which suggested a "primitive stage of self-sufficiency" which preceded a later, more advanced capitalistic agriculture, yeomanry represented a quite different approach to agriculture. Its purpose was to make a life on the land and was an end in itself. It was not a stage toward any other type of agriculture.

What a different agricultural way of life yeomanry represented when contrasted with the Squirarchial, plantation agriculture in the Old South. That style of agriculture that John S. Otto has called, "the plain folk agriculture of the Old South," was essentially yeomanesque. Otto suggests that this kind of agriculture was characterized by 1) a grazing, farmland economy with animals grazing on an "open range" in the forests, 2) a life where families lived in dispersed rural neighborhoods, with 3) occasional county-seat towns serving as centers of community concern and recreation. This was the style of agriculture, Otto says, that continued to dominate the poorer areas from Delaware to east Texas until the end of the nineteenth century (Otto 1985, 234-35).

Yeomanry has had a remarkable persistence in Southern life, particularly in southern Appalachia until well past the middle part of the twentieth century. In the nineteenth century it posed a significant challenge to the type of agriculture and way of life that developed in the Old South's plantation areas. The squire and the yeoman were different agriculturalists, a difference that James Kirke Paulding noticed as early as 1817.

> It is the old story of Mrs. Farmer Ashfield and Mrs. Planter Grundy. Mrs. Ashfield leads the tone among the Cohees (a term for those west of the Blue Ridge) squints at Mrs. Grundy, a fine lady of the Tuckahoes (those east of the Blue Ridge in Virginia). [M]y lady gives herself airs, and wears such mighty fine clothes, when she goes to the Springs. Now Goody (term for the yeoman's wife) Ashfield, for her part, don't care for fine things.
>
> As to Squire Grundy and Farmer Ashfield, they have certain snug matters of dispute to themselves. The Farmer insists upon it, at town-meetings and elections, that the Squire enjoys greater political privileges than he does, that the country of Tuckahoe has more representatives in the legislature than it ought to have, that all Squire Grundy's "negroes" are counted for voting. (Higgs and Manning 1975, 64-66)

It was a difference within the South that persisted through the Civil War, and has persisted even on into the twentieth century.

Notes

[1] See Jefferson Davis (1881, 2 vols.), E. Merton Coulter (1950), and Francis B. Simkins (1956).

[2] Allan Nevins (1950, 17-19, 73-6, 90, 103, 322-26).

[3] These are the arguments found in Carter G. Woodson (1916) and Richard B. Drake (1986, 25-33).

⁴ These are the arguments made by Thomas Jefferson Wertenbaker (1942, 167-180), Charles H. Ambler and Festus P. Summers (1958), Otis K. Rice (1985), and William G. Brownlow (1862).

⁵ For treatments of the TVA and the ARC see James Branscome (1977), Donald N. Rothblatt (1971), and David E. Whisnant (1980) and (1985).

⁶ Good discussions of English yeomanry are in Asa Briggs (1983) and Wallace Notestein (1962).

Works Cited

Ambler, Charles H. and Festus P. Summers. 1958. *West Virginia: the Mountain State.* Englewood Cliffs: Prentice-Hall.

Branscome, James. 1977. *The Federal Government in Appalachia.* New York: Field Foundation.

Briggs, Asa. 1983. *A Social History of England.* New York: Viking.

Brownlow, William G. 1862. *Sketches of the Rise, Progress and Decline of Secession, with a Narrative of Personal Adventures among the Rebels.* Phildelphia: George W. Child..

Campbell, Mildred L. 1942. *The English Yeoman Under Elizabeth and the Early Stuarts.* New Haven: Yale.

Coulter, E. Merton. 1950. *The Confederate States of America, 1861-1865.* Baton Rouge: Louisiana State University Press.

Davis, Jefferson. 1881. *The Rise and Fall of the Confederate Government.* New York: Appleton.

Degler, Carl N. 1974. *The Other South: Southern Dissenters in the Nineteenth Century.* New York: Harper and Row.

Drake, Richard B. 1986. "Slavery and Antislavery in Appalachia." *Appalachian Heritage* 14 (Winter): 25-33.

Foner, Philip S, ed. 1944. "Notes on Virginia (1781-1785), Quiery XIX." *Basic Writings of Thomas Jefferson.* New York: Wiley.

Hahn, Stephen. 1983. *Roots of Southern Populism: Yeoman Farmers and The Transformation of the Georgia Upcountry, 1850-1890.* New York: Oxford.

Higgs, Robert J. and Ambrose N. Manning, ed. 1975. *Voices from the Hills.* New York: Unger.

Inscoe, John C. 1989. *Mountain Masters, Slavery and the Sectional Crisis in Western North Carolina.* Knoxville: University of Tennessee Press.

McWhiney, Grady. 1988. *Cracker Culture: Celtic Ways in the Old South.* Tuscaloosa: University of Alabama Press.

Nevins, Allan. 1950. *The Emergence of Lincoln: Prologue to the Civil War, 1859-1861.* New York: Scribners.

Notestein, Wallace. 1962. *The English People on the Eve of Colonization, 1603-1630.* New York: Harper & Row.

Odum, Howard W. 1936. *Southern Regions of the United States.* Chapel Hill: University of North Carolina Press.

Otto, John Solomon. 1985. "Reconsidering the Southern Hillbilly: Appalachia and the Ozarks." *Appalachian Journal* 12.(Summer): 324-32.

Rice, Otis K. 1985. *West Virginia: A History.* Lexington: University Press of Kentucky.

Rothblatt, Donald N. 1971. *Regional Planning: The Appalachian Experience.* Lexington, Massachusetts: Heath.

Simkins, Francis B. 1956. *A History of the South.* New York: Knopf.

Tindall, George B. 1976. *The Ethnic Southerners.* Baton Rouge: Louisiana State University Press.

Wertenbaker, Thomas Jefferson. 1942. *The Old South: The Founding of American Civilization.* New York: Scribners.

Whisnant, David E. 1980. *Modernizing the Mountaineer: People, Power and Planning.* New York: Burt Franklin.

———. 1985. *Appalachia, Twenty Years of Progress.* Washington: Appalachian Regional Commission.

Woodson, Carter G. 1916. "Freedom and Slavery in Appalachia." *Journal of Negro History* 1 (April).

Richard Drake is Julian-Van Dusen Professor of American History at Berea College, Berea, Kentucky.

Hegemony, Alienation and Identity Reformulation: Further Thoughts on a Comparative Approach to Appalachian Studies

Richard Blaustein

When the sociologist John Shelton Reed stated that "Appalachia has always been the South's South" (Reed 1986, 42), he deftly pinpointed a key feature of the Appalachian dilemma: marginality.

Appalachia as a region is marginal to the official centers of political, economic, and cultural power in the southern states just as the South as a region is peripheral to the core of official power in the United States as a nation-state. In both cases we can observe ambiguous identity of peripheral regions with a more inclusive official sociopolitical establishment; conflicting tendencies towards acceptance or rejection of the hegemony, that is to say, the authority and legitimacy of a dominant elite which establishes cultural standards for society as a whole.

Culturally speaking, there is no such thing as the "Solid South." Though John Shelton Reed is careful to indicate the limitations of the survey data he presents in *Southerners: The Social Psychology of Regionalism,* it would appear that people who were born and raised in the Border States are much less likely to identify themselves as Southerners (42 percent) than people from the Deep South (87 percent) (1983, 13). Despite John Inscoe's recent study of Confederate loyalism in Western

North Carolina, and Tom Burton's earlier research on Confederate Home Guards in Watauga County, it would be going too far to say that Upland southerners have uniformly identified with the South; in Reed's North Carolina survey, he found that people who disassociated themselves from southern identity came from all age groups, all social classes and both sexes, but geographically they were disproportionately concentrated in mountain and hill areas in the western and north central sections of the state which were centers of strong Union sentiment during the Civil War (1983, 24). Recent studies of Appalachian self-identity by Susan Keefe (1989) and Philip Obermiller (1987) actually suggest that many southern mountaineers resist any sort of regional or sectional labeling, and mainly to avoid stigmatization. Regardless of all of the other ethnic and racial pride movements which have taken place in the United States since the early sixties, low-status marginal southern white social types like hillbillies, crackers, and rednecks are still fair game for stereotypic put-downs: "Just as rednecks seem to be the last identifiably ethnic villains, so hillbillies appear to be the last acceptable ethnic fools" (Reed 1986, 43). As Ross Spears has graphically illustrated in *Long Shadows*, his documentary film on the enduring psychic effects of the American Civil War, regional and sectional biases are still very much alive in the United States; to quote John Shelton Reed again, "As long as non-southerners think of southerners as different, southerners will be forced to think in these terms" (1983, 110).

Throughout the modern world, the vitality of regionalism, nationalism, religious, and ethnic separatism has defied the predictions of liberals and rationalists who believed that the progress of science and industry would inexorably result in homogeneous mass cultures and classless societies. Instead, the reverse seems to be happening. In capitalist and socialist nation-states alike, peripheral subject minorities are challenging the hegemony of elite establishments. The melting pot is melting, the iron curtain is rusting, the domino theory has fallen on its face, while national, regional, ethnic, and religious affiliations and animosities have proven to be stubbornly persistent. Many contemporary historians and social theorists are now convinced of the inadequacy of assimilation and mass culture theories. In their place, we are witnessing the ascendancy of models of social and cultural development founded upon the realization that ethnic, regional, and national cultures are surprisingly resilient and extremely resistant to assimilation.

In recent years, theories positing the persistence of British regional cultures in the New World have gained currency in Appalachian Studies and related branches of American social history. In part, this could be a response by British-American intellectuals to the assertion of cultural continuity by other ethnic and racial groups. If Alex Haley of Henning,

Tennessee, can trace his ancestor Kuntu Kinte to the village of Juffure in Gambia, and if art historian Robert Farris Thompson can conclusively demonstrate the continuity of specific West and Central African graphic and musical motifs in African-American folk art, (1984), is it too farfetched to propose that British-American regional subcultures might be equally resilient?

Though new regionalists as philosophically disparate as Rodger Cunningham, Grady McWhiney, and David Hackett Fischer concur that British regional subcultures have been preserved essentially intact in America, they are otherwise in far from perfect accord regarding specific historical and ethnological details. In the 1990 Winter edition of the *Appalachian Journal*, Cunningham has recently concluded that McWhiney's notion of Celtic hegemony in the American South as presented in *Cracker Culture* (1988) is not only simplistic but also accepts xenophobic descriptions of these people by hostile outsiders at face value. Though McWhiney and his colleague Forrest McDonald assert that no less than 75 percent of the settlers of the hinterlands of the Southern colonies were of Celtic origin, and these people imposed a non-English culture characterized by pastoralism, laziness, intemperance, sensuality, violence, and anarchic individualism on their neighbors (McDonald and McWhiney 1989, 1131), Cunningham contends that these people can hardly be considered Celts at all. According to Fischer, most of these back country settlers, English-speaking Protestants rather than Gaelic-speaking Catholics, came from the rim of the Irish Sea including the border country of Northern England and Lowland Scotland as well as Northern Ireland and not from historically Gaelic areas (1989, 618-21). This non-Celtic North British border culture, transported to the colonial frontier between 1717 and 1775, informed the distinctive character and image of the Appalachian South. Indeed, Fischer would argue that centuries of insecurity and violence on the borders of North Britain resulted in the psychological and cultural preadaptation of the settlers of Appalachia before they ever came to America, just as the historical experiences of the Puritans in East Anglia, the Cavaliers in southwestern England, and the Quakers in the Midlands set the stamp on the regional subcultures they brought to New England, the Tidewater, and the Delaware Valley. American history is largely a result of the dynamic interplay of these four hearth cultures.

Though Cunningham finds Fischer's version of regional determinism more agreeable than McWhiney's Celtic hypothesis, *Albion's Seed*, despite its higher degree of historical and ethnological precision, is nonetheless grievously flawed. In supporting his thesis, Fischer indulges in sweeping generalizations and outright distortions which reinforce xenophobic stereotypes. Fischer's cursory discussions of folk speech (652-55) and folk magic (708-15) are particularly distressing from the viewpoint of the folklorist; it almost seems as though he has deliberately chosen the most bizarre examples available to demonstrate just how barbaric, cruel, and superstitious these peculiar people really are. Are the vocabulary items and superstitions he presents as quintessentially Appalachian (or North British?) as he claims, or would exhaustive research uncover parallels and cognates in other British-American subcultures? And what about the purported xenophobia of the southern highlander? Fischer's characterization of Appalachians as anti-semitic (650-1) seems to be an egregious generalization from the terrible but unique ordeal of Leo Frank; what would a careful study of the geographic distribution of anti-Jewish violence in the South actually show? These may seem like carping criticisms, but what of Fischer's failure to address the ambiguity and diversity of Appalachian involvement in the Civil War (859-61)? Curiously enough, he says nothing at all about conflicts among his four hearth cultures: is this because the actual complexity of the historical event has exhausted the explanatory power of his theoretical construct?

Fischer's conception of persistent dialectic tension between regional subcultures, which posits enduring, organic relationships between a people, its homeland and distinctive linguistic and cultural characteristics, is essentially romantic. Exploring the parallels between romantic regionalism in Britain and America is ultimately more informative to the cultural historian than sifting and straining historical and ethnological facts to support a comforting counter myth. Like Rodger Cunningham, we must address fundamental questions of cultural dominance and subordination that divide core from periphery in any complex society and create identity conflicts which pull marginal, non-elite personalities between the poles of assimilation and separatism. In *Apples on the Flood*, Cunningham theorizes that a continuous history of marginality and subordination has left the descendants of the North British borders who migrated to Appalachia with an impaired sense of autonomous identity and self-worth (xxiii). This ambiguity is compounded by the ambivalence of the core culture towards its own advancement. On one hand, the primitive periphery represents backwardness, irrationality, superstition, sloth, violence; on the other, the core believes that the periphery has preserved values it believes it has lost: the primordial, the natural, organic, traditional, spiritual, spontaneous, sensual, and emotional. John Shelton Reed contrasts this peripheral "id culture" with the "superego culture" of the core: "The idea is that members of the group doing the stereotyping project their unacceptable impulses onto the group being stereotyped, and thus deny that they have those impulses" (Reed 1986, 45).

Whether we are talking about Appalachians, Celts, vanishing Indians, or any other dominated, marginal group, it is interesting that the qualities which distinguish "superego" and "id" cultures remain constant, for ultimately they are expressions of unequal power relationships:

(+)		(-)
Dominant	versus	Subordinate
Rational		Irrational
Advanced		Primitive
Hard working		Lazy
Practical		Impractical
Organized		Fragmented
Anglo-Saxon		Celt
male		female
Apollonian		Dionysian
superego		id
left brain		right brain
core		periphery
bureaucracy		folk society
United States		Appalachia

According to this formula, vanishing peripheral cultures are assumed to be displaced by advancing core cultures; historically, this has provided the rationale for the study and celebration of folk culture and indeed, for the initiation of romantic cultural revivals in general. However, before such revivals can begin, their leaders must resolve their feelings of ambiguity regarding these opposing cultural poles, neatly summed up in Malcolm Chapman's assessment of the paradoxical position of the highlanders in Scottish culture: "The highlands have long been derided as the barbarous antithesis of southern culture and sophistication, yet they have at the same time become the location of all of the virtues that civilization has felt itself to lack" (1978, 13). Like the Scottish Gael, the Appalachian highlander comes to embody the inner conflicts of core civilization," at once a fit object for the location of primitive traits, and a fit object for taming, schooling and 'improving' " (20).

This is true of the folk in general. As folklorist Alan Dundes comments, "The folk is a backward, illiterate segment of the population of which elitist intellectuals are ashamed. On the other hand, the folk represents the glorified, romanticized remnants of a national patrimony which is something for zealous intellectuals to celebrate. . . .the same situation applies in most countries. Intellectuals were both embarrassed by and proud of their folk and folklore" (Dundes 1989, 44).

Dundes proposes that the selective reconstruction or the wholesale invention of folk traditions compensates for feelings of cultural inferiority experienced by such intellectuals. The reformulation or fabrication of tradition provides a means of shedding internalized stigmatizing stereotypes and asserting a self-defined social and cultural identity. The purported revival or rediscovery of cultural traditions dating back to an unsullied Golden Age serves the same psychological function as countermythologies which reject the core culture's assertion of its own primacy and superiority; the adoption of Mother Goddess myths by feminists or Jesus-Was-Black myths by African-Americans are salient examples of what David Whisnant has seen fit to call "counter-hegemonic opposition."

By embracing the periphery and rejecting the core, such movements resolve the crisis of dual cultural loyalties experienced by peripheral intellectuals. Functionally speaking, it matters little if the cultural forms which serve as the focus of such movements are ethnographically authentic or recent fabrications as long as they fulfill the need for meaningful, positive social identity. As the British sociologist Anthony D. Smith remarks, the preservation and celebration of the cultural heritage of the periphery serves to bolster a threatened or vanishing communal personality: "The enemy within is loss of identity, self-oblivion, the end of authenticity, which erodes and corrupts the community, dividing and weakening the members and tempting them into cultural imitation and political dependence" (Smith 1979, 118). In conquering the inner enemy, which is in fact the internalized conflict between core and periphery, disaffiliated intellectuals are transformed into partisans (or patrons) of the reconstituted folk community: "They go out among the peasants and farmers, commune with nature, record the rhythms of the countryside, and bring them back to the anonymous city, so that rising urban strata may be 'reborn' and possess a clear and unmistakable identity" (106).

Folk revivalism is only one form that such counter-hegemonic movements have taken. In Appalachian Studies, we have often commented on the apparent conflict between what Jim Wayne Miller has referred to as the "action people" and the "creative folk." In recent years, that division has become less intense with the growing realization that both positions represent alternate solutions to the fundamental problem of marginality, subordination, and the consequent need for self-actualization.

Rodger Cunningham has imaginatively and constructively synthesized these seemingly disparate points of view. As Cunningham states in the final chapter of *Apples On The Flood*, the resolution of the Appalachian dilemma entails "the healing of the divided self" (Cunningham 1987, 171). His image of a borderland Merlin awaiting rebirth in his mystic womb-cavern in primordial North Britain evokes Gurney

Norman's David Ray "Divine Right" Davenport wrestling with the fiery serpent in the darkness of an abandoned mine on his Uncle Emmit's homeplace in eastern Kentucky; both suggest archetypal rituals of psychic alchemy through which the dross of the false self is separated from the gold of the authentic self and the self-actualized personality is reunited with an authentic, autonomous community.

In the end, it is probably fruitless to argue over the historical validity of the new romantic regionalism; Jo Carson has often repeated George Ella Lyon's contention that the facts and the truth are not necessarily the same thing. And, as Cunningham has observed, the real struggle in Appalachian Studies is not between the action people and the creative folk, but between the Enlargers and the Enclosers. By making us look at old questions in new ways, Rodger Cunningham is definitely one of the Enlargers. Whether we agree with all of the basic assumptions of the new regionalism or not, it is nonetheless contributing to the reconfiguration of Appalachian Studies itself.

Works Cited

Chapman, Malcolm. 1978. *The Gaelic Vision In Scottish Culture.* London: Croom Helm and McGill-Queen's University.

Cunningham, Rodger. 1987. *Apples on the Flood: The Southern Mountain Experience.* Knoxville: University of Tennessee Press.

———. 1990. "Eat Grits and Die: Or, Cracker, Your Breed Ain't Hermeneutical." *Appalachian Journal* 17 Spring.

Dundes, Alan. 1989. "The Fabrication of Folklore," in *Folklore Matters.* Knoxville: University of Tennessee Press.

Fischer, David Hackett. 1989. *Albion's Seed: Four British Folkways in America.* Oxford: Oxford University Press.

McDonald, Forrest and Grady McWhiney. 1989. "Celtic South." eds. Charles Reagan Wilson and William Ferris. *Encyclopedia of Southern Culture.* Chapel Hill: University of North Carolina Press.

McWhiney, Grady. 1988. *Cracker Culture: Celtic Ways in The Old South.* Tuscaloosa: University of Alabama Press.

Reed, John Shelton. 1983. *Southerners: The Social Psychology of Sectionalism.* Chapel Hill: University of North Carolina Press.

———. 1986. *Southern Folk, Plain And Fancy: Native White Social Types.* Athens: University of Georgia Press.

Smith, Anthony D. 1979. *Nationalism in the Twentieth Century.* New York: New York University Press.

Richard Blaustein is Professor of Sociology and Anthropology and Director of the Center for Appalachian Studies and Services at East Tennessee State University.

The Appalachian Frontier and the Southern Frontier: A Comparative Perspective

H. Tyler Blethen & Curtis W. Wood

As the title indicates, this paper originally set out to compare antebellum southern Appalachian society with that of the rural South in general. As the work progressed it became obvious that this undertaking was far too ambitious, even in general terms, given the time and space available. Its goal now is more limited: to discuss some recent revisionist perspectives from which to reexamine antebellum southern mountain society and to consider how unique that society was compared to the larger non-plantation South. The paper will focus in particular on questions of mobility and community.

The period under examination (roughly from the 1780s to 1860) is frequently referred to as the frontier or pioneer stage; those decades of initial settlement during which European culture was brought into the mountains. But this antebellum era involves more than migration, settlement, and pioneering. In fact, it contains two stages, the second constituting a time of development and elaboration during which a synthetic mountain society and economy took shape and sank deep roots.

What are the most useful terms by which to describe that syncretic society: isolated, insular, provincial, self-sufficient, subsistent, communal, egalitarian, barter, market-oriented? To what degree were the essential features of antebellum mountain society unique? To what degree were they simply more pronounced or sharply drawn, and thereby more distinctive than in the non-mountain South? What factors account for any uniqueness or distinctiveness?

The idea that mountain society is unique frequently has been used to explain the highly visible cultural survivals of the region and its more intractable problems. Arguments for uniqueness have relied on various assertions: that the southern mountain region was settled by a distinctively different class of people, or alternatively, that it was settled by certain ethnic groups whose culture was particularly adaptive to the mountain environment. Closely related is the argument based on geography: that a harsh and restrictive environment forced development along certain lines while, at the same time, forestalling alternatives and producing economic and cultural deprivation along with political isolation and powerlessness. Any student of southern Appalachian history can recognize the appeal of these ideas; however, recent research reveals a more complex picture.

One important trend has been to portray the antebellum mountain region as an integral part of the "Upland South." This interpretation, recognized by Frederick Jackson Turner seventy years ago, has recently been documented and described by Fred Kniffen, Henry Glassie, Milton Newton, James Lemon, and Robert Mitchell. Though the views of these scholars (mostly historical geographers) vary in some important respects, they stress the cultural unity of the non-plantation antebellum South from Pennsylvania to Mississippi, and they minimize diversity within this "cultural hearth." The "nearly uniform set of solutions" (Newton 1974, 150-1) of this "midland backwoods culture" (Jordan and Kaups 1989, 8-9) spread rapidly across the "Old West" frontier in the period 1750-1825. It was a cultural fusion contributed to and borne by a number of ethnic groups: Scotch-Irish, German, English, etc. The distinctive features of this cultural synthesis were dispersed settlement, the single-family farmstead, the county unit, a courthouse-town focus, an open class system, a generalized but commercially-oriented stockman-farmer-hunter economy, log construction, an extremely productive and varied food-and-feed complex, and evangelical Protestantism (Mitchell and Newton 1988, 20).

The value of this "geographer's view" is that it reminds us of the cultural unity of the frontier South, a unity which is sometimes overlooked when research is narrowly focused on the mountain region. It also encourages a greater appreciation for this remarkably dynamic phase of southern history—"the most successful forest colonization process ever devised" (Jordan and Kaups 1989, 7) —and its imprint on later southern history. Its weakness is that it accounts for continuity more successfully than for emerging regionalism and diversity.

But recent research also has revealed a surprisingly mobile, market-oriented antebellum mountain society: not a monolithic society, but one characterized by clear gradations of class and an important diversity including both isolated and accessible regions. Significant areas of the southern mountains interacted extensively with the larger society and economy and preserved a basic similarity with the rest of the South. But at the same time, some distinctive regional characteristics emerged.

The problems of travel and transportation played an important role in defining antebellum mountain society economically, politically, and culturally. The mountain environment did not pose a serious barrier to frontier settlement but presented to new immigrants a physical setting distinct enough to constitute some novelty in the settlement experience. Physical distances were measured in days or even weeks, and any travel could impose significant choices on an individual or family. Migration even over relatively short distances could mean long separation from family and friends. The single-family farmstead, the norm for mountain society, took on new meaning when farms were separated by rough, poorly maintained roads. Nonetheless, Appalachian frontier society developed a transportation system that connected it to the larger southern economy and society and which supported a lifestyle that was comparable to that in the rural non-plantation South. Frank Owsley's description of the "plain folk of the old South" provides graphic evidence of this (1949, 90-123).

The diversity of mountain society was apparent from the earliest period of white settlement. River bottoms became home to more prosperous and accessible valley communities. The families who settled the coves and hollows were affected by varying degrees of isolation, which in some cases was undoubtedly extreme. But overall, antebellum mountain society was characterized by a remarkable flow of people and a steady movement of goods. Demographic research indicates that the earliest settlers came from considerable distances, frequently from other states, and often stayed for only a short time before moving on. Even as late as 1850, a study of census records for Jackson County, North Carolina, reveals that most residents had been born in neighboring counties and that short-distance moves were still part of a typical migration pattern there. Similarly, in Washington County, Tennessee, over half the individuals recorded on any of the surviving tax lists between 1790 and 1845 did not appear on the next list, and 40-50 percent of the surnames on any tax list were missing from the next (Blethen and Wood 1987, 78-83; Dunn 1988, 1-21; Hsiung, 5-6).

Populations were remarkably fluid and mobile along the southern Appalachian frontier in the early nineteenth century. Families moved readily and frequently as the frontier shifted south and west. Often they settled on land that they never bought, and may not have even entered a claim for, before moving on. The early married life of Andy J. Wood of Jackson County illustrates that mobility:

I entered 100 acres of land on the headwaters of Cullowhee [Creek], built me a little cabin and we moved what we had to begin housekeeping with in a sled. . . . I worked very hard all day and at night I would make shoes for my neighbors or card for my wife who had toiled faithfully all day long and then did her carding and spinning at night. We stayed two years but were not satisfied with the gain we were making and in the year 1842 we decided to go to Georgia and work for gold. (Wood)

Just a few years later the family returned to Jackson County.

Places throughout the southern mountains that even in the present day seem extremely remote attracted settlers quite early. A popular presumption is that families sank their roots "where the axle broke." That explanation for the far-flung white settlement of the pioneer period is colorful, but it is not historically very plausible. Instead, we must credit the remarkable penetration of settlement into remote mountain regions to settlers in search of arable land with good water. Essential to this pattern of settlement was the mountain economy which motivated them, an economy which, though largely subsistence, was never entirely removed from a greater regional market economy.

Mountain communities in the frontier period appreciated the importance of improved transportation. Although obstacles were considerable and resources scarce, upgrading roads was a priority from the start. Once settlements were established, the settlers looked for the easiest routes to conduct their trade. In general, these routes tended to be north-south, rather than east-west. This meant that the mountain people of Tennessee, North Carolina, and Virginia found that their trade was directed not primarily toward their own states but toward the states to their north and south. These routes and the economic ties that grew from them are important in understanding subsequent developments (Blethen and Wood, 73-75, 86-87; Inscoe 1989; Hsiung 1989, 336-49). Internal improvements were one of the burning issues of the early nineteenth century, particularly in the more recently-settled areas of the south-central backcountry. The developing road network led citizens in many parts of the southern mountains to identify more with neighboring states than with the eastern seaboard and even with the capitals of their own states. Locally, county governments worked to establish and maintain public roads. Indian trails quickly became wagon roads. Private investors built turnpikes and toll roads. As new counties were created, road improvements were undertaken to connect scattered communities to their new new county seats. In fact, the system of county government and the development of mountain transportation were intimately related. By the 1830s and 1840s scheduled transportation had begun to connect many of the small towns of the southern Appalachians. Western North Carolina illustrates this growing interconnectedness. By the 1830s a weekly stage ran from Asheville to Clayton, Georgia, through Waynesville and Franklin. Another ran from Tennessee through Qualla and Webster to South Carolina. These mountain roads also gave the region good access to the Buncombe County Turnpike between Greenville, Tennessee, and Greenville, South Carolina. This network made possible interaction beyond the region which is reflected in the trade commodities regularly shipped in and out of the mountains (Blethen and Wood, 74). Rather than focusing on the isolation and impoverishment of pre-railroad mountain society, it is more useful to understand the nature of pre-railroad transportation which supported mountain life and to analyze the manner in which it met the needs of the region. Nevertheless, the fact that railroads arrived in the southern mountains decades later than in surrounding regions is of critical importance. This delay, as much a function of sectional conflict and competing economic interests as it was of the engineering and financial obstacles posed by mountain terrain, had a dramatic impact on the development of southern Appalachia.

As early as the 1820s, mountain leaders were involved in efforts to bring railroads into their region. The failure of most of these initiatives until the 1870s profoundly altered the relationship between the southern Appalachians and mainstream America. In the decades of the mid-nineteenth century, the uneven distribution of railroads widened the gap between a progressive, industrial America and an "isolated" mountain people. The highland region was once again a "frontier." From a national perspective it was "the land where time lingers," awaiting development. Its control of its own resources and its own destiny were precarious indeed.

All this leads directly to the important historical question of just how isolated the region was in the era before the coming of the railroads. The evidence for isolation is found in descriptions from travelers' accounts (Bishop Francis Asbury; Andre Michaux, etc.) and in some recent regional studies, particularly those that focus on community history (Waller 1988; Paludan 1981). Physical separation was certainly an important political reality. Local communities complained about the disadvantages in daily life of being several days removed from county courts and land offices. Their discontent was the driving force behind the creation of new counties throughout much of the nineteenth century. The mountain counties remained hidden from the attentions of their respective state governments and were sometimes even referred to as the "lost counties." This governmental attitude, however, was more a reflection of sectional conflicts within states than of genuinely crippling isolation. For mountain communities in fact had developed strong ties to the national economy and society.

Evidence of a dynamic economic life is found in the commercialized agriculture which developed in the region from an early date. The livestock economy with its annual drives to South Carolina, Georgia, and Virginia, which have been vividly described in recent literature (Dykeman 1955, 137-51; Blethen and Wood, forthcoming), burst the bonds of the subsistence economy. They gave mountain farmers direct access to southeastern markets and created local opportunities to sell corn to drovers. Trade with the outside economy stimulated the growth of mountain towns and gave rise to a class of merchants like James Patton, William Holland Thomas, and David Deaderick. There is also evidence of a more cosmopolitan cultural and social life, stimulated by antebellum tourism (Inscoe, 30-33).

Finally, in what way did the development of the community set mountain people apart from the rural South? The traditional image of American pioneer life has been that of people living in isolated, subsistence-oriented, self-sufficient family farms. Community (defined as an active network of interdependence and of shared objectives pursued collectively), when it existed, was described as marginal, with most people living in the context of rugged individualism and sturdy independence. Only recently has revisionist scholarship begun to challenge that almost mythic portrayal of our country's roots. The new version, first developed in studies of rural New England and then extrapolated to the Midwest, insists that pioneer farmers were not totally self-sufficient, but instead lived in complex webs of interdependence.

This revisionist paradigm of pioneer life is now being applied to our understanding of community in the southern Appalachians. In studying a region once upheld as the epitome of rugged individualism, and social and economic isolation, some historians are now beginning to insist upon the significance of community in the mountains. The work of scholars like Gordon McKinney, John Inscoe, Durwood Dunn, Philip Paludan, David Hsiung, and ourselves points the way to a new understanding of antebellum life in the southern Appalachians quite different from the old stereotypes of isolated and independent family farms. In summarizing these recent writings, McKinney acknowledges that most pioneer families indeed practiced subsistence agriculture and relied on their own production for all of their food. Nevertheless, he asserts that they remained dependent on the presence of craftsmen for certain skills, such as blacksmithing, milling of grain, and wheelwrighting, and on merchants for a wide variety of commodities like salt and manufactured goods (McKinney).

The key interpretive hypothesis which underlies this revisionist portrait of the southern mountains is an assertion that the Appalachian region was not socially and economically homogeneous. Rather, the new scholarship insists upon examining the southern Appalachians as a region marked by diversity. Thus, while there were some isolated family farmers, there were also towns and townspeople, as well as rural communities possessing their own social gradations and a developed sense of community and interdependence. This more sophisticated interpretation of the southern Appalachians explains how the traditional image of isolation could have arisen, while at the same time it reveals how poorly that image serves as a generalization.

One important distinction which the new scholarship has highlighted is that between urban and rural mountaineers. Not all mountaineers were the same. While there were few truly urban areas in the antebellum southern mountains, and the existing towns were admittedly small, they nevertheless created a society distinctive from the rural areas outside them.

John Inscoe, in his study of antebellum western North Carolina, has identified three types of mountain towns. The first were the older, more established towns in the foothills east of the Blue Ridge (Morganton, Lenoir, Wilkesboro). These towns were relatively prosperous and served as "gateways" between the mountains and the rest of the state. The second type were those located along the French Broad River. They were strung along the major route through the mountains, from Tennessee to South Carolina, which served as the region's economic lifeline before the coming of the railroad (Warm Springs, Asheville, Hendersonville, Flat Rock). The final type consisted of the remaining county seats west of the Blue Ridge. These were crude and frontier-like towns, which travelers delighted in belittling. Augustus S. Merrimon, a young Asheville attorney whose practice took him throughout the region, described Murphy as "a small place and poorly improved. There are several small stores here that seem to do a small business. All of them together would not make one good one." Waynesville he described as a "dirty small village and there is no place of entertainment in it fit to stay at. One would suppose it to be a large negro quarter to see it from a distance." He reserved his most unkind remarks for Jewel Hill, where Madison County's court still met. Its citizens were generally drunk, its women were "dirty, filthy strumpets," and he concluded that "I do not know any rival for this place in regard to drunkenness, ignorance, superstition and the most brutal debauchery" (Inscoe, 30-35). Carville Earle and Ronald Hoffman in their research on early southern urban history have found the development of similar types of towns across the South (Earle and Hoffman 1977, 23-51).

All of these towns, regardless of their type, created a sense of community less isolated than that experienced by the surrounding rural mountaineers. Inscoe, Hsiung, and Paludan have all stressed the connections of townspeople to the outside world and their role in linking the mountains to the greater American society. A thriving elite of business and professional men existed in them. Towns were places where merchants, travelers, and courts gathered and met. As Paludan points out, values developed in towns that were different in many ways from those held by the surrounding rural mountaineers, especially in their emphasis on looking outside the mountains to meet their needs and plans (Paludan, 26). In this way, mountain townspeople were connected to the rest of the nation. It is likely that mountain towns, though small and rudimentary, also had significant impact on the sense of rural community. But again, it is important to understand the variations that existed within the southern Appalachians. For example, Inscoe and Paludan argue that over time, small communities of rural mountaineers, like Shelton Laurel and Plum Tree Creek in western North Carolina, actually became isolated from the mountain towns (Inscoe, 53-4; Paludan, 7-8). While Paludan offers no explanation as to why this would be so, Inscoe attributes it to the growing pressures of population. Continuing immigration forced later settlers further up the mountainsides and into the coves and hollows whose distances made travel to towns more difficult. As the nineteenth century unfolded, community life in towns became more distinctive as they generated much of the area's progress, diversity, and entrepreneurial spirit (Inscoe, 25).

Just as there was diversity among various mountain communities, so too was there diversity among rural mountain people. Recent work has challenged the traditional stereotype that all mountaineers were sturdy independent yeoman farmers. McKinney and Inscoe have pointed out important variations of socioeconomic class within antebellum mountain society. Our research on antebellum Jackson County revealed a distinction between subsistence-oriented farms on which families produced for their own needs and little else, and market-oriented farms that produced a surplus and required more labor than the family could provide. Prosperous farmers in the broad valley of the Tuckaseigee River, and along Scotts Creek, grew more grain than farmers in other communities and sold it to drovers on their way to autumn markets in South Carolina and Georgia. They also maintained large herds of cattle and hogs which they both sold to drovers and took to markets themselves.

These market-oriented farmers created a demand for more labor than the family could provide. In a few cases this need was met by slaves, for there were significant numbers of slaveholders and slaves in western North Carolina, as there were in eastern Tennessee and northern Georgia. More often, it was suppled by landless laborers who worked as tenant farmers. The census of 1850 indicates that most Jackson County communities included at least a few such heads of households, identified as laborers. In the Tuckaseigee Valley community, eighteen of fifty-eight households were headed by laborers. The census does not specify what kind of work these laborers did, but it does make clear that they did not own land. Jackson County was an overwhelmingly agricultural region, and only a handful of men supported themselves by work other than farming. There is little doubt that these men identified as laborers worked on other people's farms.

A class of landless farm workers does not fit with the conventional view of a society where all men were independent farm owners. However, other research confirms the presence of dependent, landless tenants in the mountain counties of north Georgia, in Cades Cove, and in Haywood County, North Carolina (Blethen and Wood, 83-85; Bode and Gunter 1986; Dunn; Reid 1976, 69-83); and it is probable that this situation was common throughout the mountain region. Few rental contracts have been found, but a handful from Haywood County offer insight into tenant status. Tenants were probably sharecroppers rather than renters; certainly rents were rarely paid in cash. It is likely that tenants farmed pieces of land separate from the farms of their landlords. They received an agreed-upon share of the crop—often two thirds—in lieu of wages. Tenants often had other obligations required by their leases, such as to prepare new land for cultivation or to build or repair fences. Landlords probably supervised the work of their tenants and decided what they should grow and where. The Haywood County records indicate that leases were often short, for one year at a time. A tenant usually stayed with the same landlord but each year would renegotiate the terms and the lands to be leased. It appears that landlords believed that this practice was both efficient and profitable, and that it was not just a way of exploiting surplus land (Blethen and Wood, 83-85).

The lifestyle of small farmers and tenants must have been quite similar. Both cultivated small tracts of land to meet their household needs, kept livestock on the open range, and supplemented their incomes by hunting and fishing. But while tenants enjoyed a standard of living very much like that of the typical small farm owner, they were free from many of the worries connected with land ownership, particularly the payment of property taxes. And in a period characterized by considerable mobility, tenants found it easier to move on. The lifestyle of tenants and small farmers was often misunderstood and described in derogatory terms by travelers from outside the region. In 1848 Charles Lanman, a journalist, described his journey up the Tuckaseigee River:

> The river to which I alluded is the Tuck-a-se-ja, which empties into the Tennessee. It is a very rapid stream, and washes the base of many mountains, which are as wild as they were a century ago. Whenever there occurs any interval land, the soil is very rich, and such spots are usually occupied. The mountains are all covered with forest, where wild game is found in abundance. The fact is, the people of this whole region devote more of their time to hunting than they do to agriculture, which in fact accounts for their proverbial poverty. You can hardly see a single cabin without being howled at by half a dozen hounds, and I have now become so well educated in guessing the wealth of a mountaineer, that I can fix his condition by ascertaining the number of his dogs. A rich man seldom has more than one dog, while a very poor man will keep from ten to a dozen. And this remark with regard to dogs, strange as it may seem, is equally applicable to the children of the mountaineers. The poorest man, without exception, whom I have seen in this region, lives in a log cabin with two rooms, and is the father of nineteen children, and the keeper of six hounds. (Lanman 1849, 84-85)

Lanman, like many other observers, misunderstood the local economy, overlooked the importance of herding, and seemed oblivious to the existence of prosperous valley farmers. In fact, subsistence farmers and tenants in the mountains were very similar to small farmers found throughout the non-plantation South before the Civil War (Owsley, 90-123). The small group of prosperous, market-oriented farmers who hired laborers and occasionally owned slaves also had their counterparts across the rural South.

This recent research presents a more complex picture of mountain society, one which challenges long-accepted generalities and points the way to more fruitful paths for research. It also makes it much more difficult to generalize about the mountains. Finally, this recent research suggests that students of the region's history searching for an understanding of the "uniqueness" of the southern mountains might not find definitive answers in the antebellum period.

Works Cited

Blethen, H. Tyler and Curtis W. Wood, Jr. 1987. "The Pioneer Experience to 1851." ed. Max R. Williams. *The History of Jackson County.* Sylva, North Carolina: Jackson County Historical Society.

———. "James Patton: Adventures of a Frontier Merchant." ed. Robert Mitchell. *The Appalachian Frontier*. Forthcoming.

Bode, Frederick A. and Donald E. Gunter. 1986. *Farm Tenancy and the Census in Antebellum Georgia*. Athens: University of Georgia Press.

Dunn, Durwood. 1988. *Cades Cove: The Life and Death of a Southern Appalachian Community 1818-1937*. Knoxville: University of Tennessee Press.

Dykeman, Wilma. 1955. *The French Broad*. Knoxville: University of Tennessee Press.

Earle, Carville and Ronald Hoffman. 1977. "The Urban South: The First Two Centuries." ed. Blaine A. Brownell and David R. Goldfield. *The City in Southern History: The Growth of Urban Civilization in the South*. New York: Associated Faculty Press.

Hsiung, David C. "The Population Distribution of Washington County, Tennessee, 1790-1845: An Appalachian Stereotype Examined," 5-6

———. 1989. "How Isolated was Appalachia? Upper East Tennessee, 1780-1885." *Appalachian Journal* 16: 1989, 336-49.

Inscoe, John. 1989. *Mountain Masters, Slavery, and the Sectional Crisis in Western North Carolina*. Knoxville: University of Tennessee Press.

Jordan, Terry G. and Matti Kaups. 1989. *The American Backwoods Frontier: An Ethnic and Ecological Interpretation.*. Baltimore: Johns Hopkins Press.

Kniffen, Fred. 1965. "Folk Housing, Key to Diffusion." *Annals of the Associatio of American Geographers* 55.

Kniffen, Fred and Henry Glassie. 1966. *Building in Wood in the Eastern United States, A Time-Place Perspective.*. New York: American Geographical Society.

Lanman, Charles. 1849. *Letters from the Allegheny Mountains.*. New York: G. P. Putnam.

Lemon, James T. 1972. *The Best Poor Man's Country: A Geographical Study of Early Southeastern Pennsylvania*. Baltimore: Johns Hopkins Press.

McKinney, Gordon B. "Subsistence Economy and Community in Western North Carolina, 1860-1865," unpublished paper.

Mitchell, Robert D. 1977. *Commercialism and Frontier: Perspectives on the Early Shenandoah Valley*. Charlottesville: University Press of Virginia.

———. 1983. "American Origins and Regional Institutions: the 17th Century Chesapeake." *Annals of the Association of American Geographers* 73: 1983.

Mitchell, Robert and Milton Newton. 1988. "The Appalachian Frontier: Views from the East and the Southwest." *Historical Geography Research Series* 21: 20.

Newton, Milton. 1974. "Cultural Preadaptation and the Upland South." *Geoscience and Man* 5: 1974.

Owsley, Frank. 1949. *Plain Folk of the Old South*. Baton Rouge: Louisiana State University Press.

Paludan, Philip. 1985. *Victims: A True Story of the Civil War*. Knoxville: University of Tennessee Press.

Reid, Joseph D., Jr. 1976. "Antebellum Southern Rental Contracts," *Explorations in Economic History* 13: 69-83.

Turner, Fredrick Jackson. 1920. *The Frontier in American History*. Melbourne, Florida: Robert E. Krieger Publishing.

Waller, Altina L. 1988. *Feud: The Hatfields, McCoys, and Social Change in Appalachia, 1860-1900*. Chapel Hill: University of North Carolina Press.

Wood, Andy J. "Autobiography of Andy J. Wood." Small Ms. 80-38. Special Collections, Hunter Library, Western Carolina University.

H. Tyler Blethen is Director and Curtis W. Wood is Senior Research Associate at the Mountain Heritage Center. Both are Professors of History at Western Carolina University.

The Enduring Legacy of the "Southern Rebellion": West Virginia's Well-Being

David B. White

Conventional history and mainstream thought perpetuate the theme that the state of West Virginia was born in the Civil War out of the overwhelming pro-Unionist sympathies of the entire population of present-day West Virginia.

To be sure, there had existed in the Old Dominion sectionalist conflict between the more mountainous regions of the state and the lowland and tidewater areas. But the sectionalism conflict in antebellum Virginia had changed from the 1820s to the early 1860s. By the 1860s only the extreme Trans-Allegheny Northwest was at odds with Richmond's influence. Political reforms such as tax relief, voting rights and representation issues, and large appropriations for internal improvements had moved the Shenandoah Valley and Southwest Virginia areas closer to the Richmond orbit. Further, the geographic presence of the Allegheny mountains, and the commercial and industrial ties of the Northwest to Ohio and Pennsylvania (by the B & O Railroad and canal traffic) made that section of Old Virginia more northern than southern in influence. In short, the internal struggle in Old Virginia between the Trans-Allegheny Northwest and the rest of the State reflected the national struggle between the agrarian, state rights South and the industrialized, federalist North (Curry 1964).

Few areas of the nation in the late nineteenth century more typified Jeffersonian society than did the agriculture-based southern Appalachians of which present day southwestern and southeastern West

Virginia are a part. Self-sufficiency dominated, and agrarian versus mercantile or manufacturing concerns predominated. While the country was being transformed by urbanization and industrialization the southern mountains were relatively untouched:

> Throughout most of the nineteenth century there was little to attract capitalist development in Appalachia. The region's natural wealth of timber, coal, and other mineral resources was remote and inaccessible to the mercantile centers of the South and Northeast. . . . Only as the national economy entered a new stage of capitalist expansion in the years following the Civil War would the natural wealth of Appalachia attract outside capital. The sudden imposition of industrial capitalism at that time would bring dramatic changes to this rural area. By the third decade of the twentieth century, the Jeffersonian dream in Appalachia would become a nightmare of exploitation, corruption, and social tragedy. The Southern Mountains would remain a predominantly rural area, but changes in land ownership, economy, and the political system would leave the region's people dependent, impoverished, and powerless within a new and alien social order. (Eller 1979, 84)

The story of the military and political intrigue indicating how this occurred in West Virginia is both fascinating and tragic.

A closer look at the political scene in the 1860s reveals a much different pattern of sympathies than that which current historical myth holds. Of the fifty counties which comprise present-day West Virginia, Unionism was confined largely to twenty-four relatively populated and industrialized Northwestern counties in geographic proximity to the Ohio River, the Pennsylvania border, and the B & O Railroad. However, at least twenty-four other counties representing two-thirds of the total area in the future state were unquestionably Confederate in outlook and voted for secession in 1861 (Curry). [see Map, page 51]

When the Virginia legislature voted with the remainder of the Confederacy for secession, mass meetings in Northern Virginia resulted in a convention which was held in Wheeling on 11 June 1861. The agenda of the meeting concerned the dismemberment of Northwest Virginia toward the goal of separate statehood. The obstacle to this plan was Article IV, Section 3, of the U.S. Constitution which dictates the consent of the legislature to form a new state from an existing one. Of course, the Richmond government would not consent to such a proposal so a "restored" government of Virginia was formed which President Lincoln recognized as the "de jure" government of Virginia. "A rump legislature, theoretically representing the whole state but in practice representing only the northwestern counties, thereupon elected two U.S. Senators from Virginia, who were seated by the Senate on 13 July 1861. Three Congressmen from Western Virginia also took their seats in the House" (McPherson 1988, 298).

One of those elected to the U.S. Senate was John S. Carlile from Harrison County. Carlile's initial advocacy of statehood and his subsequent opposition are reflective of the mixed sentiments of the period, and also personify the growing distrust with which many moderate and conservative Republicans viewed the Radical Republicans as the war progressed (Curry; Davis 1970).

Carlile had instigated the meeting in Wheeling for separate statehood upon his return from the secession vote in April 1861. Carlile and others who led the statehood movement were "Unionists," meaning they wanted to preserve the Union *as it was* and they appeared to be motivated more by "patriotism" and the concern of "self-murder" rather than abolitionist sentiment.

However, secessionists initially recognized in Carlile a dangerous enemy, and he was vilified by Richmond editorials and states rights advocates (Davis). But by July 1862, Carlile was to become the primary obstructionist in the statehood political process. Understanding Carlile's change of heart is the key to understanding states rights and secessionist sympathies in general, and the bizarre beginning of West Virginia in particular.

> Carlile's actions must be interpreted—indeed can only be understood—in terms of Copperhead opposition to Radicalism and Lincoln's conduct of the war.... Carlile, as did all West Virginia Conservatives, consistently called for a vigorous prosecution of the war to suppress rebellion; but he was unwavering in his condemnation of "abolitionists fanaticism," whether in the form of the Emancipation Proclamation, suspension of the writ of habeas corpus, violations of freedom of the press, arbitrary arrests, or the Willey Amendment [a gradual emancipation provision of the West Virginia Constitution]. (Curry, 139)

In addition to the highly irregular course of action creating a "de jure" government and this political infighting, one must put the occurrences of the day in proper perspective. All of these events were taking place as a Union Army invaded Western Virginia. Three days following Virginia's formal secession from the Union, Major General George B. McClellan, Commander of the Department of the Army of the Ohio, invaded Western Virginia. The Union forces, far superior in number and

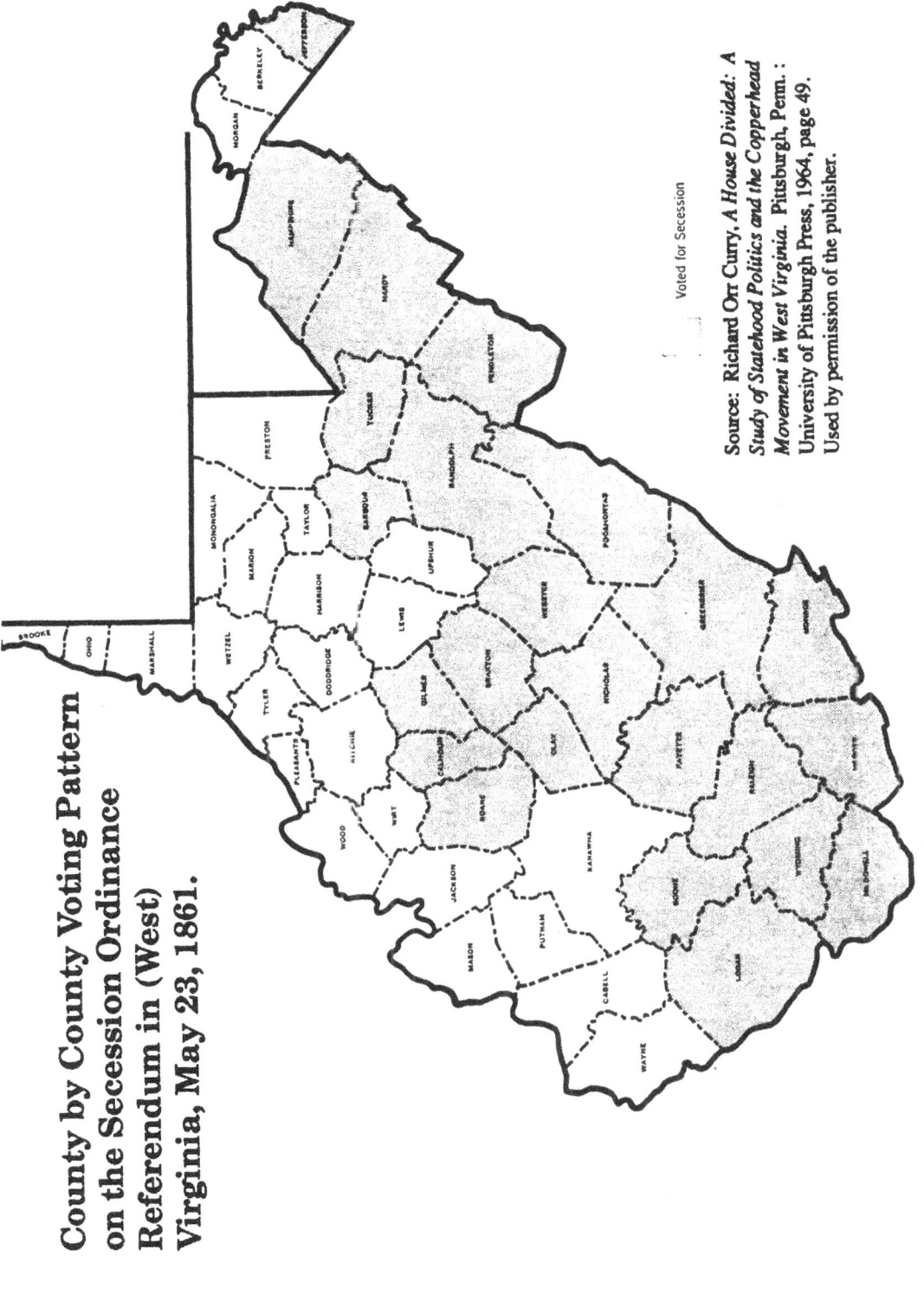

County by County Voting Pattern on the Secession Ordinance Referendum in (West) Virginia, May 23, 1861.

Source: Richard Orr Curry, *A House Divided: A Study of Statehood Politics and the Copperhead Movement in West Virginia.* Pittsburgh, Penn.: University of Pittsburgh Press, 1964, page 49. Used by permission of the publisher.

resources defeated a much smaller ill-equipped Confederate force (Catton 1961;1980; Curry; McPherson).

"This achievement was crucial to the success of the new state movement; without the presence of victorious Northern troops, the state of West Virginia could not have been born" (McPherson, 299). Or more succinctly stated by Curry, "without military occupation the reorganized government of Virginia could not have functioned effectively, and the statehood movement could not have succeeded" (7). The Union forces, portending events of the future, invaded western Virginia for strategic, as well as political reasons. The Baltimore and Ohio Railroad, the Ohio River, and natural resources were vital to Union victory (Catton 1961; Curry; McPherson).

Despite this invasion by overwhelming forces, the Confederate sympathies of much of the West Virginia population were to be painfully evident during and after the War. Indeed, during the war the military exchanges were transformed into fratricidal conflict and guerrilla war, with the reorganized "de jure" government never having effective control over more than half the counties in the state (Curry). Guerrilla war with neighbor against neighbor became the norm (Catton 1961; Smith 1927). West Virginia provided considerable numbers of troops to the Confederate cause as well.

Aided and abetted by the Lincoln administration, the clamor and political wrangling for separate statehood continued. Boundary disputes regarding what counties to be included dominated the statehood process with some factions calling for the inclusion of many southern sympathy counties to increase territory. Others balked at this option recognizing that their Unionist and industrialist interests would be subject to dominance from those opposed to these positions. Large state enthusiasts were essentially against dismemberment or had mixed feelings. Indicative that northwest Virginia was not fanatically Republican is the indisputable fact that the Republican Party polled less than 4 percent of the votes cast in the 1860 presidential election (Curry).

Carlile originally insisted that the boundaries of the new state be limited to counties which were predominantly Unionist. As noted, it appears, however, that he became increasingly disgusted by congressional interference and dictates of gradual emancipation (although slavery was virtually nonexistent in Trans-Allegheny Northwest Virginia) as a prerequisite for statehood admission. When the final senatorial vote came for statehood with the Willey Amendment intact, Carlile voted against it, but it passed. He previously had insisted on increasing the boundaries to include pro-Confederate counties. As had been concluded by Curry, Carlile and other "conservative Unionists in Northwestern Virginia became alarmed when the war for the preservation of the

Union took on the added purpose of a crusade for the destruction of slavery and the subjugation of the South" (108-109). Conservative Unionists like Carlile could not countenance this intrusion into home rule and would not vote for separate statehood unless it was on unconditional terms. Nevertheless with the process of statehood initiated, the "de jure" government in control, and the military occupation a *fait accompli*, West Virginia became a state on June 20, 1863. Lincoln reluctantly, but for pragmatic and expedient reasons, concurred (Curry).

As noted, the land and family were the dominant factors in pre-industrial West Virginia, particularly in those sections which had aligned themselves with the Confederacy. Homesteading, farming, and trapping on the land were the characteristics of life, but that changed precipitously beginning with West Virginia's new-found statehood and accelerated after the war had ceased. The stable, idyllic, Jeffersonian dream was challenged by the demands of industrialization and the discovery of rich timber and mineral deposits. Outsiders flocked to the hills for wealth. Indeed, "the 'discovery' of the resources of the region brought renewed attention to the question of ownership and title. Hundreds of ambitious speculators and agents for eastern industrial and financial interests combed the West Virginia hills surveying timber stands and mineral deposits. . . .By the turn of the century the land ownership configuration we see today was essentially in place—a configuration created for the severance of natural resources and wealth with minimal responsibility to the social, economic and physical ecology of the area" (Appalachian Land Ownership Task Force 1980, 4).

Ironically, the concerns viewed by conservative Unionists like John Carlile appear in retrospect to have been valid. Although apparently voting against their own economic self-interest and subjecting themselves to accusations of treason and disloyalty, they could not support the deal of increased capital investment for less home rule and increased radical Republican control (Curry).

Unconditional Unionists supported by Union troops prevented opposition groups from holding rallies and conventions, and continued these strategies through the imposition of loyalty oaths well after the war was over. Finally, in 1870, a coalition of Copperheads and ex-Confederates was able to give Conservatives a majority over Radical Republicans and Unionists (Curry; Foner 1988). But by this time the transition to industrialization was already in process.

The South in general was reduced to a conquered province without the services of its former antebellum leaders who were initially barred from politics. The country as a whole was prosperous but corrupt, depending on the largesse of opportune government agents and businessmen. In the South, economic recovery was impeded by vast destruction, the lack of leadership, and the presence of federal agents (Carman, Syrett and Wishy 1961, Vol I).

As the first southern state to abolish slavery, West Virginia in a sense represented the beginning of Reconstruction. Certainly its population configuration, including former secessionist counties, embodied the ingredients of what was to be widespread throughout the South (Foner 1988).

Almost every aspect of southern life was affected by the Reconstruction policies of the federal government. The course of Reconstruction was in large part determined by the outcome of the struggle between the Republican factions for the control of the nation's government. Conservatives led by Lincoln argued for presidentially-initiated moderation and forgiveness towards the South, while Radicals aligned with the growing industrial class wanted major congressionally-dictated political, economic, and social change—not without consideration of self-benefit.

> The abolitionists, who distrusted both the southern whites and the northern conservatives, had a powerful ally in the growing industrial class. The Civil War had stimulated the growth of industry and had driven planter-spokesman from Congress. If the former Confederates were now kept politically impotent, the way would be clear for the industrialists to push their schemes for transcontinental railroads, large-scale manufacturers, high tariffs, and the exploitation of the nations natural resources. (Carman et al., 719)

The war had precipitously increased the power of the federal government and had increased the riches of northeastern businessmen beyond anyone's dreams. Concurrent with this expansion however was the reality of exploitation and corruption. "With the elimination of the menace of disunion the American people increasingly devoted their energies to developing industry, exploiting the country's mineral deposits, expanding its transportation facilities, and building up its financial powers" (Carmen et. al.,699). With Lincoln's assassination and Andrew Johnson's unpopularity preventing reelection, General U.S. Grant was elected president, in effect legitimizing the industrialists' grip on the nation.

Much needed reforms were made in public education, tax laws, equal rights, and general public facilities, but the means employed often nullified the ends. And just as rapidly and as fervently as northerners had espoused reforms during the war, they became obsessed with the more practical reality of accumulating wealth. Output exceeded its pre-Civil War level manyfold, and the post-Civil War age gained the reputation of perhaps the most corrupt in the nation's history (Carman et al.; Foner; Smith). "The Grant Administration was distinctive for the incompetence of most of its officials and the uninhibited fashion in which it, in effect, turned over the North and South to the country's special interests" (Carmen et. al., 739).

The result was a business-run economy subsidized by government assistance, characterized by speculation, vast land acquisition and development, and general fraud—with the South being dominated by scalawags, carpetbaggers and radicals zealous in their vision of industrialization and progress at the southerner's expense. When reason, or accusation warranted it, the government used the ever-present military to impose it's will on former Confederate areas (Carman et al.; Foner) "The radicalism of the 1870s had lost most of the idealism that had been a distinguishing feature of the movement during the Civil War and in the years immediately following the conflict. . . .they increasingly used Reconstruction to promote the interests of northern businessmen and the Republican Party" (Carman et al., 742).

Whereas the original radical coalition had a reformer mystique, its successors were blatant spoils politicians who used Reconstruction to help themselves and their business associates. This mirrored the transformation of the Republican Party which had evolved from a militant reform movement to a front for business groups (Carman et al.; Smith 1984).

The North's victory, the subsequent subjugation of the South, and the concurrent Republican stranglehold on American industrial and political events enabled, indeed ensured, the transition from a predominantly agrarian society to one characterized as industrial capitalism. Even when the Republican Party began to lose its monolithic power because of Democratic gains and the inevitable re-establishment of southern influence, the control by industrial capitalists and northeastern business interests was unmistakably complete.

The consummation of this process appears to have been the Compromise of 1876 and the subsequent election of Rutherford B. Hayes as President of the United States. "The Compromise of 1876, engineered by old Southern conservatives and determined Southern industrialists in league with Northern bankers, brought the railroads, and industry into the region to take advantages of widespread unemployment and abundant cotton, coal and timber" (Adams 1972, 503).

The Compromise of 1876, which ended Reconstruction and any potential for positive change, was brought about by the disputed election between Rutherford B. Hayes (a Republican) and Samuel J. Tilden (a Democrat) and was ultimately settled by the support of southern Democrats who wanted an end to federal interference in local political affairs, but wanted continued business growth. With Hayes' election, the old planter and landed classes (called Bourbons) established the reign over southern politics with control by northern capitalists who wanted to exploit the region's resources (Carman et al.).

The impact of these events had a profound influence on the development or rather underdevelopment of West Virginia. From 1880 to 1930, the character of the West Virginia economy changed drastically because of the major growth in coal and other resource industries, as well as growth in manufacturing. This transformation was centered in coal counties and resulted in forceful control of the workforce rather than in increased benefits to the populace. The idyllic, independent agrarian life was transformed to one analogous to medieval serfdom with forced labor, company towns, company housing, company stores, company services, and, of course, company police/Pinkertons controlling management-labor relations. The coal industry was linked to the monopolistic sectors of the national economy and by extension the mining of coal was the appendage of the company store. Independent entrepreneurs were discouraged and prohibited, unions were forbidden, and the coal industry usurped total control of community life, which, in effect, stifled economic diversification and resulted in repression. The courts and the government were willing accomplices as well (Simon 1978; 1981).

In essence, the process of industrialization in West Virginia brought on by the Civil War and the Compromise of 1876 emulated the Reconstruction practices in the South in general. Self-sustained growth and economic diversification were blocked by the selfish motives of industrial capitalists. The social relations they perpetuated actually hampered positive growth which was, ironically, the rallying cry of those who sought an industrialized nation. "The coal industry, rather than leading the development of West Virginia by attracting other kinds of economic activity, constrained development by limiting the number of alternative profitable investment outlets" (Simon 1981, 178).

There was no internal market to generate growth other than in the northwest part of the state (the original Unionist stronghold) and this local capital initiated much development, "but it was inevitable that in the underdeveloped West Virginia economy in 1880 resources would be developed by absentee owners for export. West Virginia had lucrative natural deposits of coal, lumber, oil, and gas.... In the southern part of the state, which had remained agricultural, almost the entire initial investment had come from outside capital" (Simon 1981, 180-181). From 1860 to 1900, 50 to 90 percent of West Virginia's coal production was shipped out of state (Williams 1976).

Unrestrained absentee ownership and capitalism generated by the profit motive with minimal concern for the social, political, and economic consequences to the local populace characterized West Virginia's initial development and has had a profound impact since. The colonial political economy which was sparked in 1880, has left an indelible mark on the state. New social relationships based on exploitation versus familial patterns precipitated the violence and labor disputes which have characterized the state's history (Amsden and Brier 1977; Lee 1969; McKinney 1977; Wheeler 1976). Former farms were disrupted, and timber and coal's irresponsible extraction rendered the watersheds unstable, prone to flooding, and subject to mud slides—strip mining has only exacerbated the damage (Appalachian Alliance 1982; Munn 1975). Within a thirty-year period (by the 1920s) the original forests were almost completely depleted (Clarkson). The litany of abuses and multicausal and synergistic effects are tragic, and have been thoroughly reviewed elsewhere, (Simon 1978; 1981; White 1982; 1987) but the Appalachian Land Ownership Task Force which documented land ownership patterns in Appalachia (and West Virginia) and analyzed their impact on local communities most poignantly encapsulates the dire reality of what is West Virginia:

> West Virginia is at the same time one of the richest and poorest states in the nation. By the late 1880s the fate of independent and self-sufficient mountain settlers was altered forever by the discovery of vast natural resources wealth, especially minerals. Since that time the state's timber, minerals, water resources, and natural beauty have been bought and controlled by interests with little or no accountability for the ongoing life of the region. This tremendous concentration of absentee land ownership is the key to understanding the paradox of severe social and economic disadvantage amidst almost limitless natural resources wealth .... Well over half of the land covered by the study is owned and thus controlled by interests other than local residents. Over 50 percent of the surface of the [surveyed] sample counties (2,315,419 acres) and almost 75 percent of the minerals (3,273,242 acres) are large holdings owned primarily by absentee and corporate interests.... In the sample counties at least 30 percent of the surface acreage and 55 percent of the minerals are owned by corporations; 32 percent of the surface and 54 percent of the minerals are owned by interests from outside the respective counties; 27 percent of the surface and 41 percent of the minerals are owned by interests outside of the state of West Virginia. The 1,091,234 acres of absentee corporate surface is taxed at an average of $1.67 an acre and the 2,144,456 acres of absentee corporate minerals is taxed at an average of $1.40 an

acre. . . . The state continues to suffer from grossly inadequate housing, above average unemployment, severe ecological disruption, below average per capita income, bloated welfare rolls, and serious deficiencies in health, transportation, and educational services. At the same time, the land and its wealth have been and continue to be acquired by interests more and more removed from any responsibility for the fate of those who live on or near these holding." (Appalachian Land Ownership Task Force 1980, 1-2)

Such is West Virginia, a state born out of war and indelibly scarred ever since. There is no way of knowing whether or not West Virginia would have fared better had it retained its affiliation with Old Virginia. Virginia, like all southern states, suffered its share of indignation and subjugation after the Great Rebellion, but one must wonder whether the highly unique beginning of West Virginia's statehood initiated a process of colonial underdevelopment which may be irreversible. Given the facts, Henry A. Wise (former governor of Virginia) appears to have been correct when he declared "West Virginia was the bastard child of a political rape" (Curry, 136).

Works Cited

Adams, Frank. 1972. "Highlander Folk School: Getting Information, Going Back and Teaching It." *Harvard Educational Review* 42 (4): 497-520.

Amsden, Jon and Stephen Brier. 1977. "Coal Miners on Strike: The Transformation of Strike Demands and the Formation of a National Union." *Journal of Interdisciplinary History* 7 (Spring): 583-616.

Appalachian Land Ownership Task Force. 1980. *Appalachian Land Ownership Study: Vol. II, West Virginia*. Boone, North Carolina: Appalachian State University and New Market, Tennessee: Highlander Research and Education Center.

Appalachian Alliance. 1982. *Appalachia In the Eighties: A Time for Action*. New Market, Tennessee: Appalachian Alliance.

Carman, Harry J., , Harold C. Syrett, and Bernard W. Wishy. 1961. *History of the American People Vol. I & II*. New York: Alfred A. Knopf.

Catton, Bruce. 1961. *The Coming Fury: The Centennial History of the Civil War Vol. 1*. New York: Washington Square Press.

———. 1980. *The Civil War*. New York: The Fairfax Press.

Clarkson, Roy B. 1964. *Tumult on the Mountains*. Parsons, West Virginia: McClain Publishing Co.

Curry, Richard O. 1964. *A House Divided: A Study of Statehood Politics and the Copperhead Movement in West Virginia*. Pittsburgh: University of Pittsburgh Press.

Davis, Dorothy. 1970. *History of Harrison County West Virginia*. Parsons, West Virginia: McClain Printing Co.

Eller, Ronald. D. 1979. "Land and Family: An Historical View of Preindustrial Appalachia." *Appalachian Journal* 6 (Winter): 83-109.

Foner, Eric. 1988. *Reconstruction: America's Unfinished Revolution (1863-1977)*. New York: Harper and Row Publishers.

Lee, Howard B. 1969. *Bloodletting in Appalachia*. Morgantown, West Virginia: West Virginia University Press.

McKinney, Gordon. 1977. "Industrialization and Violence." in J.W. Williamson, ed. *An Appalachian Symposium*. Boone, North Carolina: Appalachian State University Press.

McPherson, James M. 1988. *Battle Cry of Freedom: The Civil War Era*. New York: Oxford University Press.

Munn, Robert F. 1975. "The Development of Strip Mining in Southern Appalachia." *Appalachia Journal* 3 (Autumn): 87-93.

Simon, Richard M. 1978. *The Development of Underdevelopment: The Coal Industry and its Effect on the West Virginia Economy, 1880-1930*. University of Pittsburgh, Unpublished Ph.D. Dissertation.

———. 1981. "Uneven Development and the Case of West Virginia: Going Beyond the Colonialism Model." *Appalachian Journal* 8 (Spring): 165-186.

Smith, Edward C. 1927. *The Borderland in the Civil War*. New York: The MacMillan Co.

Smith, Gene. 1984. *Lee and Grant: A Dual Biography*. New York: McGraw-Hill, Inc.

Wheeler, Hoyt N. 1976. "Mountaineer Mine Wars: An Analysis of the West Virginia Mine Wars of 1912-1913 and 1920-1921." *Business History Review* 50 (Spring): 69-91.

White, David. 1982. *A Social Epidemiological Analysis of Central Appalachian Economic Distress*. University of Pittsburgh: Unpublished Ph.D. dissertation.

———. 1987. "A Social Epidemiological Model of Central Appalachia." *Arete* 12 (Summer): 47-66.

Williams, John A. 1976. *West Virginia and the Captains of Industry*. Morgantown, West Virginia: West Virginia University Press.

David B. White is the Director of Health Administration in the Department of Education and Health Services at Saint Joseph's University, Philadelphia, Pennsylvania.

Forgotten Sisters: Mountain Women in the South

Milton Ready

As a discipline, women's history seems to construct a great many models and cults of women who never existed. Along with critical biographies and studies of clubs and social movements, models appear as a genre, a way of explaining women's roles to a larger public. A cursory reading of bibliographies in the field, for example, shows biographies of Eleanor Roosevelt, Margaret Sanger, Mother Jones, the Grimke sisters from South Carolina; Jane Addams studies of social settlements, the suffrage movement; and women in various reform movements from abolitionism to the ERA.[1] Women who are not as outstanding as, say, Lydia Maria Child or Harriet Beecher Stowe, disappear into an antebellum model similar to that portrayed by Barbara Welter. They are pious, pure, submissive, and domestic (Welter 1966, 151-74).

Unmodified models and stereotypes typically break down, telling us, as they do, of a much more complex story. In Anne Firor Scott, *The Southern Lady: From Pedestal to Politics, 1830-1930*, the figure that emerges is that of Scarlett O'Hara, the perpetually pouting adolescent belle who, transformed by the anvil of the Civil War, re-emerges as a southern matriarch, cruel and self-centered, as ambitious as any man (Scott 1970, 3-47). Such descriptions can never satisfy, of course, nor is that their intention. Wrenched out of history, Scott's southern lady reflects only one out of an immense variety of attitudes about the southern woman. Still, none of the interpretations reflect the role of Appalachian women in southern history.

Appalachian women in the nineteenth century seldom affected the depiction of southern women. Indeed, the metaphor of the changing southern women, from the belle of the antebellum period to the total woman of the Sun Belt era, stands apart from the experience of mountain women. They are, as Bill Cosby once said of the place of blacks in American history, lost, strayed, perhaps forgotten sisters of the South, even as stereotypes.

The most outstanding feature of Appalachian women in the nineteenth century is the fact that we know so little about them. While southern women in general might have kept diaries, overseen slaves, joined clubs and groups, written novels, gone to school, traveled, and even infrequently appeared in political and social events, their Appalachian sisters toiled in obscurity. Their sphere almost entirely was private, usually consisting of family, home, and church. What information is available frequently is secondary, tacit, understood only within the context of songs and ballads, folktales and stories, of "Grandma lore," and from males who talked about "womenfolk" and, at a later time interviewed them as outsiders interested in special aspects of their lives. The outline of the Appalachian women that emerges depicts still another model of the "southern lady" of the nineteenth century, one almost entirely removed from the influence of Anne Scott's portrayal.

Almost all accounts of men and women in the nineteenth century assume that they worked hard, carving out homesteads and farms in the wilderness, typically laboring from sun-up to sunset on an endless array of tasks and chores. Yet, a special case and a unique claim needs to be established for mountain women. Almost all accounts of the period—songs, stories, letters, and interviews—point to perpetual labor for women. Talking about the late 1800s, a Grandma Brown from Kentucky remembered that throughout her life, "The drudgery was unending, year in and year out" (Brown 1951, 284). Vesta Brown, a Tennessee woman, thought that when she married, "I wouldn't have to work as hard as I did at home, but I hadn't come down in the valley . . . two days before I knew I had more work to do than ever" (Winter 1965, 31). In James Still's *River of Earth*, a twelve-year-old girl soon learned that she must get up early in the morning, help her mother with breakfast and chores, make the beds, labor in the garden, help with the laundry and meal preparation, and work in the fields if another hand was needed, all while "the son in the family could eat when he wanted, [and] sleep as late as he liked unless there was a specific chore he had been asked to do" (Farr 1976, 58).

A typical mountain woman of the 1880s put in a sixteen-to-eighteen-hour day, working, cleaning, spinning, sewing, canning, washing, milking, hoeing, and, at dusk, overseeing children who brought in the cows, lit the kerosene lamps, and did the supper dishes. Almost all nineteenth-century mountain women had in common a way of life covered by one word—toil—and symbolized by the constant tools of her sphere—the needle, ladle, and hoe. They were pictured as overworked, over-burdened, always pregnant, always surrounded by children, with a babe in their arms, and a tired body and weathered face. Often they were lonely, generally unappreciated, and yearned for a shelter where there would be no work. Their refuge lay in church, in their fellow sisters who shared the same labors, and in the hymns they sang as they went about their endless tasks. A minister who promised "peace, rest, and eternal sleep" struck a resonant chord deep in the hearts of mountain women. The chorus of an old hymn reveals the hidden loneliness and despair in the lives of mountain women:

> Rest, sweet rest, and joy and gladness,
>   Comes when toil, when toil is o'er.
> Sweetest resting comes when toil is o'er,
>   'twill be joy and rest eternal
> On the other shore.

The words of the well-known song, "Sourwood Mountain," explain in part a mountain man's attitude toward women:

> Old Man, Old Man, I want your daughter
> Hey, didyum, didyum dum day
> To bake me bread and carry me water
> Hey, didyum, didyum dum day.

To him, women were helpmates and contributors, frequently more valuable than oxen and horses, but seldom esteemed more than kinfolk and hound dogs. When Alpha Baldridge, the mother in *River of Earth*, pleaded with her husband, Brack, to turn out his two worthless cousins, Harl and Tibb Logan, and his great-uncle Samp Baldridge, because "It's all we can do to keep bread in the children's mouths. . . . Even if they are your blood kin, we can't feed them much longer." Noting that they were men down on their luck, Brack replied, "I can't turn my kin out." In desperation, Alpha moved her furniture and children into the smokehouse, a place too small to accommodate any but her family, and burned the house down (Farr 1976, 57). In novels and interviews by local-colorists, mountain men frequently described their dogs in lyrical terms, almost as if they were in love with them, and their women as if they were dumb creatures prized mainly for what they could produce in the way of sons and daughters, food, clothing, and crops. In this fashion, mountain men used up their lands and women with equal neglect and thoughtlessness.

If it is valid to assert that both men and women, whether in the southern piedmont or mountains, labored long hours at arduous tasks, it is also important to note that mountain women, unlike their sisters in the lower south and their menfolk within their own culture, had little existence outside their work. Almost all accounts of Appalachian women chronicle their labor if they are young, or, if they're very old, their roles as grandmothers, as cultural agents, storytellers, and folklorists. They can be teachers but not schoolteachers, active in the church but not missionaries, and they are allowed to have opinions only on a small range of subjects—the weather, folk cures and remedies, woodlore, having children but not childrearing, family but not individual morality, local preachers, and food processing. Unlike the southern belle, the mountain women cannot be pretty, soft, sensuous, or sexually alluring, yet, by their own testimony, they enjoyed sex to such a degree that Scarlett would faint at the mention of their bawdy stories, and mountain men raged at their "Jezebel ways" and grabbed their guns.

While mountain men assembled after a meal to swap politics, stories, and drinks, women sometimes gathered to exchange news, talk about the family, and increase their knowledge of quilting, cooking, and the Bible. They also shared trashy talk. Frequently, the dirtiest old ladies were grandmothers. When, as Rayna Green observed, her grandmother stepped out of the bedroom and her sister commented that the hair on her "private parts" was thinning, granny chuckled that "grass don't grow on a race track," especially after seventeen children (Green 1977, 31). When arguing over whether older mountain men could satisfy younger women, Moms Mabley, a well-known black comedienne from Western North Carolina, maintained that, "Ain't nothing no old man can do for me 'cept bring me a message from a young man." Countless mountain mothers have warned their daughters that before they married "any ol' hairy-legged boy, be sure to look carefully at his genes" (31, 33). For women, bawdy stories served as sex education, as *double entendres* about life, as entertainment, as social criticism, and as a form of rebellion against a male-dominated society.

Early murder ballads exhibited many of the same functions. Most had women as their victims, and were sung by women, "perhaps because the songs spoke of their feelings and needs" (Smith 1978, 5). Jealousy, unfaithfulness, and unrequited romantic love dominated the themes of murder ballads. In "Tom Dooley," "Jellon Grams," and "Lula Viers," punishment, always death, comes from someone close to the victim—a family member, an ex-lover or husband, but always a male.

While it is easy to speculate that murder ballads were part of the pattern of a patriarchal society that tended to chastise women who spoke out, rebelled, ran away, and in general threatened traditional roles: they also kept alive the idea that women could disrupt society, influence men's actions, and in this fashion become folk heroes and models. When women sang ballads to each other, the message might also be to emphasize men's failures, boasts, and inadequacies, their "comeuppance for lack of comeuppance," as one woman put it.

Murder ballads give evidence of another differentiative aspect of life for most nineteenth-century mountain women—physical abuse. While it seems obvious that women in general have suffered abuse throughout the centuries, and that southern women, whether plantation belles or town prostitutes, also endured injury and assault, the mistreatment of mountain women, even in consideration of harsh frontier life and primitive living conditions, seems inappropriate, even disproportionate to their sisters elsewhere. A great many ballads such as "Tom Dooley," "Lula Viers," and "Pearl Bryant" originated in the fact that men murdered women, usually by stabbing or drowning, and, with the exception of "Tom Dooley," perhaps the most popular ballad outside the region, they go unpunished. Given the random violence of the region—family feuds and fights—it is not unlikely that women also suffered mistreatment as well. A northern Alabama farmer echoed a sentiment toward abusing women common not only to the mountains but to the South as a whole. "A woman's like a dumb animal, like a cow or a bitch dog. You got to frail them with a stick now and then to make 'em look up to you" (Fallow 1978, 49). And frail they did, with fists, sticks, whips, "tools common to their gender," in the words of an old mountain song.

Perhaps because of the unending toil and physical abuse, the rugged living conditions of mountain life, and the older tradition of arranged marriages, the apprehension, the very notion of romantic love seems inappropriate to any model of Appalachian women. For them, there were no Rhett Butlers and Robert E. Lees, no cavaliers and gentlemen, only country boys and hillbillies, men who were perpetual adolescents, immature in their feelings toward themselves and their women, failures whenever they had to deal with the outside world. Any researcher into the lives of early mountain women would be struck by the absence of any strongly romantic feelings toward men in any of the literature. From Annie Fallows Johnston to Ida Belle Marcum to Grandma Templeton Jones, mountain women talked about everything—religion, gardening, corn husk dolls, education, floods, canning, pie parties—except their men.[2] When husbands and fathers were mentioned, it was usually a commonplace comment like "We married" or "He died." Even if many of the biases inherent in any selection process are taken into account, i.e., the interviewer is a male, many questions are predictive and closed in terms of responses, mountain women are reluctant to talk about menfolk, especially if it's personal; still, the absence of emphatic, strong, spontaneous feelings toward men, even if coded in expressions like "He was a good man," seems extraordinary. While researching dialects in Cumberland County, Kentucky, Linda White found that, far from expressing romantic, even positive feelings, love, as a term, had a casual, unemotional, even negative meaning. Used mostly by women throughout southeastern Kentucky, eastern Tennessee, and western North Carolina, the term would be used to persuade, to command indirectly, as in "Do you love pickle-beans?" or "I'd love to be able to buy a new dress," or "Wouldn't you love to stay for dinner?" They don't really mean it.

Instead, nineteenth-century Appalachian women frequently found positive, loving relationships with other women, their family, their children, and their religion. On weaving days each week, women met to visit, exchange information and personal news, and, of course, enthusiastically talk and relate to each other. Visits—to family, the ill, and friends—were common, as were networks of nurses and health-care givers. Still, religion provided mountain women one of their strongest emotional outlets. At church they could "love Jesus" and be loved for it, sing and cry and clasp hands, hug and kiss each other along with anyone else, shriek for joy and weep with bliss—all with society's approval and blessing, and all on a day when little work was expected. In terms of religious intensity, but certainly not piety, mountain women appeared more emotional and less solemn or doctrinal than their lowland sisters.

Descriptions of mountain women in the nineteenth century do not disclose a southern lady like Anne Scott's. While lowland women worked hard, their sisters in the mountains labored grimly at endless tasks and chores without the help of slaves or servants or of prospects of a better life. A southern belle might be frail and delicate, but such adjectives are unthinkable for mountain women. Both sisters were domestic, presiding over a complicated household and plantation, but in the mountains the lack of domestic skills imperiled the family and community itself. Survival meant ingenuity, from growing and processing food to digging for roots in the woods. While both women were submissive in a male-dominated, patriarchal society, mountain women had almost no other significant authority figures in their lives except husbands and fathers. Purity, a virtue for southern women before and after the Civil War, had little value in the mountains. Expressions such as "planting the seed before building the fence" and "woods colt" to describe illegitimate children point to another system of values for the mountains.

Mountain women of the nineteenth century do not seem to fit the model of the southern lady depicted by such writers as Anne Firor Scott and Jean Friedman. Indeed, many of the various interpretations that could be constructed from the model because of changing conditions of race, class, and geography also seem inappropriate. What emerges, or more properly, re-emerges from composite depictions is still another model, that of Anna Maria Reeves Jarvis, a nineteenth-century West Virginia woman who became the inspiration for Mother's Day (Tyler-McGraw 1977, 28-34). The expression "but after all was she not a masterpiece as a mother and gentlewoman," working hard all her life for others, singing, sewing and quilting, suffering and redeeming all women, all society by her endless labor and love, an ideal mother and grandmother, seems a popular, yet still inaccurate description of the nineteenth-century Appalachian woman. Whether depicted as a southern lady, albeit a crude one, or as an ideal Victorian grandmother, an example for mothers everywhere, whether real or mythical, models or stereotypes, Appalachian women still do not have their story told. They remain forgotten sisters in the South.

Works Cited

Brown, Harriet. 1951. "Grandmother Brown's Move to Iowa." *The Heritage of America*. Henry Steele Commanger, et al. Boston.

Fallow, George. 1978. "A Woman's Like a Dumb Animal." *Such As Us: Southern Voices of the Times*. Chapel Hill: University of North Carolina Press.

Farr, Sidney S. 1976. "The Appalachian Woman as Portrayed by James Still in *River of Earth* ." *Appalachian Heritage* 4 (Spring): 58, 57.

Green, Rayna. 1977. "Magnolias Grow in Dirt." *Southern Exposure* 4 (Winter): 31,33.

Scott, Anne Firor. 1970. *The Southern Lady: From Pedestal to Politics, 1830-1930*. Chicago: The University of Chicago Press.

Smith, Betty to Rus Dowda. 1978 April 11. In Rus Dowda " 'He Took Her By Her Golden Curls and Throwed Her Round and Round,' Appalachian Women in the Nineteenth Century." Manuscript, Berea College.

Tyler-McGraw, Marie. 1977. "But After All Was She Not a Masterpiece as a Mother and Gentlewoman." *Goldenseal* 3 (October-December): 28-34.

Welter, Barbara. 1966. "The Cult of True Womanhood, 1820-1860." *American Quarterly* 18 (Summer): 151-74.

Winter, Oakley. 1965. "Vesta, A 'Modern Woman'." *Mountain Life and Work* 40 (Winter): 31.

Milton Ready is Professor of History at the University of North Carolina at Asheville.

Historical and Theoretical Perspectives on Appalachia's Economic Dependency

Paul Salstrom

The roots of Appalachia's economic dependency go back two centuries before the New Deal of the 1930s—back to the region's first white settlers in the 1730s. As Robert D. Mitchell mentions in *Commercialism and Frontier*, Appalachia's export-oriented production has been dependent on outside markets, and on outside investment money, from its first inception in the Shenandoah Valley of the 1730s (Mitchell 1977, 8, 153-55, 228-29, 236-37).

No such dependence, of course, characterized production within the region for use within the region. But we should bear in mind that neither family self-sufficiency, local self-sufficiency, nor regional self-sufficiency were common ideals among early settlers. It is only in hindsight—only since the 1930s re-thinking of neo-classical economics—that export-oriented development has been seen as helping to impoverish many of the world's exporters.[1]

No, it was not a commitment to avoid a "staples export" syndrome that characterized the economic values of Appalachia's early settlers, but rather a commitment to achieve what was called a "competency"—which meant enough productive property to allow one's family to maintain a comfortable living standard however that might be maintained. If production for export out of the region did help to sustain a competency (through the money or the in-kind payments received in exchange) then nothing in most pioneers' economic values prescribed the least hesitation to produce for export out of the region.[2]

And indeed, under preindustrial conditions (prior, that is, to industrialization anywhere in the United States), dependence on outside markets, and even on outside financing, was not likely to cause impoverishment. But after industrialization elsewhere in the U.S. led to far higher productivity outside Appalachia than within Appalachia in turning out many of the products consumed inside Appalachia, then what followed was "unequal exchange." What is unequal in "unequal exchange" is the amount of time and work required to produce the same unit of economic value—the same generic axe, for instance or an equivalent bushel of corn. Since work-time was required to produce equivalent economic value in Appalachia than in the industrial centers, Appalachia's market-oriented labor was thereby cheapened in economic value. And that entailed not only wage workers in Appalachia receiving lower wages, but also a cheapening of the value of the self-employed labor which went into producing axes or corn for local markets. When axes from the North got cheaper, Appalachian craftspeople had to sell their axes cheaper (or fail to sell them).

There nonetheless still remained two possible ways for Appalachia's people to avoid impoverishment. One way was for Appalachia to become a financial center. This emphatically did not occur, however. The other way to avoid impoverishment was for Appalachia's people to maintain their "competencies"—to keep their family farms of sufficient size to sustain themselves in comfort through a mixture of self-sufficiency and exchanges within local networks.

But unfortunately (from the perspective of maintaining competency), during the pioneer era of abundant land it had become customary for Appalachia's farmers to practice partible inheritance— that is, to divide their holdings among all their heirs or, at the least, among all their male heirs. This worked more or less satisfactorily so long as there remained new frontier areas in which the surplus population could re-settle. But after vast new farming frontiers ceased to open, family farms were often not large enough to support a competency.

Household economics—the economics of competency—lost some of its households due simply to changing cultural mores—a hankering for store-bought goods. Many other households, however, *tried* to maintain their competencies and yet failed. They tended to produce many children to help with the farm work, and those children in turn became adults who also produced large families to carry out the many chores. Only vast new farming frontiers could provide all the new competencies this pattern demanded, and such frontiers ceased to open by the 1890s. It was no coincidence that this was also when local products were massively driven out of local markets throughout the U.S. by competing products (both agricultural and manufactured) which were mass produced in the North and the Midwest. By this time, those farmers who could neither mass produce food nor supply specialty markets were well advised to maintain as much self-sufficiency as possible.

Recently, in Appalachian Studies, a few economic analyses have emphasized the pitfalls of export-oriented resource extraction, but of course, this by its nature is an exercise in macroeconomics.[3] Meanwhile, most *social* analyses have been quite "micro." Appalachian social analyses have emphasized family and neighborhood social mores and organization. And since the region's traditional ideology has enjoined patriarchy, evidence of de facto matriarchy (or we might call it a temporary matriarchy) has not been pondered as it deserves to be.

If, at any time during the first three decades of this century, one had toured the purely agricultural sections of Appalachia, one would have found the region's preindustrial way of life apparently in full swing. And yet many men in their prime years would have been absent, for in many cases they were out working in mines, logging camps, etc. Women were often running the home places—women, usually in their own prime years, supervising their family's subsistence farming and looking after elders as well as children in the process.[4] What this amounted to in macro terms was a process whereby subsistence farming, subsidized the industrialization of Appalachia by furnishing much of the income (non-monetized income, this was) which supported the families of industrial workers.

Permit me a disclaimer at this point. When I say that subsistence farming often "subsidized" Appalachia's industrialization, I am not talking about exploitation. Exploitation has no place in my analysis. It's not a term of reference for me. But subsistence farming "subsidized" Appalachia's industrialization by allowing many industrial operations to compete successfully in markets which they could not have entered had their wage costs been as high as their competitors' wage costs. To say this is not really the same as saying that industrialists or investors "appropriated" value created outside the market system by the families of workers. And I emphasize this because I believe that using "exploitation," "appropriation," and other Marxist categories of analysis might tend to conceal our present-day option of making constructive use of non-market economics—a subject which I will address. Granted that many coal operators, timber barons, etc., did get richer because their workers subsidized outside of market relations—but meanwhile, from the perspective of many workers, it was the industrial pay that was serving as a subsidy. Industrial pay was subsidizing their status as independent landowners by plugging gaps in their "competency" which had been opened by farm sub-division, by partible inheritance.

And where—you may wonder—where does government aid fit into this story? Well, long before the New Deal initiated direct federal aid to some of Appalachia's people, federal aid to midwesterners in the form of homestead and railroad land grants helped indirectly to impoverish Appalachia's people by hastening the exclusion of their farm and shop products from even their own local markets (not to mention markets outside the region). The immense production of food on federally-granted land west of the Mississippi River tended to make farming less profitable for everyone in the country who was already farming. Before the Midwest opened, all evidence indicates that Appalachia marketed a larger percentage of its food output than it was able to market after the Midwest's cheap food exports began invading Appalachia's stores.[5] After the mechanization of the Midwest's export-oriented farming, and then within Appalachia the creation of extractive industries to export coal and timber, etc., most of Appalachia's remaining full-time farmers continued no less dependent than they had always been on their local non-market exchanges—their local networks of voluntary reciprocity that Mary Beth Pudup has called an "informal economy" and that I call "subsistence-barter-and-borrow systems." Even most wage-earning families continued subsistence farming on the side (Hall 1986, 359-61; Corbin 1981, 33-35).

How, then, did the New Deal's relief payments interact with this situation within Appalachia? First, the relief payments made to Appalachia's unemployed and underemployed miners and other wage workers were absolutely necessary—for wage workers were obviously dependent on money income for livelihoods. But full-time subsistence farmers—to the extent that they still maintained a competency (often a very large extent)—were not dependent on money income except for their land taxes, which were low. Nonetheless, their low money income could qualify them for New Deal relief even if their landholdings and other productive assets had substantial value.

After the initial New Deal relief payments, many of Appalachia's farm people did not reapply for them but yet continued to receive relief checks. In April 1934, West Virginia's head relief administrator admitted to Harry Hopkins that local relief workers in "some counties have not investigated in six months. They keep sending checks week after week to the same people" (Beehler to Hopkins 1934). A month later that administrator warned West Virginia's relief personnel that thousands of dollars were being dispersed unnecessarily. "One rural county," he told them, "with 1,000 relief cases on April 1st [1934] which had been receiving relief for many months, found on the 20th of April that less than 300 of them had reapplied for relief"—leading the administrator to lament that "a tremendous amount of public funds had been utterly wasted" and in the process "many people pauperized thereby" (Beehler 1934, 1).

Unfortunately, the administrator did not identify the county to which he was referring, but I suspect it may well have been my present home county, West Virginia's Lincoln County. This was (and remains) a predominantly agricultural rather than industrial county. Indeed, the proportion of the population placed on relief (although not necessarily the size of their relief payments) often stood highest in the least industrial of Appalachia's counties. Already by July 1933, twelve West Virginia counties had seen over 45 percent of their households placed on relief, but only four of those counties had even 30 percent of their workforce in mining, whereas nine of them had at least 30 percent of their workers classified as agricultural. West Virginia's Lincoln County, for instance, with 84 percent of its households on relief as of July 1933, had a work-force classified as 60 percent agricultural.

The amounts of relief payments then leapt enormously during the winter 1933-1934 work relief projects of the Civilian Works Administration. After that outlay ended in the spring of 1934, Lincoln County's head relief administrator allowed hundreds of ineligible households to be reinstated on non-worker relief. During the summer of 1934, that administrator was fired and the rolls were cut back 30 percent, but, as of June 1935, 44.5 percent of Lincoln County's households were still receiving relief.

By that time, Wayne County (next door to Lincoln), had succeeded Lincoln as West Virginia's county with the highest percent of households on relief (47 percent, and receiving about $15 a month on average). Wayne County's workforce was classified as 45 percent agricultural. Lincoln County, with 44.5 percent of its workers on relief (averaging $9.70 a month) was as we've seen 60 percent agricultural. And Calhoun, the third-ranking county with 42.5 percent of his households on relief (averaging $12 a month) was 65 percent agricultural. (And it would take over $100 now to buy what $12 bought then.)

Official indifference toward the region's low-money economic networks can be surmised from official reports.[6] Of Wayne County, an October 1934 report asserted that the percent of local residents on relief "will probably run high until such time as constructive social planning makes possible the absorption of the population into self-supporting activities" (National Archives 1934, Box 311). While waiting for such planned "self-supporting activities," however, some people were being weaned by relief payments from their *customary* self-supporting activities which were not denominated in money and thus were not necessarily noticed by relief officials.

For some few farm families, admittedly, an increased money income could underwrite self-help. At the well-funded level of the Rural Rehabilitation program's, for example, federal aid did often improve farm families' long-term economic security and living standard. But Rural Rehabilitation involved large outlays of supervised credit for each family involved, and thus it could reach only a few thousand farm families per state.[7]

One of the macroeconomic regional results of massive federal aid was an increase in Appalachia's import surplus. Theoretically, relief funds were not all federally provided but included a significant contribution of state and local matching funds. Appalachian states, however, contributed far less in state and local matching funds than most states. From March 1933 through the end of 1937, $183 million was dispensed in West Virginia for relief—which in today's values would translate to over $1.5 billion. This outlay was divided among ordinary relief, work relief, the Civilian Conservation Corps, the National Youth Administration, Rural Rehabilitation programs, etc. And 87 percent of it was contributed by the federal government. Meanwhile, in the six other states that encompassed Appalachian sections, the federal contribution averaged still higher, 89 percent. But in the rest of the U.S. the federal contribution averaged much lower, below 72 percent.[8]

Not only was Appalachia's import surplus soaring, but ominously, by 1935 social workers in the mountain region were finding that (as one report put it) "most employers will not hire persons who have been on relief for extended periods" (Conley, 1935). And in May 1935, the demoralizing effects nationwide of unearned relief payments inspired the Roosevelt Administration to phase out unearned federal relief and to institute the Works Progress Administration (WPA). This was sound psychology, for subsequent studies have demonstrated that (in the words of one study) "charity wounds him who receives" (Mauss 1954, 63).[9] But in macroeconomic perspective, the WPA's work relief continued (indeed hastened with its far higher payments) the rise of Appalachia's import surplus. And it also hastened another trend—the erosion of the mountains' low-money "informal economy," the region's "subsistence-barter-and-borrow" networks. To full-time mountain farmers who often had little need for money, the WPA paid wages as high as it paid to anyone else—thirty cents an hour until June 1936, and forty cents an hour thereafter.[10] Although rural WPA employees were allowed only fifteen hours of work per week (whereas urban WPA employees were allowed twenty-four hours per week), nonetheless fifteen hours a week at forty cents an hour yielded $26 a month. And if this income was supplemented by a further $25 a month (the minimum received by families with a son in the Civilian Conservation Corps), the total of $51 would have been equivalent in today's values to $433 a month.

Please do not suppose that I begrudge those people that money. My point is that such relief payments, if made to full-time farm families, were often not serving as compensation for a shortfall in home-based competency but rather were tending to *create* a shortfall in home-based competency. Although many mountaineers admittedly remember the WPA with fondness, others do not. Claude Dillon of the Marrowbone Creek neighborhood of Mingo County, West Virginia, came to feel that "the public works programs that were prescribed to put people to work, simply took them away from farm life, took them away from the self-sufficient way to do things" (Tierney 1983, 7). And a storekeeper in Lincoln County, West Virginia, reflected later that "it was the WPA that started farming on its downhill path all around here. The WPA paid farmers to work on the roads, and work on this and that, till they started counting on that money and neglecting their land" (Ray Gene Black, interview, June 1983).

By 1942, when nine years of government aid terminated, many farm families found they had grown quite dependent on regular money income. Many of these farm families then followed the trail of government largess and took defense-related jobs outside Appalachia. From 1940 to 1960, net migration from the Appalachian region totalled 1.7 million people—which was 31.5 percent of the region's 1940 population.[11]

Now, it would be quite easy to make a case that the American economy had exploited these people more when their lives were centered at their mountain farms than it was able to exploit them later, when they had left Appalachia, and when thus their employers had to pay them a better wage, a more nearly family-supporting wage. But let me point out that to be less exploited is not necessarily to be better off. How gladly did these people undergo the transformation of their way of life? How willingly did they abandon a way of life suffused with voluntary reciprocity in economic relations and enter a way of life virtually devoid of voluntary reciprocity, a life mediated instead by binding contracts?

In any case, the question is not whether to applaud or condemn the New Deal but how to analyze it (along with the rest of Appalachia's past) in such a way as to gain insights applicable to our own situation today. Today our national economic priority should be, I believe, to minimize our horrendously bloated production of U.S. dollars—which at an alarming rate are flowing out into the hands of foreigners who can use them to buy up productive assets within the United States. To minimize the production of dollars will require that a large percentage of intra-U.S. economic exchanges be de-monetized, or at least de-dollarized. But the question then becomes *how* exchanges within the U.S. should be de-dollarized. Is it necessary that some new corporatist vision of "America, Inc." be propagated in the spirit of Louis Kelso?[12] Or can a significant portion of our intra-U.S. exchanges be de-dollarized through a revival of voluntary reciprocity—of the kind of voluntary reciprocity that pervaded rural America before the twentieth century, and which still remains common in much of Appalachia.

The contrast between the New Deal and what we now need to do is twofold. First, we should be thinking now about grassroots economic development rather than primarily (like the New Deal) about reviving U.S. markets for major U.S. commodities. The problem now isn't simply to get purchasing power into American communities but also to get competitive products to come out of American communities. One of the main ways the New Deal injected purchasing power into American communities was through public works projects—and we should not dismiss public works as necessarily contradictory to getting competitive products out of American communities. But on a cautionary note, listen to these thoughts from E.F. Schumacher's 1973 book, *Small is Beautiful*:

> Poverty means that markets are small and there is very little free purchasing power. All the purchasing power that exists already, is, as it were, bespoken, and if I start a new production of, say, sandals or shoes in a poor area, my fellow sufferers in the area will not have any money to buy the shoes when I have made them. Production is sometimes easier to start than it is to fund markets, and then, of course, we get very quickly the advice to produce for export, because exports are mainly for rich countries and their purchasing power is plentiful. (203)

Where Schumacher writes "rich countries" here, we can make his point relevant to the Appalachian situation by thinking of "rich regions" which possess plentiful purchasing power. But rather than assuming that Appalachia must produce for export only what rich regions want from us, there does exist an alternative means of starting to build up Appalachia's own internal purchasing power—and what this means is public works of the New Deal sort. Regarding this, Schumacher says:

> If you can get new purchasing power into a rural community by way of a public works programme financed from outside, see to it that the fullest possible use is made of the "multiplier effect." The people employed on the public works want to spend their wages on "wages goods," that is to say, consumers' goods of all kinds. If these wages goods can be locally produced, the new purchasing power made available through the public works programme does not seep away but goes on circulating in the local market, and the total employment effect could be prodigious. (204-5)

All well and good, but how can a local "multiplier effect" be established and maintained? Schumacher points out that:

> If I start new production in a poor country [read "region"] there can be no local market for my products unless I divert the flow of purchasing power from some other product to mine. A dozen different productions should all be started together: then for every one of the twelve producers the other eleven would be his market. There would be additional purchasing power to absorb the additional output. But it is extremely difficult to start many activities at once. (204)

Yes, it is difficult to start many activities at once. In fact, to do this in a poor area like Appalachia might well require de-dollarizing a lot of how we think about "purchasing power" within the region. To do what's needed—to start many activities at once—may well require using monies-of-account rather than dollars for a lot of our intra-Appalachian economic exchanges.

Back in 1933, when the Tennessee Valley Authority was created, the TVA's first chairman, Arthur Morgan, put his mind to this challenge in its particular Appalachian context. Here are some of Morgan's reflections from a famous speech he delivered at the University of Tennessee in Knoxville in November 1933. Like E.F. Schumacher forty years later, Arthur Morgan used shoes to help illustrate his idea:

> Suppose you want to build and operate a shoe factory in some part of this region, and in another town, furniture, in another clothes, etc. You might think "We have people here doing nothing, and they might as well be producing; they might as well be making their own goods, lifting themselves out of the economic depression. If we make shoes, we can wear more shoes; we can make shoes for each other; and so with other goods which we go without now. We can have our own economy in our little world."
>
> But suppose the shoe dealer starts to make shoes; suppose he wants to sell them over where the furniture is made; the trouble is that he is not part of the existing industrial organization; his shoes have to go back to the jobber; but the jobber already has his arrangements with a big St. Louis manufacturer, so when you buy shoes at the local store in the community where furniture is made, you find they are from St. Louis and not from the nearby community. And the furniture dealer also has to go through the ordered channels, through the wholesaler, who is connected with the big factories; and so in the shoe town he is squeezed out. Because of these deeply worn channels of trade, nearly all leading into and out of the big business and industrial centers, it seems necessary to set up a new economy if we are to

deal with ourselves and for ourselves. When we talk of balancing agriculture and industry by making things which can be consumed in this country, when we talk about having the people consume what they produce, we run into these difficulties. There are no roads going our way.

What is the answer to that situation? Does it mean that this region must always continue to be a vassal of the big centers? Is there any other answer?

No single answer will do. I do not think starting a local shoe factory, trying to serve the neighbors with shoes, will do if it is done alone. I do not think any furniture factory for local consumption is going to do a satisfactory business alone. Either the product will go into the channels of trade and when the furniture gets back here it will have 50 percent to 75 percent overhead added and it will be crowded out by the products of big industry, or else we shall have create channels for ourselves. I think it is not impossible to create new channels.

I believe that to a certain degree this region might well set up its own local economy. It can produce its own goods and deal with itself. But if a region is going to build up a new economy by making things it needs at home, it will in a limited sense have to build up a whole economy and not a fragment of an economy. If I were going to build up a whole economy, it would be somewhat in the following manner:

I would build a cooperative of some sort. I would have a central purchasing organization, a central sales organization, a distributing organization, and I think I'd have that cooperative organization have its own tokens of credit—a sort of local money.

If a local shoe manufacturer should sell shoes to a cooperative, he would get cooperative money, not United States money, at least for part of his payment. The same would be true of the clothing manufacturer, and of all the others. If a man should go to buy shoes he could use this kind of local money in which the shoes were paid for. That money would not be good at a distance, and so those who sell things for home consumption could be paid only by buying other things made for home consumption. In that way home shoes would in some degree outlaw St. Louis shoes.

I would have everybody who was producing for home consumption as part of this cooperative paid at least in part in the money of the cooperative, so there would be a kind of money that would buy the things we made ourselves but not buy the things outsiders make. In that way we would be compelled to buy from each other. Not all business would be done this way. Legal money would also be necessary. I believe this compulsion to buy from each other may be necessary in order to break across the deep worn channels of trade which all lead into and out of the great commercial centers. Such compulsion would be better than the present compulsion of sitting at home in idleness, buying nothing because we have nothing to sell.

As I think it over, I believe it is going to be almost necessary to have this element of local exchange, because otherwise, after your shoe manufacture has made shoes and has turned them in to the Cooperative he will get money for them and will buy Grand Rapids furniture; and the furniture manufacturer, after he has made furniture, unless he were paid in credits good only for home products he would buy his shoes from the St. Louis trade and not the local shoes. Soon the local money would be gone, local goods would be unsold, local factories closed, and everyone idle and unable to buy.

Now whether this thing can be done, I do not know. But if we are going to build up a local economy, if we are going to be somewhat independent of mass production, I believe we are going to have to go all the way and develop our own tokens of local credit, as well as our own distributing center, our own purchasing center, and our own credit system that will make the exchange. (Morgan 1933, vol. 1, sec. 4)

The New Deal did not make use of Arthur Morgan's suggestions along this line, and in fact he later traced his eventual ouster from the TVA partly to this 1933 speech (conversation with author, 1973; 1974). I quote the speech at such length because of its obvious relevance to the problems which still confront Appalachia almost sixty years after Morgan spoke. One bright spot among our present options is that computers have probably eliminated any need to issue a local currency in order to conduct local economic exchanges. In various parts of the U.S. and Canada, membership groups which call themselves Local Economic Trading Systems (LETS) are operating now like non-money banks which record their members' deposits that take the form not of money but of labor and goods provided to other members. Withdrawals then take the form of labor and goods received from fellow members. The groups generally expand only to about two hundred members, including individuals and households. The members receive monthly statements in the form of computer printouts which report their non-money deposits and withdrawals during the previous month, along with their running balance. Such systems are now functioning also in some cities under the name of "Service Credits" for hospital/health volunteers, whose hours of service earn them the right to that many hours of received help when and if they themselves request help.[14]

All such arrangements help to minimize the number of dollars needed for economic exchanges within the U.S. The model for such voluntary reciprocity is the informal, non-monetized networking which helped to subsidize America's initial industrialization and which we need to revive if we are to regain our local, regional, and national solvency in an increasingly competitive world.

Notes

[1] On the 1930s origin of a critique of export-oriented development, see Love (1980) especially pages 47-63.

[2] See the recent explication of these issues in Vickers (1990).

[3] See, for example, Simon (1978).

[4] See, for example, Hall (1936), pages 3-4, 13-29. On recent times, see Shackleford and Weinberg (1977).

[5] On this question of competition from Midwestern food producers, see Pudup (1988), pages 72-74. Also see Cummings (1986-87) pages 70-75.

[6] West Virginia Relief Administration, "Monthly Bulletin of Relief Statistics," Vol. 2, No. 5 (May 1935), page 13 incl. map; and Vol. 2, No. 6 (June 1935), page 19 map, in National Archives, Federal Emergency Relief Administration (Record Group 69), State Files, West Virginia, Box 312, Folder series 401. The "percent agricultural," by county taken from "West Virginia July 1933: Counties Having Very High Percentage of Families of Relief Rolls," National Archives, Federal Emergency Relief Administration (Record Group 69), State Files, West Virginia, Box 312, Special folder "Materials taken by Mr. Hopkins on his S.W. trip in August [1933]."

[7] On the Rural Rehabilitation program nationwide, see Baldwin (1968), pages 61-65, 91-94, 106-8, and 199-214. On the Rural Rehabilitation program in West Virginia see Beehler (1934), pages 1-4.

[8] Calculated from data in Heinemann (1983), pages 202-3, table.

[9] In addition, for the 1930s see Charles (1963) page 101.

[10] Surveys of the Rural Relief Situation for Johnson, Knox, and Rowan Counties, Kentucky, October 1935, National Archives, Bureau of Agricultural Economics (RG 83), Rural Relief Studies (RG 83, entry 156), Box 5.

[11] Brown and Hillary (1962), pages 55-60 including tables. For the definition of Appalachia used, see page 4 in the same volume.

[12] See, most recently, Kelso and Kelso (1986). Also see Speiser (1977).

[13] See "Credit for Good Deeds: Golden Rules of Barter," *Newsweek* 15 January 1990, page 61.

Works Cited

Baldwin, Sidney. 1968. *Poverty and Politics: The Rise and Decline of the Farm Security Administration*. Chapel Hill: University of North Carolina Press.

Beehler, William N. (West Virginia Relief Administrator) to Harry Hopkins. 4 April 1934. National Archives, files of the Federal Emergency Relief Administration (Record Group 69), State Files, West Virginia, Box 312, Folder Series 400.

———. 1934. Office of Administrator, General Bulletin. Copy in the papers of H.G. Kump (governor of West Virginia), West Virginia Collection, West Virginia University, A. & M. No. 1609, Box 45, Folder "1934, May 12-19."

Brown, James S. and George A. Hillary, Jr. 1962. "The Great Migration, 1940-1960." *The Southern Appalachian Region: A Survey*. ed. Thomas R. Ford. Lexington: University of Kentucky Press.

Charles, Searle F. 1963. *Minister of Relief: Harry Hopkins and the Depression*. Syracuse: Syracuse University Press.

Cummings, Joe. 1986-87. "Community and the Nature of Change: Sevier County, Tennessee, in the 1890s." *East Tennessee Historical Society's Publications* 58-59: 63-88.

Conley, Irene (County Worker). 1935. "Survey of the Rural Relief Situation for Johnson County, Kentucky." National Archives, Files of the Bureau of Agricultural Economics. Record Group 83, Entry 156, Box 5, Rural Relief Studies.

Corbin, David Alan. 1981. *Life, Work and Rebellion in the Coal Fields*. Urbana: University of Illinois Press.

Hall, Jacquelyn Dowd. 1986. "Disorderly Women: Gender and Labor Militancy in the Appalachian South." *Journal of American History* 73: 359, 371.

Heinemann, Ronald L. 1983. *Depression and New Deal in Virginia: The Enduring Dominion*. Charlottesville: University Press of Virginia.

Kelso, Louis O. and Patricia Hetter Kelso. 1986. *Democracy and Economic Power: Extending the ESOP Revolution*. Cambridge: Ballinger Publishing Co.

Love, Joseph L. 1980. "Raúl Prebisch and the Origins of the Doctrine of Unequal Exchange." *Latin American Research Review* 15 (3): 45-72.

Mauss, Marcel. 1954. *The Gift: Forms and Functions of Exchange in Archaic Societies*. Trans. Ian Cunnison. Glencoe, Illinois.: The Free Press.

Mitchell, Robert D. 1977. *Commercialism and Frontier: Perspectives on the Early Shenandoah Valley*. Charlottesville: University Press of Virginia.

Morgan, Arthur E. 9 November 1933. "Group Industries' Problems and Their Solution" speech at Ferris Hall, University of Tennessee at Knoxville. Copy in the TVA Technical Library, Knoxville, in Arthur E. Morgan, "Speeches and Writings."

———. 1974. *The Making of the TVA*. Buffalo: Prometheus Books.

National Archives. 8-10 October 1934. Report on West Virginia's county-by-county relief fluctuations. National Archives, State Files, West Virginia, Box 311, Folder series 400.

Pudup, Mary Beth. 1990. "The Limits of Subsistence: Agriculture and Industry in Central Appalachia." *Agricultural History* 64: 61-89.

Schumacher, E.F. 1973. *Small is Beautiful: Economics as if People Mattered*. New York: Harper & Row.

Shackleford, Laurel and Bill Weinberg, eds. 1977. *Our Appalachia*. New York: Hill & Wang.

Simon, Richard Mark. 1978. "The Development of Underdevelopment: The Coal Industry and Its Effect on the West Virginia Economy, 1880-1930." Ph.D. dissertation, University of Pittsburgh.

Speiser, Stuart M. 1977. *A Piece of the Action: A Plan to Provide Every Family with a $100,000 Stake in the Economy*. New York: Van Norstrand Reinhold.

Tierney, Michael T. 1983. "Bread on the Water: Education in an Isolated Mountain Community." *Human Services in the Rural Environment* 8 (Winter).

Vickers, Daniel. 1990. "Competency and Competition: Economic Culture in Early America." *William and Mary Quarterly*, 3rd series, 47 (January): 3-29

Paul Salstrom is Visiting Assistant Professor of History at West Virginia University.

The New Deal for Tenant Farmers: Government Planning and Indigenous Community Development on the Cumberland Plateau

Benita J. Howell

New Deal farm policy responded directly to the agricultural crisis in the Cotton Belt of the lowland South, but rural rehabilitation programs of the Tennessee Valley Authority (TVA), the Federal Emergency Relief Administration (FERA), the Resettlement Administration, Subsistence Homesteads Division, and Farm Security Administration (FSA) also reached into southern Appalachia. Mountain View, the fictitious name used here for a small farming community in Grundy County, Tennessee, was founded in 1938 by tenant farmers displaced by TVA dam construction. With indigenous organization and only modest financial and technical assistance from FSA, Mountain View survived and has remained a center of successful family-operated truck farming.

In contrast to Mountain View were the New Deal experimental communities established and run by the federal government in an effort to provide a sound economic and social basis for rural life. Families selected for these communities received impressive amounts of government assistance. Cumberland Homesteads just south of Crossville, Tennessee, and Skyline Farms in Jackson County, Alabama, were two such communities located not far from the home areas of the Grundy

County settlers. Rising political opposition forced liquidation of these and scores of similar rural communities in the late 1940s. By that time most of the communities had faltered economically; but equally important in their failure were tensions between the social vision of the planners and the cultural expectations of community residents and the general American public.

This paper compares the difficulties experienced in Skyline Farms, Cumberland Homesteads and other federally-sponsored communities with the indigenous development of Mountain View. The comparison is an interesting commentary on Appalachian community development work of the 1920s and 1930s (see Shapiro 1978; Whisnant 1983), because it points up the extent to which uneducated rural Appalachians, who were generally assumed to lack the requisite leadership skills and civic-mindedness, used traditional patterns of social and economic cooperation to form a new community with only modest federal loans and technical assistance.

Throughout the 1920s, southern agriculture was ravaged by soil depletion and erosion, the boll weevil, and a growing gap between the farmer's cost of living and low commodity prices. The Great Depression and dust bowl days of the 1930s highlighted the plight of farmers, and the national economic emergency prompted federal government action to address the crisis in agriculture (Mitchell 1947, 179-227).

Soon after President Roosevelt took office in 1933, the Agricultural Adjustment Administration (AAA) was formed, ushering in plow-ups and acreage allotments, price supports, and government purchase of surplus commodities in an effort to restore farmers' purchasing power. Policy set by the Cotton Section of the AAA was generally favorable to landowners rather than tenants; acreage reduction contracts had negative consequences for tenant farmers (Conrad 1965, 204-9). Landowners who reduced their cotton acreage did not need as many tenants to farm their holdings; furthermore, eliminating tenants or lowering their status to cropper or day laborer allowed the landowner to avoid sharing government subsidies for crop reduction with tenants. Because AAA contracts with landowners did not protect tenants from displacement, many found it increasingly difficult to rent farms in the mid-1930s, and some were left homeless. Other causes of tenant displacement were the introduction of mechanization to cotton growing and the domino effect of foreclosures on farm owners' mortgages (Woofter and Winston 1939, 22). Although the problems of cotton farming affected primarily the Deep South, commercial cotton production and attendant problems extended into the southernmost sections of Appalachia.

In north Alabama and southeast Tennessee, however, the Tennessee Valley Authority had even greater impact than federal farm policy on rural families and communities. Between its founding in 1933 and 1940, TVA constructed eight dams in the Tennessee River Valley. TVA planners hoped that flood control and abundant electric power would attract industry to the region to balance its traditional dependence on agriculture, but farmers near TVA dams paid the costs of regional progress. Some had to be relocated because their land would be flooded, while others suddenly found themselves in competition with relocatees for land to rent or buy. Many experienced social and psychological trauma as they were uprooted from home communities that disappeared forever under the rising waters of the new reservoirs.

TVA also sought to improve agriculture in the region by providing cheap fertilizer and technical assistance to increase production in areas most suited to farming, while soil conservation and reforestation programs would remove marginally productive, eroded, or worn out land from crop production (Whisnant 1980, 43-69). Coupled with the inundation of much prime valley acreage, this policy had a devastating effect on small farm owners and tenants near the dams.(McDonald and Muldowny 1982).

Rehabilitation and Resettlement: The Government Response to Displaced Tenants

The federal government responded to the problem of displaced farm tenants with outright relief and with special rural rehabilitation programs (Baldwin 1968; Mertz 1978; Woofter and Winston). The most popular program provided rural rehabilitation loans to finance the purchase of land, equipment, livestock, or subsistence goods. Along with these loans came technical assistance to develop a workable farm and home plan which would make it possible for the farm family to thrive economically, improve their standard of living, and pay back the loan. The federal lenders, first the Resettlement Administration (RA) and later the Farm Security Administration (FSA), controlled how these loans were spent by requiring that county supervisors countersign checks drawn against loan money deposited in special bank accounts (Baldwin, 195-202).

The federal government also experimented with planned communities during the New Deal (Blakey 1986, 127-30; Conkin 1959; Eaton 1950, 5-12; Infield 1945). After the turn of the century when the increasing pace of urbanization and industrial mechanization seemed threatening and the old frontier no longer offered escape, social critics romanticized the nation's agrarian past (Twelve Southerners 1930). They felt that revitalizing rural economy, culture, and society could preserve traditional American values, stem migration from rural to urban areas, and thus forestall the dehumanizing effects of industrial employment and urban life. Many currents in social science and social work in the first decades of this century reflected a common set of assumptions derived from this agrarian myth: the idealized folk image of anthropologist Robert Redfield (1930; 1947); historian Frank Owsley's (1949) documentation of the forgotten yeoman farmers of the Old South; the Country Life Commission which led to federal programs for agricultural education and extension work; the emergence of rural sociology as a discipline; and the folk school movement with its emphases on basic education, enhancement of community cooperation and quality of life, cultural revival, and economic security through a combination of improved farming and commercial handcraft production (Eaton 1937; Shapiro; Whisnant 1983). These ideas and ideals were reflected in New Deal rural rehabilitation efforts (Baldwin, 203-8; Forrest 1989) and in the planned rural communities (Campbell and Coombs 1983; Conkin).

When the Resettlement Administration was created in 1935, it inherited thirty-three subsistence homestead projects from the Interior Department (Conkin, 98-129), and thirty-four planned farm communities begun by FERA (Conkin, 133-44). The RA began thirty-five additional farm communities, including five cooperative farms, before it was succeeded as administrator of the federal communities in 1937 by FSA (Banfield 1951, 18-20). These projects were created with long-term federal involvement in mind, but political pressure to dismantle the more controversial New Deal programs mounted as the national economy recovered. By the mid-1940s, Congress had declared its intention to terminate the planned community projects (Conkin, 185-207). The projects ended and their assets were liquidated over the rest of the decade. Cumberland Homesteads, begun as an Interior Department subsistence homestead project, and Skyline Farms, a FERA relief project for displaced tenants, were two of these short-lived experimental communities located not far from Grundy County and the original homes of the families who established Mountain View.

Cumberland Homesteads (Krechniak 1956) and other projects in the subsistence homesteads program grew out of the belief that stranded miners and industrial workers could best be helped by putting them back on the land where they could combine subsistence farming for home consumption with cash income from wage labor in industry. Two hundred fifty-one homesteads were created south of Crossville, Tennessee, between 1934 and 1937 and settled by families who came from all walks of life, some from other sections of the state and nation. WPA workers cleared the land and built barns, which the project families occupied while helping to build their own homes. These were attractive four- to seven-room stone houses with electricity, modern bathrooms, and up-to-date kitchens. Between 1934 and 1939, labor credits and cash payments were applied toward eventual purchase of the homesteads, but the exact terms of lease-purchase agreements were not spelled out to the government's tenants. Long-term federal ownership was being used to block development that did not fit into the community plan, and to prevent financial speculation on the improved land. In addition to their uncertainties about land ownership, the families at Cumberland Homesteads were saddled with a sizeable debt for their spacious, modern houses. Because the planners assumed that wage work would provide most of the families' income, the landholdings were small; many tracts contained fewer than ten acres.

Several cooperatives were established to provide cash income, among them a dairy, cannery, sorghum mill, and coal mine; but the real hope was to attract private industry to the area. Social planners hoped to convince industry to locate in rural areas where jobs were needed, but in the absence of adequate services and transportation this plan was unrealistic. Efforts to attract outside industry to Cumberland Homesteads never bore fruit, nor did the local cooperatives succeed. Without opportunities for cash income, many homesteaders were stranded on landholdings too small for raising livestock and too poor and rocky to support truck crops. The Cumberland Homesteads families were in effect locked into the government's community plan so that there was little they could do on their own initiative to adjust to circumstances.

The government tried to save the situation for Cumberland Homesteads and similar subsistence homestead communities by extending WPA jobs, subsidizing community cooperatives, and offering direct subsidies to the industries it was trying to attract to the communities. This latter action, in particular, brought complaints from the public and Congress that the subsistence homesteads were proving too expensive and were bringing government into undesirable competition with private enterprise. For Cumberland Homesteads, construction of Watts Bar Dam, Douglas Dam, and Oak Ridge finally created jobs within commuting distance; this outside source of income enabled many of the original homesteaders to purchase their places when the government began selling out in 1945. At Skyline Farms, the shift to private ownership was not so smooth.

Skyline Farms (Campbell and Coombs) was planned to give displaced tenant farmers a chance to improve their lot through cooperative farming in a carefully planned community. Before the settlers arrived, relief workers had already cleared the land, put in roads, and built a house, barn, and smokehouse for each forty to sixty acre farm. Families were chosen for this project from the relief rolls, but the applications were carefully screened in an attempt to find families of good character who already had farming skills. The successful applicants moved into a house, were issued food stamps and clothing, draft animals, seed, and fertilizers. The community planners intended to train participants in cooperation as well as in home management and the latest farming practices. The community was organized into a number of cooperative associations, for example: a commissary co-op, a produce marketing co-op, and later a co-op to build and operate a hosiery mill. The community included a progressive, non-graded school, a pre-paid health plan, and an array of social events and group craft activities which the planners believed would develop cooperative spirit and create community cohesion.

Under mounting pressure from the critics of New Deal social and economic experimentation, administration of the experimental communities was shifted from one government agency to another, and in the process policies were constantly changing. It never was made clear to the settlers at Skyline Farms exactly when or how they would receive title to their land, but they believed their labor and rental payments were being applied towards purchase. Skyline Farms also experienced economic difficulties. The hosiery mill was a costly failure, even after a private concern was contracted to run it, and the farming operations failed to thrive. When federal ownership was liquidated, any tenant who was in debt to the government was ruled ineligible to buy his farm. Because many of the farmers had outstanding production credit loans, they found themselves evicted from their homes. Families who had stuck with Skyline Farms for as long as twelve years through the frustrations of government management and economic uncertainty felt cheated out of the equity they thought they had been building through rental payments.

Establishment of the Mountain View Community

Mountain View (Lane 1985), although created by private citizens rather than government plan, was a consequence of TVA activities in the region. According to TVA statistics (1940), 1,952 farm families, or 12.2 percent of the entire population of Jackson and Marshall counties in north Alabama, were displaced by the Guntersville Dam project; 649 rural families in the Chickamauga reservoir area in southeast Tennessee faced relocation, and the project affected others indirectly through inflated land prices. By the late 1930s, federal land acquisition coupled with rising private demand for land had pushed real estate prices beyond the reach of tenant farmers who had weathered the worst of the Depression and now hoped to buy their own farms. While "150' by 500' lots in Chickamauga Farms, fronting the paved road to the new

(Chickamauga) dam" sold for $350 (*Chattanooga Times*, 11 September 1938), the same $350 could purchase seventy acres of recently cut-over timber land north of Chattanooga in Grundy County, part of a twelve thousand acre tract put on the market when timbering was completed in 1937. This offer attracted East Tennesseans from Bradley and Meigs counties, part of the Chickamauga Dam impact area, and families from Marshall County in north Alabama who were affected by construction of the Guntersville Dam.

While the obstacles the Mountain View settlers faced were daunting, their new start meant a way out of a hopeless situation. Many of the women took their first look at the desolate area and would have left, but as one said, "We had nothing to go back to." In 1935 and 1936 when TVA conducted social surveys prior to relocation, most farmers in the Guntersville purchase area produced cotton and food for home consumption on small farms averaging thirty-three cultivated acres. Only 30.8 percent of those farming were owner-operators; 40.7 percent were tenants, 21.8 pecent were sharecroppers, and 6.7 percent were farm laborers. In 1935, net real income (cash and produce) of tenant farms averaged only $507 as opposed to $645 for owner-operated farms (TVA 1940).

The Chickamauga purchase area contained parts of Bradley, Hamilton, McMinn, Meigs, and Rhea counties in Tennessee. Throughout this five county area, which includes metropolitan Chattanooga, only about 16 percent of the work force was engaged in agriculture. Those who did farm raised primarily corn and hay, and many gained an income principally from dairying, raising livestock, or growing truck crops. Acres in cultivation averaged 38.9 for all farmers, although tenants actually managed larger farms than owner-operators, cultivating fifty acres on average. Nevertheless, in 1936 the net real income for these tenant farms averaged only $715 as opposed to $969 for owner-operated farms (TVA 1940).

The Mountain View settlers were able to take advantage of rural rehabilitation loans to obtain seed, feed, and fertilizer. As stipulated in the terms of these loans, they worked closely with the county FSA supervisor to develop a diversified farming program and monitor each year's income and expenses; a home management supervisor taught the women modern canning methods and other domestic skills. Loans were not granted for land purchase in Mountain View, however. Federal policy supported the reforestation of marginal crop and pasture land, not the continued clearing of forest for crops; thus the new Mountain View farms did not seem a promising risk to the federal lenders. Mountain View was established in a period of great opportunity, however, just as Grundy County agriculture was beginning to recover from the effects of the Great Depression. Between 1930 and 1935, the number of farms in the county had risen from 524 to 964 as workers displaced from other occupations went back to the land to eke out a living. Average farm size had fallen from seventy-nine acres in 1930 to only forty-five acres in 1935, and the percentage of tenant farmers had risen from 22 percent to 31% percent By 1940 the county had only 623 farms, but these had become more viable economic units as average farm size increased to seventy acres. The rate of tenancy as opposed to full or part ownership had fallen to 20 percent (U.S. Census 1945).

Between 1929 and 1939, the number of Grundy County farms growing vegetables for sale had been reduced by almost half, from fifty-two to twenty-seven, and acreage in truck crop production had fallen from seventy-nine to twenty-seven acres (U.S. Census 1945). Growth in Chattanooga and an expanding wartime economy created new markets for farm products. Once the Mountain View farmers had cleared sufficient acreage and their good results with cabbage and other truck crops became apparent, government agencies no longer considered their farms poor financial risks. By the late 1940s and early 1950s, some of the Mountain View farmers finally were able to obtain land purchase loans from the Farmer's Home Administration to increase their land holdings. By this time, however, the community's success already was fairly well assured. Largely through their own efforts, with only modest financial and technical assistance from New Deal programs, the citizens of Mountain View had established themselves economically. They also developed strong social bonds between families through cooperation and intermarriage, and built their school and church into focal institutions of community life.

Indigenous Forms of Cooperation in Mountain View

Stimulating cooperation was an explicit goal of the New Deal planned communities (Baldwin 1968, 203-27; Conkin), but if Edward Banfield's (1951) assessment is accurate, the social engineers' efforts to induce cooperation were largely ineffective. Banfield studied the social organizational aspects of the Casa Grande cooperative farm in Arizona, one of the most economically successful of the experimental projects. Participants in the Casa Grande project received food, shelter, all the material accoutrements of a decent standard of living, jobs, technical training, and the benefits of the community life planned for them, yet there was constant grumbling. Every incident and every decision aroused factionalism. The residents resisted participation in clubs and other activities which project managers organized to stimulate community cooperation and cohesion. Banfield concluded that the grumblers and non-cooperators were trying to regain a sense of self-respect and assert status claims, that they resorted to this behavior because the stigma of relief, the regimentation of the project, and social engineering of daily life blocked more constructive means of self-validation. Resentment of government intervention and the atmosphere of discord and factionalism caused many participants to leave Casa Grande, and the same was true of other less collectively-oriented projects like Skyline Farms.

The Mountain View farmers were grateful for their rehabilitation loans but didn't like being in debt to the government. They paid off the rehabilitation loans as soon as possible, even though they cooperated closely and enthusiastically in programs suggested by FSA county supervisors and have continued to work well with their county agricultural extension agents. Self-validation was hardly at issue in Mountain View, however, when every family that stayed on the mountain was fulfilling dreams of independence and showing a somewhat skeptical county populace that they had the right stuff to succeed.

Aside from negative psychological consequences which may have been inherent in the kind of social engineering being attempted in the experimental communities, cooperation might also have been inhibited by more fundamental factors such as group composition. Social workers carefully screened candidates for government projects and selected families whom they judged to have desirable skills and potential for rehabilitation. Since the projects aimed to supplant maladaptive cultural patterns with new ones, common background, experience, values, and beliefs were not considered important. These were precisely the common denominators the Mountain View families shared.

Although only some of the Mountain View settlers had been acquainted with one another before the move, all were poor ex-tenant farmers with similar aspirations, and all were Baptist. Several Guntersville residents saw the Grundy County land advertised for $5.00 an acre in *The Progressive Farmer*, and two who decided to buy became agents for the land company. One tenant farmer from Guntersville who had lost a farm in East Tennessee during the Depression, visited relatives there and struck a deal to sell an old Tennessee acquaintance a portion of the acreage he had just bought.

Five families from Alabama and three from East Tennessee selected themselves and one another to form the nucleus of the Mountain View community. Interestingly, if they had been relief families eligible for Skyline Farms they probably would have been passed over because the household heads were well into middle age, and fathers of large families. But marriages between their grown children soon reinforced the bonds of shared background, values, and goals, knitting Mountain View into a complex network of neighbor and kin relationships typical of older rural settlements. Moreover, these older household heads and their wives had accumulated the experience and wisdom necessary to organize community-wide cooperation.

Their first goals were to obtain an elementary school from the county and build themselves a church. Although the county provided teachers and built the school building using a National Youth Administration labor force, community women formed an active Parent-Teacher Association (PTA), organized money-raising projects to pay for extra furnishings and supplies, and took over the responsibility of providing a hot lunch program. When county-wide consolidation closed the school in 1963, the community took steps to retain ownership of the building. It became the property of the Pleasant Ridge Baptist Church and became a center for church and community social activities.

Even more than the school, the church has been the symbol of community identity and cohesion. The first church-building project was aborted when it became apparent that the man who donated land for the church intended to name it for himself. Once they obtained land from a disinterested party, community members, who had jointly saved money to buy materials, contributed their labor to erect the building. Buying a heater and a second-hand piano were projects taken on by the community women's club. While this club was first organized by the FSA home supervisor, the women themselves kept it active after her position was cut. It later became their Home Demonstration Club.

As in traditional rural settlements of the region, the church became not only the spiritual center of the new community, but its social center also—the site of revivals and singings, monthly birthday dinners, holiday celebrations, family reunions, and the like. In the case of federally-sponsored communities like Skyline Farms, the doctrine of separation of church and state prevented federal project managers from actively promoting the formation of churches, so the opportunity to build community using this traditional arena of social activity was lost to them. Campbell and Coombs make it clear, however, that the planners of Skyline Farms were steeped in country life and folk school ideas and had a theoretical commitment to developing community spirit through other means: folk music, recreation, traditional handcrafts, and collective enterprise. Unfortunately, their approach ignored or discounted the existence of traditional patterns of cooperation which operated effectively in Mountain View. (See Hicks 1976, 103-7 for a similar critique of the War on Poverty in Appalachia.)

Banfield's observations at Casa Grande and events at Cumberland Homesteads and Skyline Farms suggest that the Mountain View settlers were lucky to have as little direct government support as they did.

Unlike the residents of Cumberland Homesteads and Skyline Farms, the Mountain View settlers were able to fit the size, location, and character of their landholdings to their needs through buying and selling parts of their original tracts and expanding their landholdings. Looking back fifty years to the beginnings of their community, the residents of Mountain View often speak of themselves as pioneers in a wilderness. Like pioneers, they endured many hardships in the early years and only gradually added modern conveniences to their homes. Paying off their mortgages to the land company and buying more land were more important to them than fancy housing. In contrast residents of Cumberland Homesteads and Skyline Farms were provided many amenities on the assumption that the economic development schemes planned for those communities would work, and that residents could easily handle the debt they incurred by participating in the projects. Neither Skyline Farms nor Cumberland Homesteads implemented its economic plan successfully; only outside developments saved the situation for residents of Cumberland Homesteads.

The Mountain View farmers pursued traditional flexible strategies for supplementing farming with other sources of income. In the early years, some of the men worked seasonally at coke ovens located in Grundy County or took factory jobs in Chattanooga, Tullahoma, or Oak Ridge. "Public work" was a temporary expedient if a crop failed, a building burned, or if cash was needed for some specific purpose—to buy more land or complete a building project. Among the various income-producing activities that regularly supplemented farming were timber cutting, hewing crossties, operating a sawmill or a charcoal kiln, and selling furs or medicinal roots.

For the people of Mountain View, however, this traditional diversified subsistence strategy was a means to achieve a new goal of successful commercial truck farming. The Alabama families first tried growing cotton, the crop familiar to them, but found the growing season too short. Then they tried corn, soybeans, and potatoes, but there were not strong markets for these commodities. Almost by accident, one farmer experimented with cabbage, discovered how well suited it was to the cool, moist plateau climate, and was gratified by the price he received in Chattanooga for his crop. Others followed his lead, gradually adding other vegetable crops and expanding their marketing to Nashville. By the 1960s certain crops, notably pimento peppers, were grown for canners as well as produce wholesalers. Sound financial management begun with FSA assistance, readiness to experiment, and cooperation with agricultural extension agents were important in this transition to commercial farming (Tennessee Agricultural Extension Service 1935-1940). Cooperation within the community was critically important also.

Initial land purchases spread out the pioneer families across the top of the mountain. Through land swaps, subdivision of the larger tracts, and later purchases, however, the families brought themselves into closer proximity, realizing that they needed one another to survive. For women as well as men, swapping labor was a means of efficiently accomplishing onerous tasks and heavy labor, beginning with the work of clearing land and building houses and barns. To assist in land clearing, members of the community pooled cash to buy a stump-puller which was considered common property and available to all. Barter of services and surplus commodities was an essential ingredient in the local economy until the shift was made from subsistence to commercial farming. One man with blacksmithing skills, for example, repaired tools and equipment for his neighbors and might receive syrup or firewood in return. As the truck farmers became more prosperous and increased their cultivated acres, they began to invest in tractors and other expensive equipment. For tasks that were not mechanized, like planting cabbage seedlings, women and young people from the community were now paid to supplement family labor. But informal economic cooperation persisted in the form of joint equipment purchases, usually involving relatives, and equipment swapping throughout the community.

At first everyone in Mountain View was poor and struggling to pay off a mortgage. But from the 1950s on, those who were able to expand their operations and become most successful as commercial operators have continued the pattern of cooperation. They still share equipment with part-time farmers who cannot afford their own. They also handle cooperative purchasing of seeds, plants, fertilizer and the like, for any farmers in the community who want to participate. And at times they assist young people trying to get started in farming to secure loans. By the 1980s, the operator of the largest farm in the community began pushing for a formally organized Vegetable Growers Cooperative. A specific project he advocated was a community packing shed which would help individual growers increase their leverage in marketing and free them from some of the pressures of grading, packing, and shipping their produce.

Conclusion: Social Engineering vs. Indigenous Community Development

The New Deal experimental communities were a worthwhile experiment in providing training and skills rather than just short-term relief, but their planners failed to win over either their clients or the general public to their views of cooperation, in fact achieving less cooperation than the unplanned community did drawing on its own supposedly inadequate traditions. Historians of the New Deal agree that rural rehabilitation loans were generally a popular and successful program (Baldwin, 199; Blakey 1986, 124-5). These loans held out to tenant farmers the possibility of regaining control over their lives and destinies, while social engineering in the government projects only replaced the landlord with a more benevolent master. Pervasive government control denied the independence that has always been a prime attraction of farming; philosophically the social visionaries who planned these projects operated on the premise that individual enterprise and cooperative spirit were incompatible values.

Mountain View, on the other hand, began with traditional modes of informal community cooperation such as mutual aid and barter of services, and transformed these into more modern guises—equipment swapping, cooperative ownership, and cooperative purchasing. The idea for a formally organized vegetable marketing cooperative developed naturally out of this context. The county agricultural extension agent then became a facilitator—someone to help the community explore its options and locate start-up funds. The focal point of community social interaction was the church, but although all of the pioneer founders shared similar religious values and identified as Baptists, in time there were disagreements between fundamentalist and more liberal viewpoints which produced schisms in the mid-1960s and again in the mid-1980s. Ambivalence about taking on leadership roles and resentment of those who'd assume leadership (phenomena observed by Hicks in "Little Laurel") played a role in the schisms. Although Pleasant Ridge Baptist Church still symbolizes the community and its history for the children of the pioneers, they realize that it can no longer be an all-inclusive community institution. In search of another forum that would encompass the whole community and address general issues such as Neighborhood Watch, they began a Community Club in 1985. Interestingly, members of the pioneer families took the initiative getting the club going but nominated "outsiders" to serve as officers, people who moved to Mountain View ten to fifteen years ago and have gained the confidence and respect of the pioneer families (cf. Hicks, 97). Thus, throughout its history, Mountain View has worked hard to maintain the ties of social and economic cooperation which were essential to the survival of individual farms and the community in the early years.

The Mountain View families, working out their own destiny without benefit of social engineering, faced physical hardships and risks that were unknown in the government projects; but they likewise faced possibilities to improve their lot immeasurably through their own persistence and hard work. Their experience revealed no dichotomy between individualism and cooperation; they found traditional patterns of economic and social cooperation to be effective and adaptable means of enhancing the security of each farm family and forming a supportive community for all of them.

Works Cited

Baldwin, Sidney. 1968. *Poverty and Politics: The Rise and Decline of the Farm Security Administration*. Chapel Hill: University of North Carolina Press.

Banfield, Edward C. 1951. *Government Project*. Glencoe, Illinois: Free Press.

Blakey, George T. 1986. *Hard Times and New Deal in Kentucky, 1929-1939*. Lexington: University Press of Kentucky.

Campbell, David and David Coombs. 1983. "Skyline Farms: A Case Study of Community Development and Rural Rehabilitation." *Appalachian Journal* 10(3): 244-54.

Conkin, Paul K. 1959. *Tomorrow a New World: The New Deal Community Program*. Ithaca: Cornell University Press.

Conrad, David Eugene. 1965. *The Forgotten Farmers. The Story of Sharecroppers in the New Deal*. Urbana: University of Illinois Press.

Eaton, Allen H. 1937. *Handicrafts of the Southern Highlands*. New York: The Russell Sage Foundation.

Eaton, Joseph. 1950. "The FSA Cooperative Farms." *Cooperative Group Living, An International Symposium on Group Farming and the Sociology of Cooperation*. Eds. H.F. Infield and J.B. Maier. New York: Koosis.

Forrest, Suzanne. 1989. *The Preservation of the Village. New Mexico's Hispanics and the New Deal*. Albuquerque: University of New Mexico Press.

Hicks, George L. 1976. *Appalachian Valley*. New York: Holt, Rinehart, Winston.

Infield, Henrik F. 1945. *Cooperative Communities at Work*. New York: Dryden Press.

Krechniak, Helen and Joseph Krechniak. 1956. *Cumberland County's First Hundred Years*. Crossville, Tennessee: Centennial Committee.

Lane, Patricia G. 1985. "Mountain View. An Ethnographic Account of Cooperation and Conflict in a Tennessee Community on the Cumberland Plateau." Knoxville Tennessee Anthropological Association Miscellaneous Paper No. 10.

McDonald, Michael and John Muldowny. 1982. *TVA and the Dispossessed: The Resettlement of Population in the Norris Dam Area.* Knoxville: University of Tennessee Press.

Mertz, Paul E. 1978. *New Deal Policy and Southern Rural Poverty.* Baton Rouge: Louisiana State University Press.

Mitchell, Broadus. 1947. *Depression Decade: From New Era Through New Deal, 1929-1941.* (Economic History of the United States, vol. 9) New York: Rinehart.

Owsley, Frank L. 1949. *Plain Folk of the Old South.* Baton Rouge: Louisiana State University Press.

Redfield, Robert. 1930. *Tepoztlan, a Mexican Village: A Study of Folk Life.* Chicago: University of Chicago Press.

———. 1947. "The Folk Society. *American Journal of Sociology* 52: 293-308.

Shapiro, Henry D. 1978. *Appalachia on Our Mind.* Chapel Hill: University of North Carolina Press.

Tennessee Agricultural Extension Service. 1935-1940. Annual Reports of Extension Agents. Typescripts on file, University of Tennessee College of Agriculture.

Tennessee Valley Authority. 1940. Department of Regional Planning Studies. "Social and Economic Characteristics of Six Tennessee Valley Reservoir Areas." Typescript on file, University of Tennessee Library.

Twelve Southerners. 1930. *I'll Take My Stand: The South and the Agrarian Tradition.* New York: Harper.

U.S. Census Bureau. 1945. Census of Agriculture.

Whisnant, David E. 1980. *Modernizing the Mountaineer.* Boone: Appalachian Consortium Press.

———. 1983. *All That Is Native & Fine. The Politics of Culture in an American Region.* Chapel Hill: University of North Carolina Press.

Woofter, T. J., Jr. and Ellen Winston. 1939. *Seven Lean Years.* Chapel Hill: University of North Carolina Press.

Acknowledgements

I am most grateful to the people of "Mountain View" and to Pat Lane, whose information on the community is incorporated in this paper. Pat and I became acquainted with "Mountain View" during a community history project completed in 1984 with support from the Tennessee Humanities Council. I presented an earlier version of this paper to the community during that project. Pat Lane continued research in Mountain View and completed her M.A. thesis the following year (Lane 1985); it is the primary source for the detailed descriptions of economic and social cooperation which are included in this paper. Thanks also to Jerry Walling and George Smith of the Agricultural Extension Service, who provided information and made AES reports available for study.

Benita J. Howell is an Associate Professor of Anthropology, University of Tennessee, Knoxville.

Lawrence Augustus Oxley: The Beginnings of Social Work Among Blacks in North Carolina Counties

John L. Bell

A remarkable event occurred in North Carolina in 1925: the creation of the Division of Work Among Negroes. Housed within the State Board of Charities and Public Welfare, this agency's purpose was to study black social problems, help blacks organize local social work agencies, and to support needed statewide agencies for blacks. This Division of Work Among Negroes was the first such state agency in the United States, and it became a model of its type. It secured black social workers in forty counties, encouraged the formation of charitable organizations, secured improved hospital care, mediated racial conflicts, pressed for prison reform, fought lynching, sought improved child care, helped wayward juveniles, enforced school attendance laws, and sponsored unemployment relief in the depression. Although the Appalachian counties of North Carolina had few blacks, this division was active in Buncombe County. The purpose of this paper is to examine the organization of statewide social services and the activities of the Division of Work Among Negroes in the Appalachian counties.

This division's effectiveness in providing black social services would not have been possible without a changing climate of opinion on social issues. Before 1900, few people understood how black social problems had an impact on the larger society. Public opinion in the South began to change as the National Conference of Charities and Corrections, later called the National Conference on Social Welfare, held periodic meetings in the South: at Louisville in 1883, Atlanta in 1903, Richmond in 1908, and Memphis in 1914, and focused attention on these problems. Prior to 1900, these national conferences looked condescendingly at the South, offering gratuitous solutions to its social problems, but the Atlanta conference of 1903 affirmed that the South was best suited to solve its social problems, and this affirmation spurred southern welfare workers to action. Social melioration was also a theme of the Southern Sociological Congresses that met in racially integrated sessions in Nashville, Atlanta, and Memphis before World War I to discuss the plight of blacks (Wisner 1970, 125-34).

Public opinion also began to change in North Carolina when an annual state social welfare conference, meeting the first time in 1912, spurred the state to social action. The 1916 conference proposed a State Board of Charities and Public Welfare be charged with starting statewide social welfare programs rather than giving passive supervision to local initiatives, as it had been doing. A.W. McAlister and Alfred M. Scales, both of Guilford County, secured the creation of such a board in the 1917 legislature, supposedly the first proactive state welfare agency in the nation. This board had five subdivisions: county organization, child welfare, institutional supervision, mental health, and publicity. It appointed for each county a three-member board to advise the state board and local officials (Shivers 1935, 226-28; Bruno 1957, 298-99).

Although the founders of the state board desired to improve black social conditions, the legislature would not fund black social services. Still, black speakers at the state conferences highlighted the need. A.M. Moore, who worked with Governor Thomas Bickett during the war to assure an equitable distribution of defense jobs to blacks, addressed the 1920 conference on their needs. Moore pleaded with the conference to help end lynching, restore the ballot, improve housing, abolish Jim Crow transportation, encourage white ministers to preach against racial injustice, provide equal access to education, obtain better benefits for black veterans, secure justice in the courts, and to end derogatory references to blacks. That he could speak so frankly indicated daring on his part and receptivity in his white listeners (North Carolina 1920, 28-33).

Moore's pleas fell on the receptive ears of the Commissioner of Charities and Public Welfare, Kate Burr Johnson. A native of Morganton in the mountain county of Burke, Johnson was the first woman appointed to head a state agency in North Carolina. She took assorted courses at Queens College, the University of North Carolina, and the New York School of Social Work, but she never took a degree. She learned leadership by presiding over women's clubs and heading the state office of child welfare. Appointed commissioner in 1921, she supervised one social worker, two stenographers, and an annual budget of $15,000. When she resigned in 1930, she supervised a staff of sixteen and a budget of $30,000, and she had secured grants of $114,000 to support social services for blacks and rural people, no little achievement (Raleigh 1930, 1952).

One grant which Kate Johnson secured (in 1924) was $60,000 from the Laura Spelman Rockefeller Fund. Half of this three-year grant went to establish and operate the Division of Work Among Negroes, an agency of her board. The division's purpose was to study black social problems and then help blacks organize locally to solve them (Raleigh).

To achieve these objectives, Kate Johnson's main task was to find an able person to head the division. She found a well-qualified person at St. Augustine's College, an Episcopal school for blacks in Raleigh. Her choice was thirty-seven-year-old social sciences instructor Lawrence Augustus Oxley, an "able and conscientious" (North Carolina 1929a, 7) man who headed this work for nine years until he became a member of President Franklin D. Roosevelt's "Black Cabinet." Born in Boston, Oxley attended a preparatory school in Cambridge and was later tutored by Harvard instructors. He enlisted in the army in World War I and rose in rank from private to first lieutenant. Serving as a special agent for the War Department, he investigated the morale of black troops in training camps. Postwar opportunities drew him to work in the Harlem YMCA, with the War Camp Community Service as a field investigator, with the Episcopal National Student Council, and finally to St. Augustine's in 1920 (*Who's Who* 1950, 404-5; *Washington Post* 1973).

Oxley was well prepared to work in the state's twenty-two Appalachian counties, but he was greatly hampered by the small black population and the racial attitudes of county officials. Some 30,000 blacks called Appalachia home in 1920, and about 38,000 in 1930, in each case, less than ten percent of the population. Although every Appalachian county had some blacks, only six counties had over 2,000: Buncombe, Burke, Henderson, McDowell, Rutherford, and Wilkes. By 1930, nearly half of the black Appalachian population was located in Buncombe County. Oxley's plan for social services required blacks to organize, set their own agendas, and hire a black social worker. Most counties did not have the size and concentration of black population to do this. So Buncombe's large black population, located mainly in Asheville, made it a focal point of Oxley's work in Appalachia (United States 1920, 735-45; 1930, 975-90).

The racial attitudes of county officials also made it difficult to organize social work in Appalachia. As part of a child welfare study, Oxley surveyed the racial attitudes of clerks of court, superintendents of schools, farm agents, and county doctors in fourteen Appalachian counties with the fewest blacks (Rosenwald Study 1929). The forty officials surveyed unanimously believed blacks to be inferior beings who should be segregated from whites. Looking at education for blacks, about half of these officials believed that blacks could benefit from elementary education only, but about a sixth wanted no black schools at all, feeling that education only ruined blacks for menial work. Surprisingly, three officials wanted "educational and economic equality of opportunity" for them (Rosenwald Study). When asked about blacks owning land, six officials opposed it; the other thirty-four wanted blacks to own land, but in segregated areas; they believed that land ownership helped make blacks better citizens. The whites in two counties, Graham and Mitchell, were hostile toward blacks, and encouraged visiting blacks to depart before sundown. An official in Mitchell County wanted to employ a black cook, but he feared for her safety if he brought her in. The towns of Jefferson and Morganton prohibited blacks from owning land inside the town limits, so patterns of residential segregation were well established. Only a fourth of these county officials wanted blacks to vote; the other three-fourths opposed their voting. Officials in Cherokee, Macon, Jackson, and Yancey counties believed their black inhabitants to be above average in intelligence and behavior, and race relations were thought to be good.

As a result of the survey, Oxley discovered few major social problems. The clerks of court reported no dependent children who were wards of the county. Black families took care of their own orphans. Children also were well behaved. The few delinquent children to appear in juvenile court were sent home with their parents to be whipped, a punishment never ordered for white children. This parental whipping was thought to be effective because there were few repeat offenders. School attendance was generally better than in white schools, and the pupils were generally "courteous and bright." One problem that emerged was a different standard of sexual mores. Two county officials noted that sexual liaisons between married black leaders and single women did not hurt the reputations of either. These liaisons did, however, result in a higher rate of venereal disease than among similar classes of whites (Rosenwald Study).

The poor racial attitudes of mountain whites caused the first major problem for Oxley. In October 1925, Governor Angus McLean called him to defuse an explosive situation in Asheville. Since the 1890s, Asheville had attracted thousands of tourists and health-seekers, especially tubercular patients. Growing population and a real estate boom fostered a mushrooming construction industry. From 1920 to 1925 some 3,000 black workers from adjoining states flocked to jobs in Asheville, and they were inclined to crime. During 1925 some 70 percent of blacks convicted of crimes in the county courts were from nearby states (North Carolina 1929, 13).

These conditions produced two rapes and an assault on white women by black men in September and October, 1925. These incidents outraged the white community, and a lynch mob ransacked the county jail in September searching for a black suspect whom the sheriff had moved to Charlotte only minutes ahead of the mob (Asheville 20 September 1925). Officers arrested 43 of the 200 in the mob, and 15 of them were later convicted and imprisoned (North Carolina 1929b, 53-54). In October a black man raped one white woman and assaulted another, and he was apprehended and identified. Again a lynch mob assembled, but the white victim refused to accompany the mob to the jail to identify the accused, and it disbanded (Asheville 27 October 1925).

White community feeling ran high over these incidents, and black leaders, before the second rapist was apprended, were mortified to read in the 29 October 1925 Asheville *Citizen* an editorial addressed "To Asheville Negroes." The editorial charged that the *Citizen* had appealed for help from the black community to apprehend the second rapist, but blacks had made "no substantial answer to an appeal, which should have stirred you. YOU HAVE FAILED IN YOUR DUTY." The editor believed that blacks had "inherited channels of communication that carries news swiftly and secretly to the Negro community." "YOU MUST DO SOMETHING," demanded the editor. "There must be no other assault on a white woman by a Negro—one more and peril will stare you in the face—a fearful peril. It will be no respecter of persons—the powers and influences which have restrained it will no longer avail." (Asheville 29 October 1925) The editor did not specify what the peril would be, but it seemed clear that it would take the form of indiscriminate, violent attacks on Asheville's 9,000 blacks.

Black leaders were swift to react to this "negro-baiting." Representatives of Asheville's "better class" of blacks met on October 29, 1925, with a *Citizen* reporter and argued that they could not be held accountable for the actions of some 3,000 black workers recently arrived in the city. These "boll weevils," as the newspaper called them, had "shown a tendency to run riot and have exercised a bad influence on their fellows". (Asheville 30 October 1925). The black leaders pleaded "for Asheville to distinguish between the race and the individual" because they could not guarantee the good behavior of 3,000 itinerants (Asheville 30 October 1925). On October 30 these black leaders met with the city commissioners and presented a resolution condemning the *Citizen* editorial. The commissioners endorsed the leaders' plans for a mass meeting of blacks to be held the next Sunday to discuss ways of cooperating with law enforcement officers (Asheville 31 October 1925).

The Sunday mass meeting was anticlimactic. Blacks voiced "open resentment" that they were not employed on the city police force. The main speaker was Lawrence Oxley, sent by Governor McLean to defuse the hostility of blacks. Oxley stressed the need for "straight and sane thinking," and he urged the crowd to "co-operate to the fullest" with city officials. He also cautioned people to be "careful in the matter of making radical statements that have no foundation in truth" (Asheville 2 November 1925). The meeting adjourned without taking any formal action, and feeling in the white community subsided. Oxley's exact role in averting disaster is not fully known. It is known that he spent a week in Asheville working behind the scenes until danger passed. Although some of the black press criticized his role, others credited him with restoring sanity to the town.

Closely related to this Asheville situation was Oxley's study of capital punishment of blacks in the state. Describing lynching as an extra-legal form of capital punishment, Oxley showed that lynching was subsiding. No blacks were lynched in the state from 1922 to 1928. He attributed this result to the strong resolve of governors Thomas Bickett, Cameron Morrison, and Angus McLean to oppose mob violence. His case study of an Asheville mob showed this gubernatorial resolve. In September 1925, a mob stormed the Buncombe County jail to seize and lynch Alvin Mansell, the suspect in the first rape case indicated above. The mob destroyed jail property and released prisoners to find Mansell, but the sheriff had whisked him away to Charlotte just minutes before the mob struck. Officers were able to identify and apprehend 43 of the 200 people in the mob. After their trial, Judge A.M. Stack sentenced four of the leaders to three to eight years in state prison and eleven of them to county road terms up to one year, and to another five he gave suspended sentences. In sentencing the men, Judge Stack said, "God save the state that has to depend on mobs to protect its women.... What the officers needed down there that night was a few machine guns" (North Carolina 1929b, 54). Some 6,000 Buncombe County petitioners pleaded with Governor McLean to grant clemency. The governor refused, saying that "those who are asking for clemency for these men should remember that the crime they committed was one of the most serious known to our law—serious because the sovereignty of all the people of the State was trampled under foot and insulted by the mob.... Our people are determined to suppress mob violence at any cost" (North Carolina 1929b, 55).

This mob violence was directed against Alvin Mansell whose case Oxley used to demonstrate the injustices of the court system in his publication, *Capital Punishment in North Carolina*. In 1925 the seventeen-year-old Mansell moved from Pickens, South Carolina, to Asheville to live with his older sister and work in a sanatorium. Having only a fifth grade education, the 120-pound Mansell had an I.Q. of fifty-three and the mental age of a nine-year-old. The thirty-five-year-old white woman who accused him of rape sold flowers at the sanatorium where he worked. After walking a mile away from the sanatorium one morning, she alleged that a mulatto attacked her. After the attack she walked to a friend's house where, before a deputy sheriff, she described her assailant as being a thirty-five-year-old mulatto wearing a blue shirt, yellow trousers, and a felt hat. Later that afternoon she went to the sanatorium and identified Mansell as her assailant although he did not match her earlier description in any particular. A court-appointed attorney defended Mansell, but the judge denied his motion for continuance to have time to secure witnesses. Mansell testified in his own behalf, denying his guilt and saying that he never left the sanatorium until mid-afternoon. Co-workers corroborated his testimony. The prosecutor introduced no evidence other than the victim's testimony, and nothing to corroborate her charges. After considerable deliberation, the jury found Mansell guilty, and the judge sentenced him to death.

Some four thousand Buncombe citizens, believing a miscarriage of justice had occurred, petitioned the governor for clemency. At this point, Lawrence Oxley's duties required him to prepare the facts of the case for presentation to the governor, for the Division of Work Among Negroes reviewed all requests for pardons and clemency for black prisoners. Oxley pointed out discrepancies in the victim's description of her assailant. Two doctors who examined her and the deputy sheriff who first questioned her, none of whom the prosecutor called to testify, found her earlier statements at sharp variance with her testimony in court. Six patients at the sanatorium, none of whom testified at the trial, also contradicted her testimony. Six jurors, reading the affadavits of these witnesses after the trial, requested the governor to commute Mansell's sentence to life because they had reasonable doubt of his guilt. Even a prosecuting attorney, after reading the new evidence, appealed to the governor for clemency. After considering the new evidence and appeals, Governor Angus McLean commuted the sentence from death to life in prison. McLean refused to pardon Mansell because he believed that the jury could have heard the new evidence and still found Mansell guilty (North Carolina 1929b, 99-102). To Oxley, this case was an example of the miscarriage of justice that gave a higher percentage of death sentences to blacks. From 1909 through 1927, he discovered, the state convicted 198 people for capital crimes, 147 of them black and 51 white. Of these 198 convicted, 94 were electrocuted, 81 blacks and 13 whites (North Carolina 1929b, 54-5, 19-20).

While seeking justice for blacks, Oxley also worked on the county level helping blacks organize themselves to identify and solve their own social problems. To do this, Oxley needed the leadership provided by educated, middle-class, black citizens, concentrated in an urban area for ease of communication. By 1930, Asheville's black population numbered 14,255, about 40 percent of all blacks living in the mountains. It was an ideal place in the Appalachian counties for Oxley to focus his efforts. Accordingly, in 1925 Oxley encouraged the county to employ its first black social worker, Douglas Clarke, one of thirteen such workers in the state. By the summer of 1926, blacks had Faith Cottage operating to care for unwed mothers. Oxley also secured the appointment in 1925 of a seven-member state advisory board to Kate Johnson. Included on the board was Dr. L. O. Miller, an Asheville physician who led the opposition to the Asheville *Citizen's* race-baiting in 1925. Oxley also encouraged the development of the YWCA in Asheville. Its director was Adela F. Ruffin, who replaced Dr. Miller on the state advisory board in 1927 (North Carolina 1924-1926, 40, 109, 132; 1926-1928, 110). Because of the extreme individualism of Asheville blacks, Adela Ruffin felt that she had experienced an uphill struggle to organize the community for social improvement. "Asheville is a small *town* grown quickly--*too* quickly—to the *size* of a city. It has the problems and responsibilities of a city — without wide vision. It is a smug town. . . . ," complained Ruffin. "Its thinking is individualistic — to a surprising degree because, in most cases, the *individuals* have had so much training that we expect them to be different" (Ruffin 1927).

Given the purported lack of social vision in Asheville, Oxley was able to help this mountain area develop some vision and compassion. In 1931, as the economic depression deepened, Governor O. Max Gardner requested Oxley's services to help organize blacks for relief work across the state. Governor Gardner believed that all relief work should come from local effort, and that the relief efforts should be segregated where possible, white agencies helping whites and black agencies helping blacks. To assist the governor, Oxley secured the appointment of a statewide advisory council of blacks and twelve district committees. Dr. L. O. Miller of Asheville was on this statewide committee also. One of the district committees was in Asheville, and it sponsored community mass meetings to enlist the active support of leaders (North Carolina 1930-1932, 100-101). One person on the committee acted as an agent to determine relief needs, and to minister to them through existing public agencies. The committee also contacted every employed black person to secure contributions to the Community Chest, the United Welfare Drive, and the Associated Charities. County and city agencies cooperated with white and black relief groups to operate a wood lot, community gardens, a small cannery, and street cleaning to provide relief for the unemployed. In return for working three days a week, the unemployed were given groceries adequate to feed their families for a week (Raleigh 1931; 1932). By 1933, the Reconstruction Finance Corporation made some $5 million available to North Carolinians for unemployment relief. Oxley found it possible to enroll blacks in work relief programs "only and when trained, intelligent Negro workers are appointed as members of staffs of local relief agencies." He tried "to place such Negro leaders in strategic places throughout the State" (Oxley 1933) and thus help blacks get relief money. Oxley's relief efforts constituted a model national program and won for him appointment to an advisory relief council to President Hoover.

Oxley provided other minor services for the Asheville area, especially as a contact person in state government. When the city cut teachers' pay in 1933, black teachers were not told the reason, and they were afraid to ask the white superintendent whether the cuts applied to both races. The teachers asked Oxley to get the needed information in Raleigh. Oxley also secured from the American Legion, to which he belonged, gifts for some forty-three black patients in the veterans' hospital at nearby Oteen. Oxley also referred requests for mountain summer experiences for black children to people in Asheville who took children into their homes in the summer (Swepson 1933; Oxley 1931; 1929).

While Oxley's local initiatives were beneficial to Asheville, his work to establish and support statewide agencies and institutions also promised assistance to Appalachian blacks. A major concern of Oxley's was the rehabilitation of juvenile delinquents. In 1925, the Federation of Colored Women's Clubs contributed $25,000 to establish the North Carolina Industrial Home for Colored Girls at Efland. This home had a dormitory for twenty girls, and facilities for teaching domestic science and sewing. Juvenile courts committed twelve girls there in 1926. Oxley and an association of white women lobbied the legislatures from 1927 to 1933 to have the state assume control of the facility, but they were able to secure only a $2,000 annual appropriation. The state had more interest in the rehabilitation of delinquent boys, for the 1925 legislature created the Morrison Training School at Hoffman. The $25,000 appropriation provided for the purchase of 300 acres and the erection of four buildings to which the courts assigned 200 boys in 1933 and put 280 on the waiting list. The training school used a farm and a model dairy to teach the boys initiative and self reliance (Sanders 1933, 8-9).

Assistance for crippled children was another concern of Oxley's. In 1921, the state established an orthopedic hospital at Gastonia, but it was for whites only (Brown 1928, 157). In 1925, Benjamin N. Duke contributed $15,000 to this hospital to build a ward for twenty black children. The need was so great that he contributed $25,000 more to add thirty more beds by 1933. Social workers helped to organize local clinics to screen children whom the hospital might help (Sanders 1933, 9, 40-41).

Another need was training for black social workers. Mecklenburg County hired the first black social worker, Hattie Russell, in 1919. By 1933 local governments employed about forty black social workers across the state. This was a completely new field for blacks, few of whom were educated in social work, and most of whom had, at best, only some college. Oxley's Division of Work Among Negroes sponsored annual three-day institutes to train social workers. The 1926 institute, for example, enrolled seventy-three students who listened to inspirational speakers and attended classes (North Carolina 1924-1926, 111-13). The classes were on the history and objectives of social work, community organization, case work and record keeping, school attendance, juvenile court, and mental defectives.

Oxley also helped to meet the need for formal social work education. The Atlanta School of Social Work, established in 1920, was the first such school for blacks in the South. The University of North Carolina School of Public Welfare also was established in 1920, but it enrolled only whites. Its faculty did, however, teach at the annual institutes and contribute to the founding of a religious school of social work at St. Augustine's College in Raleigh. This school was the Bishop Tuttle Memorial Training School, established by the Women's Auxiliary of the Episcopal Church in 1925. Requiring two years of college for admission, the school provided a three-year curriculum, and some twenty students were graduated by 1930 (Ross 1978, 427, 433, 463; Shivers 1935, 209-11; North Carolina 1924-1926, 114; 1932-1934, 88).

Oxley's work in North Carolina ended in 1934 when he accepted an offer from Secretary of Labor Frances Perkins to work in her department to improve employment opportunities for blacks. From 1925 to 1934 Oxley had directed a model state program to provide much-needed social services for North Carolina blacks. Included in this program were services for blacks in Appalachian counties. Concentrated mainly in Buncombe County, these services included mediation of racial conflict, support for anti-lynching activities, better treatment of blacks in the criminal justice system, inclusion of mountain blacks on state advisory committees, securing the employment of black social workers, and encouraging local unemployment relief. Oxley also encouraged the development of statewide social services agencies open to Appalachian blacks. These included training schools, an orthopedic hospital, and social work education. This period of Oxley's leadership ushered in a new era of society's concern for its black citizens.

Works Cited

Asheville Citizen. 20,22 September 1925; 23, 24,28, 29, 30,31 October 1925; 2 November 1925.

Brown, Roy M. 1928. *Public Poor Relief in North Carolina.* Chapel Hill: University of North Carolina Press.

Bruno, Frank J. 1957. *Trends in Social Work, 1874-1956: A History Based on the Proceedings of the National Conference of Social Work.* New York: Columbia University Press.

Bunche, Ralph J. 1973. *The Political Status of the Negro in the Age of FDR.* Ed. Dewey W. Grantham. Chicago: University of Chicago Press.

Kirby, John B. 1980. *Black Americans in the Roosevelt Era.* Knoxville: University of Tennessee Press.

North Carolina. 1920. State Board of Charities and Public Welfare. *Bulletin* 3 (April-June 1920). Raleigh, North Carolina.

———. 1924-26. State Board of Charities and Public Welfare. *Biennial Report.* Raleigh, North Carolina.

———. 1925. State Board of Charities and Public Welfare. Division of Work Among the Negroes. Special Report, 1 January to 31 March 1925, in Commissioner's Office, Subject File, 1891-1952, Box 6, Records of the Department of Public Welfare, North Carolina State Archives, Raleigh, North Carolina (hereinafter cited as DPW).

———. 1926-1928. State Board of Charities and Public Welfare. *Biennial Report.* Raleigh, North Carolina.

———. 1929a. State Board of Charities and Public Welfare. *North Carolina's Welfare Program for Negroes.* Special Bulletin Number 8, Raleigh, North Carolina.

———. 1929b. State Board of Charities and Public Welfare. *Capital Punishment in North Carolina.* Special Bulletin Number 10, Raleigh, North Carolina.

———. 1930-1932. State Board of Charities and Public Welfare. *Biennial Report.* Raleigh, North Carolina.

———. 1932-1934. State Board of Charities and Public Welfare. *Biennial Report.* Raleigh, North Carolina.

Oxley, Lawrence A. 1925. Correspondence to Gertrude Weil, 6 November 1925, Commissioner's Office, Subject File, 1891-1952, Box 5, DPW.

———. 1929. Correspondence to Charles C. Middleton, 19 June 1929, Division of Work Among the Negroes, General Correspondence-M, Box 230, DPW.

———. 1931. Correspondence to J. M. Caldwell, 18 November 1931, Division of Work Among the Negroes, General Correspondence-C, Box 230, DPW.

———. 1933. Correspondence to Oscar DePriest, 8 April 1933, Division of Work Among the Negroes, General Correspondence-D, Box 230, DPW.

Raleigh *News and Observer*. 19 February 1930; 26 February 1930; 29 May 1951; 18 January 1931; 8 February 1931; 1 November 1931; 2 January 1932.

Rosenwald Study. 1929. "Attitudes Toward the Negro" in Alleghany, Ashe, Avery, Burke, Cherokee, Clay, Graham, Haywood, Jackson, Macon, Madison, Mitchell, Watauga, and Yancey counties; Commissioner's Office, Subject File, 1891-1952, Interracial Cooperation, Box 6, DPW.

Ross, Edyth L., ed. 1978. *Black Heritage in Social Welfare, 1860-1930*. Metuchen, New Jersey: The Scarecrow Press.

Ruffin, Adela F. 1927. Correspondence with Lawrence A. Oxley, 13 January 1927, Division of Work Among the Negroes, General Correspondence-R, Box 230, DPW.

Sanders, Wiley Britton. 1933. *Negro Child Welfare in North Carolina: A Rosenwald Study*. Chapel Hill: University of North Carolina Press.

Shivers, Lyda Gordon. 1935. "The Social Welfare Movement in the South: A Study in Regional Culture and Social Organization." Ph.D. diss., University of North Carolina.

Swepson, Beulah M. 1933. Correspondence to Oxley, October 9, 1933, Division of Work Among the Negroes, General Correspondence-S, Box 230, DPW.

United States. 1920. Bureau of the Census. *Population* (1920), 2: 735-745.

———. 1930. Bureau of the Census. *Population* (1930), 3: 975-990.

Washington. *Washington Post*. 5 July 1973.

Who's Who in Colored America. 1950, 404-405.

Wisner, Elizabeth. 1970. *Social Welfare in the South From Colonial Times to World War I*. Baton Rouge: Louisiana State University Press.

John L. Bell is a professor of history at Western Carolina University in Cullowhee, North Carolina.

Religious Freethinkers in the Southern Highlands

Henry J. Weaver

I must be contented to be a Unitarian by myself, although I know there are many around who would gladly become so. . . . I trust that there is not a young man now living in the United States who will not die a Unitarian.

The writer of the above quote was far more skilled as a farmer, inventor, political philosopher, statesman, diplomat, and Chief Executive of the United States than as a prognosticator of religious denominational popularity. Thomas Jefferson's talents did not include predicting accurately the dominant religious movements of the future, especially those in the southern Appalachians that spread to the west and south from his "Little Mountain" home facing the Blue Ridge in Albemarle County.

This paper will focus on the Unitarian and Universalist traditions that so attracted Mr. Jefferson and those traditions' experiences in the southern Appalachian region. Included is a look at Old World roots, the American foundings of both Unitarianism and Universalism, and some things that other denominations' scholars had to say about the two strains of religious "free-thinking." There is a brief state-by-state sketch about freethinking's history. The paper concludes with a short history of the religious experience of freethinking in the Holston Valley of upper East Tennessee from the time of Dr. William Hale in the mid-1800s to the end of the 1980s.

The Christian view of church and state began in the benevolent protectorship of Constantine, the first Christian Emperor of Rome. Under him, Clement of Rome reminded the faithful that salvation is not by wisdom or works, but by faith. Soon, Tertullian warned against the infiltration of Greek heresy (Murch 1962, 10). Greek philosophy, widely accepted by the intelligentsia throughout the Roman Empire in New Testament times, had a tremendous influence upon religion. Religious philosophies seeking a satisfactory theory of God, explanation of nature, and codes of conduct formed the basics of many religious approaches that some branded as heresies and other viewed as viable alternatives (Murch, 9). In A.D. 190 Victor of Rome claimed to be "universal bishop," but he was ignored by most other churches (Mattox 1961). Departures from the emerging orthodox faith (a belief in the three-part nature of God, or "Trinitarian" view) were largely responsible for the convening of the Council of Nicea (A.D. 325) and five other general church councils, at the last of which was held in A.D. 680. (Murch, 11). At Nicea, the doctrine of the Trinity was adopted by the established church—by means more political than religious. Thereafter, those who stressed the unity of God (later known as "Unitarians") were branded as heretics by the now-dominant Trinitarians (Provost). It's been an uphill battle for Unitarians ever since.

From the fourth century A.D. on, the Greek-based idea of the unity of God spread across Western Europe. Incumbent in this philosophy was the idea that the Unitarian God is a God of mercy and *universality*. All humans, not just specified "elect" can expect to be lovingly viewed by that Diety. The Second London Confession, usually referred to as the "Confession of 1689," deserves note because it influenced future Baptist beliefs and led to the English rise of Unitarianism. The "Confession" was very dogmatic and became a kind of hyper-Calvinism. Its immediate effect was to seem to freeze the genial Christian spontaneity of Baptist thought, and brought a stiff formalism of expression. Soon, many Baptist leaders, as well as whole churches turned to the philosophies incumbent in Unitarianism, beginning about 1690 (Paschal 1930, 36-7). The great migration from the British Isles to the United States in the late eighteenth and early nineteenth centuries found the seeds of Unitarian and Universalist theology taking widely scattered roots in the young nation. Both strains sought to provide Christians with a relevant, rational alternative to Trinitarianism. By enshrining reason, experience, and conscience at the heart of Christian life, and by declaring that revelation and salvation must be measured by human character rather than by dogmatic pronouncement, Unitarians genuinely sought the revered Christian loyalties and energies of a disenchanted with the orthodox, but productive and inventive segment of the American people (Mendelson, 163).

John Murray arrived in coastal New Jersey in 1770, and is considered the American founder of the universal forgiving theology that became the Universalist Church (Miller, 3). Another coastal town,

Newport, Rhode Island, was the birthplace of William Ellery Channing in 1780. A watershed date for the modern American Unitarian Church is often considered 5 May 1819, when Channing preached on "Unitarian Christianity" at an ordination in Baltimore (Mendleson, 158-59). Unitarians tended to cling to the Atlantic seaboard and to their New England origins. If they ventured beyond, they settled in urban rather than rural environments.

Universalists, on the other hand, although also associated historically with New England, were much more inclined to venture into the frontier (Miller, 233). In the lands of the frontier, the early itinerant Universalist preachers "rode the circuit," or wandered the country side much as did their counterparts in Trinitarian denominations. Their arrival was often greeted by indifference, if not hostility, and their influence ended with their departure. Yet they doggedly made their rounds and occasionally planted religious seeds that later matured into societies and churches that made all the effort seem worthwhile.

The majority of Universalist itinerants in the pre-Civil War period were obscure even in their own day, and completely unknown to later generations. Appearances, particularly in the Midwest and South, were often unscheduled and the "discourses" strictly impromptu. Above all, the Universalists in the pioneering days of the denomination were handicapped by the lack of central or even regional headquarters to which to turn for material support. They had to depend on their own limited resources and ingenuity to a much larger extent than did most other itinerant preachers (Miller, 235).

George Rogers (1803-1846) is an excellent example of the stressful life style of early Universalist itinerant preachers. Although he basically preached in the western Pennsylvania and southern Ohio regions, he also traveled and preached in the mountain sections of five states from Kentucky to Alabama. While in Tennessee, he saw and heard Andrew Jackson as "Old Hickory" made his triumphant return home after completing his second term as president in 1837 (Miller, 238). Rogers died of consumption at the age of forty-two, literally worn out. Meanwhile, a small but constant stream of converts who abandoned orthodoxy became Universalists, and an even greater number became Unitarians in the urban settlements of the upland South.

Other denominations, predictably, did not react with great calmness to such conversions. In rural North Carolina in the 1780s, a Baptist minister named John Stancil became a Universalist and was described as being "arch, cunning, and insinuating, carried away many with his craft through the subtlety of Satan" (Paschal, 500). A Primitive Baptist lay scholar equated Unitarian denial of Christ's divinity to elements he found repulsive in Arianism, Roman Catholicism, and Mohammedanism

(Islam), (Hassell 1973, 380). He went on to condemn a Universalist college president who was described as seeing "the whole creation in one vast restless movement, sweeping toward the grand finality of universal holiness and universal love" (Hassell, 592). The Primitive Baptist who criticized Unitarianism dismissed that possibility, stating he only believed in the old-fashioned Bible, unmixed with Pagan philosophy and could see no such grand finality. Jacob Bower, a Baptist itinerant preacher who was a rare reverse convert from Universalist to Baptist, recalled in his autobiography of trying to sell Bibles to a houseful of Universalists. He was asked, "Are you one of those hell fire and brimstone preachers who go around heaping that on people and preach up Eternal Damnation to a part of the humain [sic] family? We are all Universalists in this timber and you cannot sell us any of your Bibles" (Sweet 1964, 224). No less a Christian churchman than Bishop Francis Asbury wrote John Wesley in 1783, stating among other things, "that the Calvinists and Universalists very much retard the work of God. . . .by keeping people from seeking 'heart religion'" (Sweet, 15).

For several decades after the American Revolution there was something of a revolt against prevailing orthodoxy that led to the limited acceptance of Unitarianism, Universalism, and Deism. The French Revolution became a popular topic of conversation, and the religious skepticism associated with that movement attracted in the West (remember, the southern mountains were "the West") numerous advocates of French "infidelity." The American Tract Society and other publishing houses printed and spread the religious literature of the Presbyterians, Congregationalists, and Unitarians, and concentrated on religion in the West.

The Great Revival of the early 1800s was a watershed in the religious history of the South and originated in the mountains. It predetermined the eventual failure of the dominance Thomas Jefferson had predicted for Unitarianism. The deistic liberalism of the post-revolutionary era soon faded into the past, leaving only a few areas to continue to grow and most to wither. John Boles, in his definitive work on the Great Revival period, writes that Unitarianism (and presumably Universalism) was too philosophical to satisfy the emotional needs of the people—rural and mountain people were always an emotional lot, despite their often calm facade (189-90). In the religious denominational haggling after the Great Revival, one Baptist wrote about the Disciples of Christ leader, Alexander Campbell, "If I had evidence of his being a Christian, I should call him a spiritual Bastard; but that name is not appropriate. There is not a meeting-house except those of the Universalists or Unitarians that will admit him to their pulpit" (Posey, 58-59). One can discern from these examples that Unitarians and Universalists were not always the recipients of great Christian love, understanding and patience. Of all those who criticized the movements, "Parson" William Brownlow of East Tennessee was perhaps the most severe. Brownlow was a combination Methodist preacher, politician, military rabble-rouser, and newspaper editor. His vicious attacks on Presbyterians, Congregationalists, Unitarians, and Universalists to a large degree stunted their efforts to grow in many parts of the southern mountains (20-21).

Despite the widespread opposition created by orthodox Christian denominations, somehow the principles of Unitarianism and Universalism persisted. A scholar of the Disciples of Christ wrote that "in areas that scriptural teaching was not positive and clear, that Christians were free to follow their own private judgement" (Harrell 1966, 30). This distinction was theologically important to the disciples of Christ—the union of Disciples and Stoneites who were suspected of Unitarianism. Long before William James penned the thought below, American religious freethinkers were practicing his philosophy:

> I am done with great things and big things, great institutions and big success, and I am for those tiny invisible moral forces that work from individual to individual creeping through the crannies of the world like so many rootlets, or like the capillary oozing water, yet which, if you give them time, will rend the hardest monuments of man's pride.

William Ellery Channing's 1819 Baltimore sermon was an effort of greater subtlety than is widely acknowledged. There was not a single premise in the Calvinist system that Channing did not isolate, examine, discard, and replace. He did it as follows:

- Dogmatic scripturalism was supplanted by a Bible accountable to human reason and experience.
- The Trinity was superseded by a unified, integral Creator-Father.
- Divine-human Christ became a stable, homogenous, suffering and conquering teacher; the Jesus of Nazareth's dusty roads.
- God, capable of perpetrating the horrors of total depravity and predestination, was replaced by a paternal diety whose moral perfection was both *understandable* and *imitable* in human terms.
- The ancient Anselmic notion that man, by sinning against

an infinite being, was poisoned by an infinite guilt
was supplanted by the situational argument that a
person's guilt must be measured by his/her nature and
power of choice.
- The supreme object of religious practice, therefore, was
not to avoid punishment, but to cultivate and communicate
virtue. (Mendelson, 162)

Often called "heretical sects," Unitarians and Universalists, basing their beliefs on the image of a one-part Diety and ultimate salvation for all, struggled to survive in America in the years between 1770 and 1860. By the time of the War Between the States, they had grown sufficiently in strength and influence to become institutionalized as full-fledged churches providing a viable Christian alternative to the dominant theology of orthodox Trinitarianism. Ranging beyond ideas of the unity of God and universal salvation, both churches plunged into matters of social ethics, established academies and colleges (Harvard and Tufts, but none of note in the southern mountains), participated in such reform movements as temperance, women's rights, the abolition of slavery, and capital punishment. A quietly pervasive force in American society came out of the roughly parallel traditions of Unitarian and Universalist religious liberalism (Miller, coverleaf).

While it is possible to overstate the ethical effects of Unitarianism and Universalism, even the most liberal Trinitarian denominations should be careful in claiming too much credit for social justice achieved in this country in the last century-and-a-half. Rarely do Trinitarians give due credit to freethinkers in matters of social justice and, to this day, members of the so-called "Moral Majority" delight in castigating religious freethinkers with the label "secular humanists" which, to the Jerry Falwells of modern America, is a buzz-word for a legal dirty name. While most liberal Trinitarians do not agree with the Moral Majority namecallers about freethinkers, they have not noticeably rushed to embrace the freethinkers high-priority concerns about social matters. An example is the nuclear arms insanity. Virtually all Unitarians and Universalists have had the nuclear arms race as a top social concern since August 1945 and the atom-bombing of Japan. It is instead a "come and go" issue with most Trinitarians—at least in their formal declarations. In formal meetings, much more of Trinitarian time has been spent on such "life and death" issues as banning dancing on college campuses, outlawing abortions, not ordaining women, selling and buying church property, seeking more extensive tax exemptions for church activities, and closing adult bookstores while more obscene situations exist all around in the living conditions of the disenfranchised. It is not argued that many Trinitarians (probably the majority) are not interested in social justice to the degree that are freethinkers. It is rather obvious, however, that the social concerns of church members do not proportionately equal that of Unitarians and Universalists, demonstrated by the historical lack of social activism by the orthodoxy. Individual salvation and "gettin' right with God" seem to overshadow the blessed message of deep concern for all life taught by Jesus of Nazareth.

Russell E. Miller, Professor of English and History at Universalist Tufts University, Chairman of the Department of History, and University Historian/Archivist, published in 1979 the to-date definitive history of the Universalist Church's first century in America, 1770-1870. The following sketches about freethinkers in those states that contain the southern Appalachians are taken from his work. There are few other well-documented accounts of freethinkers in the region prior to this century for reasons stated earlier in this paper. Mainly, the hardships, and the lack of regional headquarters support of the early itinerant preachers, stunted the growth of freethinking.

Maryland: the state's large Roman Catholic population joined with the effective opposition provided by the German Reformed Church to limit freethinkers' growth mainly to Baltimore. Attempts failed to establish the denomination on either the Eastern Shore or the mountainous western part of the state (723).

Virginia and West Virginia: Numerous efforts were made to form churches by freethinkers in the Shenandoah Valley, but with modest successes. A problem was the large-scale presence of Dunker congregations, who also believed in universal salvation and preferred to retain their German pietistic designation. Considerably more success was experienced on the Eastern Shore for a time, but ultimately, freethinkers did not flourish in urban or rural areas. The liberal scholar, Clarence Gohdes, wrote: "Had Thomas Jefferson lived in the 1840s, he would have bowed his head in futile rage as the power of religious conservatism (initially fueled by the Great Revival) cast a blacker and blacker cloud over the scattered lights of liberalism in the South" (Boles, 190). The few groups of freethinkers that were found in what became West Virginia were located mainly in the northern neck around Wheeling. They probably came to the area via an entirely different migratory pattern than did most of the peoples of the Southern mountains. The most distant from the central Virginia itinerant freethinking preachers was W.R. Chamberlin, who used Abingdon as a base and travelled up and down the "Great Valley." Between 1848 and 1850 he preached once a month at four designated stations. There is no way to know for certain, but it is reasonable to assume that his work may have played some part in the later conversion of Dr. William Hale of Free Hill, Tennessee, to Universalism. Free Hill is in upper east Tennessee, and as part of the "Great Valley Extended," is only about fifty miles from Abingdon. The flow of information put out by Chamberlin could well have influenced Hale long after Chamberlin moved to Cincinnati in 1850 after he "was nearly starved out." Religious legacies are often hard to determine, but a geographical and cultural knowledge of the area portends the possibility of some tie between Chamberlin and Hale.

Tennessee: Until late in the nineteenth century, Universalism was the only evident form of freethinking in this frontier state, and was strictly a bootstrap operation. George Rogers was of some renown as an itinerant preacher, and others came up occasionally from Alabama or down from Kentucky and concentrated their efforts on non-mountain counties. Later, churches grew in the "Valley Extended" areas of what are now Tri-Cities and Knoxville. Chattanooga got some attention from Alabama-based freethinking ministers (731-33).

Kentucky: the Cumberland Gap route into the Bluegrass and the Ohio River route down to the western parts of Kentucky saw the majority of freethinker growth in "Kentuck." George Rogers travelled in the eastern mountains in 1836-37, and had little success. Among sects present, he discovered the "Live Forevers," who believed in man's eventual rejuvenation. They apparently saw nothing in Universalism more attractive than what they already possessed in the way of religious belief (733-35).

North Carolina saw virtually no organized freethinker presence in the mountains. The Piedmont saw little influence either, but the Coastal Plain has a rather extensive history of Universalism. Towns like Richlands and Swansboro in Onslow County, Clinton in Sampson County, Chinquapin in Duplin County, and Edenton and Halifax in the northeast corner of the state, nourished fairly substantial Universalist congregations (753-64). A very probable explanation lies with the migration patterns of various ethnic groups. The coastal freethinkers almost surely can trace roots to the English Baptists that converted to Universalism in reaction to the hyper-Calvinism brought about by the Second London Confession (1689).

South Carolina: While there was a large settlement of Dunkers who possessed theology similar to Universalists, freethinkers never made it to the mountainous counties of northwest South Carolina.

Georgia: The Georgia experience was much like that in South Carolina. The nearest to the mountains with a recorded effort is the town hall in Athens (described as "the headquarters of unorthodoxy in Georgia") (751-58).

Alabama saw sort of a leap-frog effect as Universalists from South Carolina migrated there through Georgia and settled in the non-hilly parts of the state. In 1853, J.M.H. Smith of Huntsville, in mountainous Madison County, claimed to be the only public advocate of Universalism in all of northern Alabama.

Mississippi: While Mississippi is hardly a mountainous state, it does touch the southern end of the Appalachians and the story of freethinkers there before the modern years was repeated in the same pattern as in most other states of the south; namely, isolated pockets of believers in a one-part Deity and universal salvation. They were scattered over a rural landscape, largely without organization, and depended on roving preachers who were small in number and often were based in other states. The congregations were usually the county-seat towns that were normally the larger communities and served as political as well as commercial headquarters (769-70).

The preceding information illustrates the rather hit-and-miss nature of the formal history of organized freethinking churches in the southern mountains. For reasons already twice discussed, there is a dearth of information about specific church efforts in the mountains, however, there is not a total void. Through the excellent initiative and primary source scholarship of Mrs. Ida Metz Hyland of Johnson City, Tennessee, the writer is able to give considerable detail—more than I will include in this paper—about the history of the freethinkers' experience in the Holston Valley of upper east Tennessee from before the War Between the States to the 1980s.

The beautiful and highly liveable hilly terrain of the Holston River Valley is geologically a part of the "Great Valley (Shenandoah) Extended." Western European religious thought has travelled with pioneers down the Valley from the original Colonial America settlements of Pennsylvania, Delaware, and Maryland since the first half of the eighteenth century. The ancestors of Dr. William Hale brought Universalist views to the Holston Valley from York and Lancaster counties in Pennsylvania by 1795. William Hale was born in northeastern Tennessee in 1838, and died in Washington County in that same area in 1906. Trained in medicine, he served as a full-time doctor for a number of years, and later in life was a part-time physician and a Universalist lay preacher. Finally, in 1877, he because the first native-born Tennessean licensed to preach by the Universalist Church. He operated out of his home in the area called Free Hill, quite possibly a rural community of freethinkers, near the present-day town of Gray. A church was organized in 1880 with fifteen members. For the rest of his life, Dr. Hale balanced medicine and preaching. Hale also wrote about Universalism. In 1879, he wrote a series of articles entitled "Rise and Progress of Universalism in East Tennessee by a Universalist Pioneer," which appeared in the *Universalist Herald*, published in Alabama and currently on file in the State Department of Archives and History in Montgomery. In the article, Dr. Hale wrote that his uncle, Aman Hale was an early pioneer to the area, taught school, and was a Methodist preacher who converted to Universalism because of a belief in "final restoration." As a consequence, he was "handled roughly by some of the brethren." Dr. Hale considered his uncle the first professed Universalist in Tennessee (Hyland to Miller 1978).

Dr. Hale was reared a Methodist and converted to Universalism in about 1860. This conversion happened after theological debates with his father while his father was reading a religious tract entitled, "Freedom in the West" (Hyland 1982). The War Between the States no doubt played a role in Dr. Hale's beliefs. Elderly family members recall he was drafted into the Union Army and served as a doctor in several campaigns, he met and conversed with Clara Barton, later of Red Cross fame. Captured by the Confederates, Hale escaped from a Tidewater Virginia prison camp and, after a harrowing time afloat on Chesapeake Bay, was repatriated by the Union Army. He made his way home and sat out the rest of the war (Hyland 1982).

From 1865 until licensing by the Universalist Church in 1877, Hale preached on many topics. He often preached from the steps of, and handed out leaflets from, the courthouse in Jonesborough, the oldest town in Tennessee. Jonesborough has great symbolism within the basically Calvinist Presbyterian "Lost State of Franklin." A frequent theme was "King Alcohol bribes the tongue and leads you to utter folly" (Hyland, 5). Dr. Hale led a full family life, had nine children by his first wife, and a pleasant last few years with a second wife after his first wife died. He died on October 12, 1906, at home at Free Hill in his sixty-ninth year. Death was credited to valvular enlargement of the heart (5). With his death, so died leadership of the Universalist Church in the area for over a half-century.

In 1958, with rapid industrialization like Tennessee Eastman to the Holston Valley, and academia bringing in more people with a scholarly bent for work at East Tennessee State University, a group of independent, religious-minded individuals formed the Holston Valley Unitarian

Church. Institutionalized freethinking religion was once again in that part of the southern mountains. In 1968, Dr. Hale's long-obscure gravestone was discovered by a church member and Mrs. Hyland was told of the location. It has since served as an inspiration for the church, and Mrs. Hyland launched her investigation into the life and times of her freethinking predecessor in the Holston Valley. In 1978, a new church building was dedicated within a few miles of Dr. Hale's old haunts and, in 1979, a corner of the church sanctuary was made into a memorial to Dr. Hale and his spiritual legacy to the present congregation.

In conclusion, it can be firmly stated that, while the formal experience of freethinkers in the southern mountains has often been hit-or-miss, off-and-on, and always uphill in the moral climate of the area, it *has* been a quietly pervasive presence with surely positive moral results. John C. Campbell sensed this when he wrote of something he experienced while doing mission work in the north Georgia mountains in the early 1900s. He was superintendent of a Union Sunday School and taught the Men's Bible Class. He recalled that the class contained men of diverse beliefs including

> a lone Universalist who waged a losing battle against all his fellow-members, steadfastly united through their belief in eternal punishment. The death of the Universalist brought the first break in the ranks of the Sabbath School class, and relaxed, too, for the time being the rigid hold of dogmas. The Missionary Baptist gave evidence of his kinship to the departed by making his rough casket. The Old School Presbyterian and the Campbellite combined their funds to send to the county-seat for black-calico and nickel nails to adorn the pine box fashioned by Baptist hands. The Methodist loaned his mules for the funeral cortege. The wives of other members united in making or loaning garments of mourning for the bereaved widow and daughters; and all lamented a brother and neighbor lost to class and community. (Campbell 1969)

So, what does the history and the continued presence of freethinkers mean for the southern mountains? I think of human beings, on this cinder of a planet out at the edge of the universe, not knowing where they came from, why we are here, or where we might go after death—and yet we still laugh, and cry, and feel, and love. "Love," Thornton Wilder wrote, "will have been enough; all those impulses of love return to the LOVE THAT MADE THEM [writer's capitalization]. Even memory is not necessary for love. There is a land of the living and a land of the dead and the bridge is love, the only survival, the only meaning" (Morris 1981).

Works Cited

Boles, John. 1972. *The Great Revival, 1787-1805.* Lexington: University Press of Kentucky.

Campbell, John C. 1969. *The Southern Highlander and His Homeland.* Lexington: University Press of Kentucky.

Harrell, David Edwin, Jr. 1966. *Quest for a Christian America: The Disciples of Christ and American Society to 1866.* Nashville: Disciples of Christ Historical Society.

Hassell, Cushing Biggs. *History of the Church of God, From Creation to A.D. 1885 including especially the History of the Kehukee Primitive Baptist Assn.* Middletown, New York: Tilber Beeke's Sons, Publishers. Revised and completed by Sylvester Hassell and reprinted by Old School Hymnal Co., Inc., Conley, Ga, 1973.

Hyland, Ida Metz. 1979. *Unitarian-Universalism in East Tennessee.* Johnson City, Tennessee.

———. 11 April 1982. Conversation with author.

Mattox, F.W. 1961. *The Eternal Kingdom, A History of the Church of Christ.* Delight, Arkansas: Gospel Light Publishing Co.

Mendelson, Jack. *Channing, The Reluctant Radical.* Boston: Unitarian Universalist Association.

Miller, Russell, E. *The Larger Hope, The First Century of the Universalist Church in America, 1770-1870.* Boston: Unitarian-Universalist Association.

———. 10 September 1978. Letter to Ida Metz Hyland.

Morris, Willie. 13 September 1981. *Parade Magazine.* New York.

Murch, James DeForest. 1962. *Christians Only, A History of the Restoration Movement.* Cincinnati: Standard Publishing Co.

Paschal, George W. 1930. *History of N.C. Baptists.* Raleigh: The General Board of the N.C. Baptist State Convention Vol. 1, 1663-1805.

Provost, Gary. *A Brief History of Unitarian-Universalism.* Boston: Unitarian Universalist Association, pamphlet.

Sweet, William W. *Religion on the American Frontier, The Baptist, 1783-1830.* New York: Cooper Square Pub. Inc., Vol. 1.

Henry J. Weaver is a graduate student in Appalachian Studies at Appalachian State University. He was the winner of the 1988 Appalachian Studies Association student paper competiton at the Radford University conference.

Two-Party Politics in Appalachia?

David Sutton

W. J. Cash wrote in his *Mind of the South* in 1941 that the Democratic party "ceased to be a party in the South and became the party of the South, a kind of confraternity having in its keeping the whole corpus of Southern loyalties...." To Cash, the Democratic party had so smashed the Republican party in the region that "it either ceased altogether to exist or continued to exist only as a Federal-job-ring...."(Cash 1941, 129, 132).

Cash's portrait of the South failed to account for the diversity within the region and made no allowance for the dissenting experience of Appalachia. While students of southern political history recognized Republican strength scattered along the Appalachian highlands, some described the influence as comparable to that wielded by the Democrats in the lowlands and blackbelt. Leonard Ritt writes, for example, that "very little research has been published on the politics of the "Other Solid South,"—the highland areas of the southern Appalachians"(Ritt 1967, 2).

Still a third point of view argues that a picture of Republican hegemony over the Appalachian region glosses over the significant variations in the degree of interparty competition in the mountain counties (Ritt; Sutton 1982). Many of the Appalachian counties, especially in North Carolina and Virginia, have been and are now highly competitive. Virginia's 9th Congressional District, for example, which covers all of southwest Virginia west of Roanoke, is known as the "Fighting Ninth", in part because of its tradition of fiercely competitive two-party politics.

North Carolina's westernmost 11th District which switched party hands four times in the 1980s (1980, 1982, 1984, 1986) is considered the decade's most volatile congressional district. The Smoky Mountain district is the only district in the nation to throw out its incumbent representative in four consecutive elections. The jinx ended in 1988 when James McClure Clarke, the incumbent, won 50.4 percent to 49.6 percent.

The highly competitive nature of North Carolina's 11th, however, is not typical of congressional and presidential races in the United States today. The electoral order of the country has evolved into a highly distinctive two-tier system in which one party, the Republican, wins the White House, and the other party, the Democratic, runs the Congress. Instead of the two major parties competing vigorously for the presidency and the Congress, the United States has an electoral order in which the Republicans have a decided edge in contests for the presidency and the Democrats have a lock on the House of Representatives (Shafer 1989, 3-4).

Accordingly, the thesis of this paper is that presidential and congressional elections in the South and in Appalachia are not characterized today by Democratic dominance, Republican hegemony, or by vigorous two-party competition, but by the Republican party sweeping the presidential vote and the Democratic party the congressional vote.

A key proposition of the paper is that the contemporary electoral order has emerged in American politics because many voters, especially in the South and Appalachia, choose to split their tickets between a presidential candidate of one party and a House candidate of the other party. This cross-cutting voting in recent years has resulted in an extended period of divided control of government. From 1954 to the present, American elections more often than not have failed to resolve the question of who will govern, and instead have produced a system approaching dual sovereignty of the government with Republicans controlling the White House and Democrats the Congress (Sundquist 1988-89, 613-35).

The paper will examine first recent election results in the region to ascertain the degree of support for its major thesis, and to explore the disparity in the frequency of split-ticket voting in Appalachia and the South and the rest of the country. Second, possible explanations for the split-ticket voting will be offered. Finally, the consequences of this cross-cut nature of American politics for Appalachia will be examined.

For this paper, the unit of analysis is the congressional district. Election results for twenty-one congressional districts in central and southern Appalachia were studied. In all but one of these congressional districts, a majority of the counties in the districts are defined as "Appalachian counties" by the Appalachian Regional Development Act. The one exception is Virginia's 6th District through which runs the

Shenandoah Valley. Only four of the district's nine counties are defined by law as Appalachian.

The congressional districts included in this analysis are: all four congressional districts in West Virginia; the 5th and 7th districts of eastern Kentucky; the 6th and 9th districts of southwestern Virginia; the 5th, 10th, and 11th districts of western North Carolina; the 7th and 9th districts of northern Georgia; the 4th and 5th districts of northern Alabama; the 1st district of northern Mississippi; and the 1st. 2d, 3d, 4th, and 6th districts of the eastern half of Tennessee. Prior to 1982 and reapportionment, Tennessee had only four congressional districts in the Appalachian region. Consequently, there were only twenty congressional districts in the analysis of 1980 election results as opposed to twenty-one districts in the study of 1984 and 1988 results. Data for the district vote for president and general-election returns for House members are taken from various editions of the National Journal's *The Almanac of American Politics* and Congressional Quarterly's *Politics in America*.

This analysis begins with a discussion of the marked Republican superiority in presidential elections. From 1968 through 1988, Democrats have had only one electoral college success. Jimmy Carter's victory in 1976 represents the only presidential contest during this time that the Democratic party's presidential nominee was able to win the South and most of central and southern Appalachia. Carter, with his rural southern background, carried sixteen of Appalachia's congressional districts in 1976. Although Carter in 1980 also won, although by a narrow margin, a majority of the Appalachian districts (eleven for Carter to nine for Ronald Reagan), he carried only one Southern state—his native Georgia.

Republicans, on the other hand, have had three landslide vote victories (1972, 1984, and 1988) and four lopsided electoral college wins in the South and nation (1972, 1980, 1984, and 1988). In 1984, Ronald Reagan captured nineteen of the twenty-one Appalachian districts. He lost only Kentucky's 7th District (49 percent to 51 percent) and West Virginia's 4th District (49 percent to 50 percent). George Bush swept the eleven states of the South in the 1988 presidential election and won seventeen of the twenty-one congressional districts in central and southern Appalachia. Bush only lost Kentucky's 7th District and the 1st, 3d, and 4th Districts of West Virginia.

Although the Republican party has become established as the dominant force in presidential elections in the South and Appalachia, Democrats continue to enjoy a decided advantage in races for the U.S. House of Representatives. In 1980, Republicans won 42 of the 115 House seats in the eleven states of the old Confederacy plus Kentucky, or 36.5 percent. Almost a decade later, after reapportionment, Reagan, and a Bush sweep of the region, found the Republicans with 42 seats but only 34.1 percent of the region's 123 seats (after the 1982 reapportionment) in 1988. In House elections in the decade of the 1980s, Republicans went nowhere in the South, and in Appalachia experienced significant losses.

Republicans in central and southern Appalachia could boast of an almost even split in the region's House delegation in 1980—eleven Democrats to nine Republicans. In 1984, Reagan swept the nation and the South, capturing forty-nine of the fifty states. As noted earlier in the paper, he won nineteen of the twenty-one Appalachian districts in this study. Yet, the Republican party's portion of the region's twenty-one member House delegation shrank to only five representatives, or 23.8 percent. The 1984 election results show a remarkable disconnection between presidential and House voting in the region.

Although Bush won in seventeen of the congressional districts in 1988, his party captured only four of the region's twenty-one House seats, or nineteen percent. The four victories were in the most impeccably Republican districts in the region—the 1st and 2d Districts of Tennessee, the 5th District of Kentucky, and the 10th District of North Carolina. In three of the twenty-one districts, Republicans allowed the Democratic candidate to win unchallenged even though George Bush carried them (the 2d in West Virginia, the 4th in Tennessee, and the 4th in Alabama).

A comparison of current Republican congressional strength in the region to its influence twenty years earlier, strikingly illustrates the extent of the debacle Republicans have suffered in House representation. In 1968, Republicans held eight of the area's twenty House seats, or double the number they have at present.

What is the significance and extent of split-ticket voting in American politics today? *Congressional Quarterly* notes that if Republican candidates had won every congressional district that George Bush did in 1988, their party would command a better than two-to-one advantage in the House of Representatives. Instead, because of split-ticket voting, Republicans are on the downside of a three-to-two deficit (Cook 1989, 1710-16).[1] In earlier times, congressional results were tied closely to the presidential vote. But today ticket-splitting is certainly in vogue, especially in the South and Appalachia.

As Table 1 shows, in 1980 only four districts split their tickets between a presidential candidate of one party and a House candidate of the other party. In 1984, the number of split-ticket districts jumped dramatically to fourteen of the twenty-one districts, or 67 percent. All fourteen split-ticket districts were of the Republican presidential/Democratic House variety—a result congruent with the new electoral order.

Table 1

Presidential-House Voting in Appalachia

1980 Voting (20 Districts)

Straight Ticket Districts				Split Ticket Districts			
Reagan / Republican House		Carter / Democratic House		Reagan / Democratic House		Carter / Republican House	
#	%	#	%	#	%	#	%
7	35	9	45	2	10	2	10

1984 Voting (21 Districts)

Straight Ticket Districts				Split Ticket Districts			
Reagan / Republican House		Mondale / Democratic House		Reagan / Democratic House		Mondale / Republican House	
#	%	#	%	#	%	#	%
5	24	2	9	14	67	0	0

1988 Voting (21 Districts)

Straight Ticket Districts				Split Ticket Districts			
Bush / Republican House		Dukakis / Democratic House		Bush / Democratic House		Dukakis / Republican House	
#	%	#	%	#	%	#	%
4	19	4	19	13	62	0	0

Source: Calculated by the author from information in the 1982, 1986, and 1990 editions of *Congressional Quarterly's Politics in America* Washington, D.C.: Congressional Quarterly.

In 1988, one out of every three congressional districts nationwide had a split result. As Table 2 shows, split-ticket voting in 1988 was the heaviest in central and southern Appalachia with thirteen of the twenty-one districts, or 62 percent exhibiting a split result. Once again, voters in the thirteen districts went Republican for president while electing a Democrat to the House.

Table 2

Split Ticket Congressional Districts in 1988

	Total Districts	Split Ticket Districts		Bush / Dem. House	Dukakis / GOP House
	#	#	%	#	#
Appalachia*	21	13	62	13	0
Non-Appalachian South**	106	51	48	50	1
Non-Appalachian and Non-South	308	84	27	72	12
National Total	435	148	34	135	13

*Appalachia includes all four congressional districts in West Virginia; Georgia's 7th and 9th; Virginia's 6th and 9th; Alabama's 4th and 5th; Tennessee's 1st, 2nd, 3rd, 4th, and 5th; and North Carolina's 5th, 10th, and 11th.

**The remainder of the districts in the eleven states of the Old Confederacy plus Kentucky.

Table 3

Appalachian Democratic House Members Elected in Districts Carried by Bush in 1988

	Bush %	Dem. House %
Ed Jenkins, Ga. District 9	71	63
George "Buddy" Darden, Ga. 7	70	65
Marilyn Lloyd, Tenn. 3	62	57
Jim Olin, Va. 6	61	64
Stephen Neal, N.C. 5	60	53
Bart Gordon, Tenn. 6	60	77
Jamie Whitten, Miss. 1	59	78
Ronnie Flippo, Ala. 5	59	64
James McClure Clarke, N.C. 11	59	50
Jim Cooper, Tenn. 4	57	100
Tom Bevill, Ala. 4	57	96
Rick Boucher, Va. 9	54	63
Harley Staggers, Jr., W. Va. 2	52	100

Two of the Democrats—Ed Jenkins and George "Buddy" Dardin of Georgia—had to survive a Bush sweep of 70 percent of their district's vote. In nine other districts, Bush won by 55 percent or more while the Democrat was being elected to the House (see Table 3).

After Appalachia, the next highest frequency of split-ticket voting was the non-Appalachian South with 51 of 106 districts having split results, or 48 percent (Table 2). In the rest of the country, there were split presidential - House results in 84 of the 308 districts, or 27 percent. Clearly, ticket-splitters in the South and Appalachia are playing a major role in giving the country its divided government.

What explains the success of the split-ticket Democrats and of Democrats in general in House races? While the contemporary Republican party has achieved an ideological consistency which allows it to run a national campaign for the presidency, the Democratic party is perceived as multiple mini-parties that coalesce and divide depending on the issues at hand. At the congressional level, the heterogeneity of the Democratic party works to its favor in winning a House majority in the different geographical regions and demographically diverse districts. Democratic congressional candidates can be their own "enterprise" and adapt themselves to the prevailing ethos of their region. The key to their success is their ability to focus on local concerns—a skill that is more likely to be present in a coalition than in an ideologically consistent party (Elving 1989, 2674).[2] Thus, the strength of the Democratic party in congressional elections becomes its weakness in presidential contests, and the strength of Republicans in presidential politics becomes a handicap at the subnational level.

A second factor which works to the benefit of Democratic candidates is that elections to the House of Representatives, for the most part, are not about ideology or foreign affairs, but about social welfare and service provision. On these issues, Democratic candidates excel. Marilyn Lloyd of Tennessee's 3d is the "Oak Ridge congresswoman" who guards the Oak Ridge National Laboratory and the defense-and energy-related contractors working around it. Harold Rogers of Kentucky's 5th district pushes forward the Cumberland Gap Tunnel and is a tiger on tobacco and coal issues while his colleague Chris Perkins of Kentucky's 4th fights for dollars for badly needed highway and bridge construction in his district. West Virginia's Nick Rahhal introduces bills to make it easier for miners suffering from black lung disease to claim benefits while Georgia's Ed Jenkins introduces measures to protect textile companies and workers from cheap imports. Mississippi's Jamie Whitten is touted by congressional observers as a shrewd trader in appropriations pork and a true believer in government's pump-priming potential.[3]

What are some of the possible consequences of divided government for the people of the Appalachian region?[4] First, as each political party has entrenched itself within its own governmental stronghold (the executive for Republicans and the Congress for Democrats), American politics has come to be about the efforts of each party to strengthen its particular institutional bastion and to undermine the institution controlled by its political adversary. In short, institutional combat has supplanted electoral competition as the desired form of political struggle in the nation. The Democrats attacking the drinking habits and sexual conduct of Defense Secretary designee John Tower, and the Republicans castigating the personal finances of House Speaker Jim Wright and Whip Tony Coehlo, are examples of weapons of institutional combat used by the parties to de-legitimate one another (Ginsberg and Shefter 1989, 33-4).

Political campaigns become devoid of substance and the parties fail to offer voters any coherent rationale for why they deserve their votes. In other words, more and more politicians are providing voters with little opportunity or reason to participate in politics. As a consequence, the proportion of the electorate that votes in presidential and congressional elections has been dropping steadily over time. The decline in political participation, however, has not been uniform throughout the electorate. There is a large gap between the voting rates of Americans with more education, higher incomes, and white-collar occupations and those of working class and poor Americans. The disproportionate participation of those in the top one-third of the income scale results in public policies which cut top-bracket income tax rates, and provide more stringent needs tests for transfer programs for the poor. Consequently, the decade of the 1980s in the United States has been characterized by upper-tier Americans significantly expanding their share of the national wealth and low income persons losing ground.

In the current electoral order, neither party is likely to make a major effort to bring into the electorate working class and poor Americans who presently stand outside the political process. A greater electoral mobilization of these groups would, most likely, create an electorate more receptive to a variety of broad social welfare initiatives. Each party can now win a part of the government, and expansion of the electorate could threaten that advantage. Moreover, current congressional and presidential politicians have learned their political skills in a low-voter environment.

Still another consequence of this electoral order is that politicians in each branch of government are compelled to focus on the implications of programs and policies for institutional struggles (Ginsberg and Shefter 1989, 13-4). The Tennessee Valley Authority (although the brainchild of a Republican senator from Nebraska) is perceived as a part of the New Deal legacy. The Appalachian Regional Commission, earmarked for termination by the Reagan Administration, is remembered as the first piece of Lyndon Johnson's Great Society legislation and part of his War on Poverty. The social welfare establishment is perceived as an important institutional bastion of the Democrats in much the same way that the defense establishment is seen as being Republican. Republican administrations have come to accept unprecedented deficits as the chief constraint they can impose on Democratic congressional power. Thus, non-power programs of the TVA and the economic development programs of the ARC have limped along this decade on minimal funding. There is little evidence there will be any major new investment of social capital by government in Appalachia for education, housing, health care, or community development under the current divided government and its concomitant political deadlock and disarray.

Notes

[1] See also Richard E. Cohen (1989) pages 1048-54.

[2] Also see John A. Ferejohn and Morris P. Fiorina (1985) pages 112-14.

[3] The information on campaign issues and legislative interests of various Appalachian congressmen is taken from various editions of *Congressional Quarterly's Politics in America.*

[4] For an excellent paper on the consequences of the present electoral order on American politics and public policy, see Benjamin Ginsberg and Martin Shefter (1989).

Works Cited

Cash, W. J. 1941. *The Mind of the South.* New York: Alfred A. Knopf.

Cohen, Richard E. 1989. "Lonely Runner." *National Journal* (29 April): 1048-54.

Cook, Rhodes. 1989. "Key to Survival for Democrats Lies in Split-Ticket Voting." *Congressional Quarterly Weekly Report* 47 (8 July): 1710-16.

Elving, Ronald D. 1989. "Defining Democrats: Party or Coalition?" *Congressional Quarterly Weekly Report* 47 (7 October): 2674.

Ferejohn, John A. and Morris P. Fiorina. 1985. "Incumbency and Realignment in Congressional Elections." *The New Direction in American Politics*. Eds. John E. Chubb and Paul E. Peterson. Washington, D.C: The Brookings Institution.

Ginsberg, Benjamin and Martin Shefter. 1989. "Mobilization, Demobilization and the Power of the American State." Paper presented at the Annual Meeting of the American Political Science Association, 1 September 1989, Atlanta, Georgia.

Ritt, Leonard G. 1967. "Presidential Voting Patterns in Appalachia: An Analysis of the Relationship Between Turnout, Partisan Change, and Selected Socioeconomic Variables." Dissertation, University of Tennessee.

Shafer, Byron E. 1989. "The Notion of an Electoral Order: The Structure of Electoral Politics at the Accession of George Bush." Paper presented at the Annual Meeting of the American Political Science Association, 1 September 1989, Atlanta, Georgia.

Sundquist, James L. 1988-89. "The New Era of Coalition Government in the United States." *Political Science Quarterly* 103 (Winter).

Sutton, C. David. 1982. "Party Competition in the South's Forgotten Region: The Case of Southern Appalachia." Eds. Laurence W. Moreland, Tod A. Baker, and Robert P. Steed. *Contemporary Southern Political Attitudes and Behavior*. New York: Praeger Publishers.

David Sutton is Professor of Political Science at Appalachian State University, Boone, North Carolina.

Political Culture in Jesse Stuart's Appalachia and the South: From Agrarian to Industrial Development

Glen Edward Taul

The political culture of Jesse Stuart's Appalachia and of the South traveled similar paths. As in the South, Stuart's Appalachian culture had been shaped by the experiences of both the Civil War and the Great Depression. Both were being transformed from an individualistic, agrarian orientation to a progressive, industrial one. Despite strong influences of modernization to conform to a predominate culture, the agrarian ideology in the South and its Appalachian region continued to be an influential force in the political culture.

The culture that Stuart describes in his prose existed approximately from 1900 to 1970. The roots reach experientially to the Civil War, but the taproot is embedded in the European heritage of the first settlers. The ideology of the people, as reflected by Stuart, has a traditional, grassroots orientation that is associated with an agrarian society. Its antecedents are located in the feudal history of Scotland; in the experiences of the Ulster Scots; and the oppressive conditions of the Palatinate Germans (Taul 1978, 141). When immigrants settled the Appalachian frontier, they adapted many of their customs and folkways to the rigors of frontier life. Characteristics of individualism, intense partisanship, factionalism, and clannishness, which emerged from these customs and folkways, became established in an era of isolation from the developing modern culture of the lowlands (Taul, 141). A manifestation of this adaptation is the Appalachians' adherence to a grassroots rural government. In feudal Scotland, the powerless central government of the monarchy was unable to maintain peace and promote economic prosperity because of the factional nature of the political culture. Powerful overlords continually fought among themselves, and cooperated with the king only when it furthered their personal ambitions. Appalachians generally believe that public affairs should be administered by a decentralized system within small political units. Basic problems of government are essentially local, and local problems are better resolved by local initiative. This belief produced a fragmented political system where factionalism also reigned (Taul,147-149). In the antebellum period, a homogeneous society developed in the Tug Valley from a variety of ethnic backgrounds. The mountain environment forced a blending of all cultural groups. Social cohesiveness was enhanced as the original influx slowed to a trickle. These families were prolific, intermarried extensively, and established complex kinship networks. The mountains insulated inhabitants from the economic, social, and political forces that were transforming the rest of America. By the Civil War, their differences in house styles, farming, dress, religious worship, and political allegiances were almost imperceptible (Waller 1988, 21). This process was probably repeated throughout Southern Appalachia.

Family and land were the foundations of this agrarian society. The social structure was more egalitarian than the economically developing regions of America. Economic activity was virtually the same for everyone, and poverty was almost unknown. Social differentiation was determined by the quantity of land, animals, and the production of home manufactures. This differentiation did not, however, inhibit economic and social interaction (Waller, 21-23).

The extended family has been the primary organizing unit of the community since the first settlements. Local political factions and other community institutions developed as extensions of the family. These institutions served as important agents for social control by legitimizing and sustaining the mores of the community, and they reflected the importance of personal relationships and local autonomy in their operation and structure. These personal relationships generated intense loyalties and also fueled rivalries (Waller, 81; Eller 1982, 9, 30).

The mountain political culture reflected the values and social patterns of most pre-modern societies. The different stages of the democratic process were a series of social events. The culture valued intimate social interaction and community spirit in conducting their public affairs. Political leadership was given on the basis of kinship ties, personality characteristics, and oratorical skills. Elections had a high rate of participation because campaigns and election days, with their speeches, intense competiveness, direct contact between voters and candidates, personal confrontations among candidates, and *viva voce* voting, were the height of entertainment and social interaction. In fact, the annual elections were the most important social event of the year for residents within a voting district because they formalized neighborhood networks that bound families together for the rest of the year (Eller, 9, 11-12, 36, 37; Waller, 26).

County courts, the traditional form of local government in the South, were the most important and relevant governmental entity of the antebellum mountain political culture. The county courts, which performed the executive, legislative, and judicial functions of government, were the central foci for ordering community affairs, from land distribution to poor relief. Local officials and residents exercised almost complete control over their communities. Conflicts were resolved at the local level by individuals sharing similar perceptions of authority and justice (Waller, 23-24).

A local official, elected by his family, or an alliance of families, put kinship interests as his most important debt. Nepotism became a privilege of election; it helped to cement the power of a family group. The power of a family group over individual lives was more overt than that of the government. The "system" was inefficient and incompetent, and it fragmented authority within local government, but it encouraged heavy participation and a feeling of local control (Eller, 30-31). This was part of the Jeffersonian and Jacksonian political ideology that dominated agrarian societies.

The qualities of traditional grassroots political culture are portrayed as predominant in Stuart's Appalachia. Partisan loyalties are influenced by family ties. As in *Foretaste of Glory*, Stuart often identifies parties by the families who dominate local politics. The Greenough and Dinwiddie families alternately, have controlled politics in Blake County for more than 150 years; people join either the "Greenough Party" or "Dinwiddie" Party when they register to vote (Stuart 1946, 9).

In this context, a winning combination for a candidate appears to be oratorical skill, a competitive, individualistic spirit, attention to local issues, use of Machiavellian campaign tactics, and the support of dominant families. Family patriarchs are the brokers of local political power. Dusty Boone, in "As the People Choose," blends these qualities to win the race for county prosecutor. To win, he must gain the endorsement of two patriarchs whose families have been feuding for seventy-five years. His purpose in running is to end the Boone-Reffitt feud. Since neither patriarch will work for him if he reveals his platform, he resorts to lying, deception, and vote buying (Stuart 1974, 135-6).

Dusty first receives Uncle Tobias Boone's endorsement by emphasizing his familial relationship; he does this by revealing the scars Boone supposedly received fighting Reffitts (but actually were inflicted when he ran into a barbed wire fence), and by saying that his opponent, the incumbent, boasts that he will get both the Boone and Reffitt votes. He next gains Uncle Roosevelt Reffitt's support by denying his kinship to Tobias: he says his opponent expects to receive the Boone vote, he points to the battle scars Reffitt received while fighting Boones, and promises to deliver "chop" (cracked corn) for Uncle Roosevelt Reffitt's stills a few days before election day (Stuart 1974, 128-48).

Candidates emphasize their commonality with the people by stressing their lifestyles, and parochial issues. They promise direct personal benefits to an individual or group. A candidate for county judge, in "Road Number One," promises to construct gravel roads up every hollow. In "Uncle Casper," a senatorial candidate, in addition to promising improved roads and schools, pledges to place destitute drunks in "feather beds," provide old age pensions for men, homes for widows and orphans, and double the amount of food for indigents. He also will support laws to prohibit the carrying of pistols and bowie knives and those to re-establish the school trustee system (Stuart 1950, 133; 1974, 2-3).

Although he lives in the county seat, Blake County Judge Allie Anderson, in *Foretaste of Glory*, cultivates a lifestyle with which rural people identify. His has a home just a block off Main Street with modest furnishings, a large family, and a large garden along with cows and hogs. He belongs to the church that most hill people attend. And he does not swear, smoke, or drink. As he feeds his hogs each evening, people from the county come to talk about farming and to seek favors. They would rather talk with Judge Anderson there than his plushly furnished courthouse office, because, despite his peculiar style of city living, the rural people see him as "just a common man." This strategy has revived the nearly defunct "Greenough Party" (Stuart 1946, 25-7).

Election day has the characteristics of a festive community holiday celebration. It is the finish line for an intense contest. Candidates and their loyalists will commit fraud to win, and partisans observe the tabulation of votes to insure fairness. In the "Voting Goodlaws," Oscar Kimble, a county road foreman and a "Greenough Party" election worker, gets the maximum benefit from the Goodlaws' large family by proxy voting. One Goodlaw votes, and then votes again (in another precinct) for his brother who is in the hospital. Another Goodlaw comes by party headquarters to get his promised pint of whiskey before voting. After he votes, he votes again for another brother (who is late in arriving from Ohio, where he has lived for two years). When the Ohio brother arrives and discovers that his brother has already voted for him, he becomes angry and threatens to expose all of them unless he votes. Oscar finds a cousin Goodlaw who has died, but has not been purged. The Ohio brother votes for him (1974, 271-84).

In the days when paper ballots were used and votes were counted by hand, people congregated in and out of the courthouse to await the results. As days become weeks counting votes, in "He Saw the Sun This Time," Greenough and Dinwiddie partisans become irritable. Several attempts are made to invalidate the election results of a Greenough precinct by Dinwiddie supporters. When the results favor the minority Greenough, Sheriff Simpleton, a Dinwiddie election judge, threatens to invalidate the votes of three large Greenough precincts because of improper signatures by election judges. The sheriff is stopped by a determined Greenough partisan who says, "We'll count the votes or fight! ...If they are thrown out we'll be counting the dead instead of votes" (1970, 22-26)

Mountaineers saw themselves as law abiding. The court system was respected as vital in the smooth functioning of mountain communities. Its embodiment of social authority was recognized as long as mountaineers perceived its decisions as being rooted in local customs and traditions, and reflecting community values. The grand jury, in "Before the Grand Jury," was the guardian of these customs, traditions, and values. It asks Jasper Higgins about his knowledge concerning public decency and safety. It questions him about people carrying concealed deadly weapons, uttering public profanities, or selling poison moonshine. Jasper admits to knocking a boy unconscious when he interrupted a school program one night, yelling that he was the meanest man since Adam. Everyone in the schoolhouse was afraid of the boy, so Jasper challenged him; no sheriff was around to maintain peace. In its agrarian sense of justice, the grand jury vindicates Jasper. It agrees with his defense: "where there's not any Law to protect a man, there shouldn't be any to prosecute him. We have to protect ourselves in this County. You know that." He is not indicted (Stuart1956,).

Even in an agrarian society partisanship determines decisions. Jasper complains before the grand jury that if a man is murdered, he is sentenced to one year in the penitentiary. "Steal a chicken, you get five years in the pen. No pardon on chicken stealin', but you have a chance for a pardon if you belong to the right party when you kill a man. They need your family vote. The family turns against them unless the killer gets a pardon. Sometimes it's already waitin' in the courtroom soon as the man is sentenced" (Waller, 90; Stuart 1956, 200-4).

The agrarian flavor comes through especially in Stuart's descriptions of hangings and trials. Both events have the elements of being exciting, entertaining, and festive. Both provide opportunities for socializing. During court day, in *Beyond Dark Hills*, people descend into the county seat to trade, to sell, and to listen to trials. Everyone seems to take a personal interest in the cases being tried. The seats, windows, and aisles are filled with people waiting to be entertained (1972, 215).

In "Sunday Afternoon Hanging," execution of criminals is a public affair. People come from surrounding counties to watch. "Everybody got to see it and laugh and faint, cuss or cry, do just as he damned pleased about it." People get drunk, bands play, men have dates, and refreshments are sold. They like to hear the condemned confess their "sins," or trade insults (Stuart 1956, 100-1, 112).

The county judge presides over a fragmented local government. He is the chief administrative and legislative officer of the county. Other county officials—county clerk, sheriff, jailer—are also elected. Each of these semi-autonomous individuals maintain a proprietary attitude toward their offices and lack direction either at home or from the state capital.

The county judge is usually under-educated, lacking especially in any legal training for the judicial duties of the office. His powers are enhanced if he happens to be the governor's county patronage man. This is the profile of County Judge Toodle Powell in "Road Number One." Judge Powell is elected on the promise to gravel every road in the county. With a majority of the magistrates belonging to his party, he can deliver on this promise; he fails because of his incompetence in managing the county's affairs (Stuart 1950, 123, 141).

As in the post-Civil War and the modernized Appalachian region, agrarian values and social patterns are or have been very evident in the southern political culture. These elements were established in the colonial and antebellum periods. There was a strong tradition of individualism. Local autonomy and a decentralized political system were valued over a federal or national government. Personalities overshadowed issues: the voters preferred personal contact with candidates and government officials. Electoral and governmental politics were a prized past-time, and a favorite source of entertainment (Grantham 1988, 55, 84).

Unlike the southern Appalachian region, the South was essentially undemocratic in values and practice. The centralizing forces of a commercial economy, however, had a greater effect. It created distinct class divisions in which a wealthy, powerful elite maintained control through undemocratic means. Qualifications for voting and holding office were generally limited to propertied whites, and legislative districts were mal-apportioned where the older seaboard regions held a disproportionate share of power. The vigorous two-party system that emerged during the 1830s was essentially a division between agrarian elites about whether or not government resources should be used to aid commercial development. Even some parts of Appalachia wanted government aid to construct railroads through their areas (Grantham xi; Durden 1985, 6, 45-46).

The Civil War and the Great Depression altered the direction of politics in both regions. Throughout the post-Civil War and post-depression periods, a rural, provincial orientation remained. After the Civil War, single party politics (Democratic in the South and Republican in Appalachia) developed and industrialization sharpened class differences, concentrated wealth into fewer hands, disrupted the traditional culture, and caused social conflict. These trends continued in the post-depression period, but single party politics and the individualistic character declined.

Southern mountaineers were the largest group of Southern whites who remained Republican until the 1950s. The Republican party became established as the dominant party after Reconstruction; before 1860, allegiance to either Democrats or Republicans depended on personal considerations. The war had awakened mountaineers to the common interests that needed to be defended. Support for the Union or Confederacy depended on whether or not either government could preserve the independence and autonomy of the mountaineers, or on the nature of the commercial links to the planter and regional economy. Most mountaineers supported the Republicans because they were credited with saving the Union, they promised government assistance to help the South recover from the war's devastation and financial chaos, and the Republican party was not controlled by the power elite of the lowlands (McKinney 1978, 3, 14, 12, 29; Waller, 29-31).

Political affiliations were influenced by the Civil War in Stuart's Appalachia. The family and social environment that emerged from this conflict shaped the political character for two succeeding generations. In "Two Worlds," Shan Powderjay and his siblings "were children of indecision" (Stuart 1969, 18). His parents argue about the North and South, Lee and Grant, Methodists and Baptists, and Republicans and Democrats. His maternal grandfather is an ex-Confederate and a Democrat, and his paternal grandfather, an ex-Union soldier and a Republican. "Each world was a powerful voice beckoning us to follow" (Stuart, 18).

The Great Depression and the New Deal altered political alignments again in the mountains as well as in the South. Blaming Hoover for the Depression and the ready acceptance of Democratic relief programs, a once heavily Republican region was split into Democratic and Republican subregions (Caudill 1963, 207). The family of Press Tussie formerly voted a straight Republican ticket, but became Democrat when government relief was first offered. "It looked like too good a thing to pass up," says Press (Stuart 1943, 37).

In states like Kentucky, a three-party system developed. Statewide, the Democrats generally have controlled politics since the Civil War, with the Republicans giving strong opposition. There usually were two opposing factions within the Democratic ranks. Stuart's father, Mitchell, comments on how Republicans have been the minority party since the Civil War. Even when there has been a Republican governor in Kentucky, the Democrats have controlled the legislature. "And with one party in power all my lifetime, the net results are that we stand on the bottom of everything" (Stuart 1960, 120). Of course, he is probably expressing the frustration that a legislature, dominated by the Bluegrass and western regions of the state, has continuously ignored the needs of the state's eastern region.

As the commercial culture grew to replace agriculture as the basis for the region's economy, jobs in the public sector became more important and were a source for building local political organizations. Press Tussie's ability to control votes in his family is dependent on his success in gaining benefits from New Deal programs for most members of his clan. Road construction was another major source of patronage, especially after World War II, when rural Kentuckians demanded all-weather roads. Nearly bankrupt local governments depended on state funds to finance their construction. But the local men, in "Road Number One," who built the roads were hired more for their party affiliation than for their skills in operating equipment (Stuart 1943, 47-48; Caudill, 269; Stuart 1950, 142-143).

Welfare benefits and roads were sources for federal and state largesse to communities but education was the major source on the local level. Bitter political battles were fought for the right to control these jobs. Whoever backed the winning candidate for governor became the administration's local patronage person. Governor Warburton, in "Governor Warburton's Right-Hand Man," faces a dilemma when he comes to Blake County to pick his patronage man. For the first time, the two factions of the "Greenough Party" backed the same candidate. If the governor chooses either the county clerk or another Greenough leader, he will alienate the loosing faction. He retains the loyalty of both by choosing an independent voter (Stuart 1950, 195-204).

The commercial culture that developed between the Civil War and 1920 conflicted with traditional relationships and obligations. It recognized contracts as inviolable and enforceable without reference to circumstances surrounding an agreement. Traditional culture considered terms of a bargain within the context of customary rights. A commercial culture was antithetical to someone who was illiterate, who thought and behaved in oral face-to-face terms: it required cash and a literate populace. The cash-free economy and illiterate environment of a traditional culture created many exploitative situations. There is a dispute over the "ownership of the law" in this kind of environment. Traditionalists expected the law to uphold customary rights and obligations. Modernizers viewed the law as a means to protecting economic development and profits (Waller, 47-48).

Stuart portrays this conflict in the *Trees of Heaven*. A conflict between the law and the individual comes to focus in Anse Bushman, who defines ownership in terms of a deed and cash purchase. He declines morally when he attempts to manipulate the law. When he buys the Sexton land at a courthouse auction, he changes his image as an upright, law-abiding citizen to one who is against the community, only because the hill people oppose the sale of any land by court order. He declines further when he uses the law to evict Boliver Tussie, a squatter, from the land. Boliver's family is allowed to stay as sharecroppers, with his intention to manipulate them for his own profit. Boliver's family is eventually evicted because Anse wants Boliver's tobacco crop for himself.

The New Deal, and the welfare system it established, has corrupted the traditional values and social patterns of the mountain culture. It has divided families like the Tussies. Press Tussie is patriarch of the Relief Tussies while Press' brother is head of the other Tussie faction. The New Deal also promotes waste, lethargy, and needless "rest," as in the case of Peter Farmer. He is participating in a government program that loans him more money than his farm is worth, and pays him not to raise tobacco, corn, or cane. The furrows of the once-plowed fields are welded together, and the plows are becoming rusty from disuse. Peter's brother chastises him for being a "sellout" because "there is not the honor of sweat" in what he is doing (Stuart 1943, 47-8; 1966, 61, 69-70; 1971, 3, 5-8).

The New Deal poses a direct threat, for some, to the traditions of an agrarian political culture. It threatens local autonomy and the ability to decide how one should live. For Rev. Ezekiel Wrenhouse the blue eagle of the National Industrial Recovery Act is evil. It represents a despotic government trying to tell him what he can do.

In "A Pilgrim Out in Space," the preacher's small assistant is prevented from buying eggs at the usual store because "it's not fair to the Government of America! Look at the window! . . . Where is the Blue Eagle!" says Jerry Sprouse. When Rev. Wrenhouse finds out what has happened, he confronts Sprouse and his friends, and tells them that he will buy his eggs where he pleases. After viewing the NRA symbol in the other store, he holds an all night vigil of prayer. By morning he has received a "vision" similar to one described in Revelations 13. He concludes that Roosevelt and the NRA, which have the number 666, have the "Mark of the Beast."

A Democrat for all of his life, Rev. Wrenhouse immediately begins campaigning against FDR. He campaigns full time, publicizing his vision and talking to any audience wanting to listen. He dies before the election, but his county votes two-to-one against FDR while the surrounding counties go the opposite direction for the "Mark of the Beast" (Stuart 1971, 156-73).

In *The Land Beyond the River*, Stuart tells the story of how the welfare system has had a corrosive effect on the dignity, pride, and individualistic spirit of Appalachians. The Perkins family is wedded to traditional ways when they move across the river into Ohio to begin life anew. In their former Appalachian home, they were subsistence farmers who were forced to depend on government commodities, losing their pride and economic stability. They regain their pride as tenant farmers in Ohio.

Just as the Perkinses begin to put their lives back together, a series of events cause significant change in their lives: the father (Gil) is partially disabled by a snakebite; Gil's wife (Sil) has her twelfth child; and their beneficit landlord dies. Worried about providing for the needs of his large family, Gil succumbs to the tempting advice of Uncle Dick and enters the welfare system.

The traditional values weaken their hold on the family, especially with the children. The oldest two rebel against the family. They shift from their fundamental religious beliefs as Free Will Baptists to the more liberal Presbyterian. Cassie-Belle changes her name to Clarissa Jo at Ohio State University because her former Appalachian name hindered her adjustment to the new life. Pedike, as he begins working at the Dupont Chemical Plant, vows to keep his pride and never go on welfare. He will not follow the ways of his parents and have more children than he can feed and educate (Taul 1978, 144-46).

Similar developments occurred in the southern political culture after the Civil War. A single party system evolved, but Democrats dominated it. The party organization was amorphous and transitory, dependent on the ascendancy of particular leaders and factions at any given moment. The New Deal encouraged the fragmentation of the Solid South. The national Democratic Party was changing in character. The importance of the South was receding, and the old assumption that support of the Democrats was synonymous with the defense of the "Southern" position also began to erode. The growth of centralized government and creation of the welfare state disturbed conservative southerners, who were inclined to attribute their apprehensions to Roosevelt's leadership. In 1948, the Dixiecrat Revolt resulted from Truman's promise to expand the welfare program and boldly sponsor federal civil rights legislation. The revolt was also a manifestation of the broader regional conservatism that was a defensive reaction to rapid economic and social change (Grantham 1988, 26, 123-24).

There were also some contrasting trends in the two regions: the rate of decline for voter participation was slower in Appalachia. Although the power of the planter and commercial classes increased in both regions, the egalitarian ideal of Jeffersonian democracy prevailed in Stuart's hill region.

Stuart's prose fails to reflect significant trends within his region and in the South, which also affect Appalachia. He does not write about the impact of coal mining and the development of company towns on the political culture, nor do his characters talk about their attitudes toward African-Americans, and consequently, the civil rights movement of the 1960s.

Despite the centralizing forces of modernization, the political culture of the South and Stuart's region still favors an agrarian democracy. This democracy is oriented to the individual and local autonomy. It means a small government with direct access to candidates and officeholders, and is conducted on a direct, personal, intimate, informal basis. It is a belief that rural government is more efficient, effective, and democratic than a big distant government administered by a bureaucracy of a select group of men. Local government is for the common man; officeholders need no special training or qualifications. Their willingness to serve the community and conform to its system of values is enough.

Works Cited

Caudill, Harry M. 1963. *Night Comes to the Cumberlands: A Biography of a Depressed Region*. Boston: Little, Brown.

Durden, Robert F. 1985. *The Self-Inflicted Wounds: Southern Politics in the Nineteenth Century*. Lexington: University Press of Kentucky.

Eller, Ronald D. 1982. *Miners, Millhands, and Mountaineers: Industrialization of the Appalachian South, 1880-1920*. Knoxville: University of Tennessee Press.

Grantham, Dewey W. 1988. *The Life and Death of the Solid South: A Political History*. Lexington: University Press of Kentucky.

McKinney, Gordon B. 1978. *Southern Mountain Republicans, 1865-1900: Politics and the Appalachian Community*. Chapel Hill: University of North Carolina Press.

Stuart, Jesse. 1943. *Taps for Private Tussie*. New York: E.P. Dutton.

———. 1946. *Foretaste of Glory*. New York: E.P. Dutton.

———. 1950. *Clearing in the Sky*. New York: McGraw-Hill.

———. 1956. *Plowshare in Heaven*. New York: McGraw-Hill.

———. 1960. *God's Oddling: The Story of Mick Stuart, My Father*. New York: McGraw-Hill.

———. 1966. *My Land Has A Voice*. New York: McGraw-Hill.

———. 1969. *Come Gentle Spring*. New York: McGraw-Hill.

———. 1970. *Seven by Jesse*. Terre Haute: Indiana Council of Teachers of English, Indiana State University.

———. 1971. *Come Back to the Farm*. New York: McGraw-Hill.

———. 1972. *Beyond Dark Hills*. New York: McGraw-Hill.

———. 1974. *Thirty-two Votes Before Breakfast: Politics at the Grass Roots, as Seen in Short Stories*. New York: McGraw-Hill Book Co.

Taul, Glen Edward. 1978. "Kentucky Politics in Jesse Stuart's Prose." Master's Thesis, Baylor University.

Waller, Altina L. 1988. *Feud: Hatfields, McCoys, and Social Change in Appalachia, 1860-1900*. Chapel Hill: University of North Carolina Press.

Glen Edward Taul is a doctoral student in history at the University of Kentucky and works for the Christian Appalachian Project in Lancaster, Kentucky.

A Cure for the Malaise of the Dislocated Southerner: The Writing of Jesse Stuart

Edgar H. Thompson

Walker Percy, in his essay "Southern Comfort," asserts that the South has entered "the American mainstream and the old southern vein of oddities and exoticas" (1980, 348) have finally played themselves out. Though we might agree with Percy's assessment, the specific traits and qualities that anchor this new South and its literature in the American mainstream are not immediately clear. W. J. Cash, however, gives us some idea what these traits might be when he contends that throughout the highland and lowland South "it is easy to trace . . . a fairly definite social pattern . . . a complex of established relationships and habits of thought, sentiments, prejudices, standards and values, and associations of ideas" common to the region (1969, viii).

It seems to me that these social patterns and habits of thought that Cash talks about come in large part from what Randall Stewart calls the Tidewater and the Frontier traditions in literature and geography. Both traditions commonly include a sense of place, a sense of community, and a sense of justice. An awareness of the positions within social classes is evident in both traditions, but in the Frontier tradition, an individual's social position is not given much importance. Even though both traditions have similar features, there are also elements which differ greatly. Stewart described them as follows:

TIDEWATER (TUCKAHOE)	FRONTIER (COHEE)
Good manners and decorum	Crude behavior
Wit and an interest in polite literature and art	Slapstick and anti-intellectualism
Courtliness, sophistication and restraint	Rough-and-tumble behavior
Subtlety	Straightforwardness

Randall Stewart places Thomas Wolfe and Jesse Stuart in the Frontier tradition, writers like Eudora Welty, John Crowe Ransom, and Allen Tate in the Tidewater tradition, and William Faulkner and Robert Penn Warren somewhere in between (1975, 420-421).

Scholars have long used the traits of these two traditions as a way to separate the South and its literature into highbrow and lowbrow, with the Tidewater tradition most often being associated with the highbrow, the "real" South and "true" southern literature, i.e., writers like Welty, Ransom, and Tate. However, at this time in history, what is *now* accepted as outhern is changing, and this new concept of the South is broader than it used to be. As ties with the past are cut—by the distance from "home," by the loss of the "home place," and by the death of loved ones—many southerners, whether highland or lowland, feel alienated and disconnected from their past. The "successful grandchildren [of people who lived such a life close to the land] . . . are [now] going nuts in Atlanta condominiums" (Percy, 438). Economics prevent many of these people from actually picking up and moving "back home." Still, this economical reality does not remove the need, the tremendous desire that people feel to somehow capture what is being lost, and to understand what all of this has meant in the past and what it means now. It is at this nexus that the writing of Jesse Stuart becomes important. He provides a fictional world that captures enough of the substance and traditions of both the highland and the lowland South to reassure the current generation of dislocated southerners by his messages, his images, and his vision. At a time when many highland and lowland southern writers are trying to determine "how you hold onto what you have in the past world but live beyond it and balance the two" (Hoffert 1989, 49), Stuart is already there to provide at least a glimpse at what the past was, and it is this vision that has the potential to help us come to grips with the malaise of dislocation people presently feel.

At first glance, it would appear that the majority of Stuart's work clearly falls into the Frontier tradition, and thus we might assume that it has little relevancy for those who come from or find themselves living within the confines of the Tidewater tradition. However, if you look closely, there are some Tidewater traits in Stuart's work that give it a broader perspective. I am not trying to claim that Jesse Stuart is a southern writer in the Tidewater tradition; however, his writing does contain many of the "down home" elements that displaced highland and lowland southerners are trying to reclaim.

To illustrate my point, I want to use one of Stuart's most popular yet also one of his least literary and most frontier-like novels, *Hie to the Hunters*. Consider the plot of this book: Jud "Sparkie" Sparks, from the Plum Grove Hills, rescues Didway Hargis, son of a wealthy Greenwood merchant, from a beating by spitting tobacco spittle with pin-point accuracy into the eyes of Did's attackers. Sparkie then convinces Did that he doesn't have to put up with this kind of abuse and invites Did to come home and live with him. Sparkie's parents, Peg and Arn, are happy to see Did. They won't turn away a stray hound from their door, so they are not about to turn away Did.

As Did spends time in the hills with Sparkie, he undergoes a metamorphosis, which John T. Flanagan succinctly describes as follows:

> When Sparkie . . . takes young Did Hargis out to the mountain cabin of his parents, Did is rather puny, pale, nervous, unaccustomed to strenuous physical exertion. It is only a matter of weeks before Did, eating coarse food and deprived of all the amenities of a comfortable town home, is able to hoe corn, plow, drive a mule, follow a trap line, scythe brush, and skin animals to the complete satisfaction of his mentor. (1977, 80-81)

Did has many adventures with Sparkie, including learning how to coon and fox hunt, going to mountain dances, and engaging in a harvest cornshucking, a Plum Grove community event on the Sparks' land. The cornshucking ends in an all-out battle between the hill folks and Did's father and his men who have come from town to rescue Did. In the end, Did's father's group loses.

Finally, the last attempt by Mr. Hargis to take Did home ends with Mr. Hargis and his men side-by-side with the Plum Grove men as they try to save Peg Sparks' barn; it was set on fire by a barn burner who plagued the hills during a feud between the farmers and the fox hunters. After the fire is out, when Mr. Hargis talks with Did, he treats him as an adult who is able to make up his own mind. Mr. Hargis agrees that if Did will come back and finish school, he can spend his summers in the hills with Sparkie, Peg, and Arn. Thus, Did becomes an active participant in both the town and the hill cultures.

This book clearly illustrates traits of the Frontier tradition. There is *roughness* and *crudeness of manners*, e.g., Arn smokes a pipe [not very genteel], their language is coarse though not profane, etc. There is *rough-and-tumble behavior* in many places, for instance when all the men wear guns in holsters to the big dance, when dogs are poisoned and barns burned, when both men and women get involved in the "knock down, drag out" fight at the Sparks's cornshucking. There is certainly *anti-intellectualism*, which is revealed early in the book. When Did and Sparkie first meet and Sparkie finds out that Did is in his second year of high school, he says, "Ye're high up in larnin'.... To look at ye, one wouldn't think it" (Stuart 1938, 8). Sparkie had only gotten to the Second Reader when he quit school. Sparkie and Peg and Arn, who are essentially illiterate, value more practical things like hunting and farming and making a living off the land. There is certainly *no courtliness or sophistication*, and the characters in this book are presented in a straightforward manner, with little or no *subtlety*. All of these things are of the frontier.

However, there is also a love of humor, e.g., the laughter when Did first appears in Sparkie's "hand-me-down" clothes. Though perhaps not *wit*, it isn't slapstick either. It is just human. Further, the people from Plum Grove always treat Did warmly, readily welcoming him into their midst. This behavior surely demonstrates *good manners, decorum*, and *a sense of community*.

There is *justice* and *restraint*. In the opening event of the book, Sparkie comes to Did's defense because he is outnumbered in a fight, thus, illustrating a sense of fair play. Another example is how the hill people treat Did as an adult who is free to make his own decisions. Thus, they will not let Mr. Hargis "bully" Did into returning to Greenwood. To allow this to happen wouldn't be fair or just. Instead of fighting immediately, however, they show great "restraint" in avoiding violence, until they are left with no alternative; e.g., when they are surrounded by Mr. Hargis and his men in the corn field. In fact, the people from town are exhibiting more frontier-like behavior than the people from Plum Grove. They have no choice but to fight their way out. Thus, there are also elements of the Tidewater tradition, in a universal sense, in Stuart's work. Actually, a book as simple and straightforward as *Hie to the Hunters* is not totally at odds with Lee Smith's conception of a southern novel; i.e., a book characterized by "leisurely development, care lavished upon developing characters, the importance of place, and the use of history" (Hoffert 1989, 48), though surely Stuart's characters could use some fleshing out.

In sharp contrast to many southern writers, who seem obsessed with exploring "the darker recesses of the human heart" (Percy 1980, 349),

Stuart inspires his readers by pointing out what is most basic and fundamentally good in life, particularly a life lived close to the land, close to the old home place, close to one's roots. Since so many contemporary southerners feel that these qualities have disappeared, reading the work of a writer like Jesse Stuart helps them to reclaim and to celebrate these qualities, at least vicariously. It is this vicarious connection with the past that, I believe, has allowed Jesse Stuart's writing to survive and to remain popular. Even though Stuart may not be a writer of the same skill and stature as William Faulkner, much like Faulkner, Stuart was trying "to talk about people ... men and women in their universal humanity" (Brooks 1983, 2), and in so doing he captured qualities universal to both the highland and lowland South. Stuart's genuine love of family, of friends and acquaintances, of the land, and of local customs, his sense of fair play and justice, his eternal optimism in the face of despair and adversity, the simple descriptions of home, i.e., the people, the food, the smells, the behaviors, all connect him to both Tuckahoes [plantation farmers] and Cohees [mountaineers].

A vision such as Stuart's is frequently dismissed as lacking artistic depth and social importance. As Jim Wayne Miller points out, however, "literary works not overtly concerned with political and social conditions have often made contributions to social and political awareness" (1980, 66). In fact, historian Henry Steele Commager claimed that "the image of the American past and with it our national identity was ... to an extraordinary degree a literary creation by poets and storytellers ... " (66).

As novelist John Gardner once said:

> Great [literature] can make us laugh or cry, in much the same way life can, and it gives us at least the powerful illusion that when we do so we're doing pretty much the same things we do when we laugh at Uncle Herman's jokes, or cry at funerals. Somehow the endlessly recombining elements that make up works of [literature] have their roots hooked, it seems, in the universe, or at least into the hearts of human beings. Somehow the [literary] dream persuades us that it's a clear, sharp, edited version of the dream all around us. Whatever our doubts, we pick up books at train stations, or withdraw into our studies and write them; and the world—or so we imagine—comes alive. (1984, 38)

And this is what happens when we read Jesse Stuart. A literary dream is created, and a fictional world comes alive for us. It is a world that may not exist in reality, but a world quite real, at least in our mind's eye. This world is made vivid and rich by the images and details of plain living evoked by Stuart's writing. In a time when we are suffering malaise, dislocation, and mourning the disappearance of the homeplace and the loss of the home-folks, reading what Stuart wrote soothes us and takes us home, at least for a while.

Works Cited

Brooks, Cleanth. 1983. *William Faulkner: First Encounters*. New Haven: Yale University Press.

Cash, W. J. 1969. *The Mind of the South*. New York: Vintage.

Flanagan, John T. 1977. "Jesse Stuart, Regional Novelist." *Jesse Stuart: Essays on His Work*. Eds. J. R. LeMaster and Mary Washington Clark. Lexington: The University Press of Kentucky.

Gardner, John. 1984. *The Art of Fiction*. New York: Alfred A. Knopf.

Hoffert, Barbara. 1989. "Writer's Renaissance in North Carolina." *Library Journal* 114:18, 44-48.

Miller, Jim Wayne. 1980. "A Post-Agrarian Regionalism for Appalachia." *Appalachian Heritage,* Spring 1980, 58-71.

Percy, Walker. 1980. "Southern Comfort." *Popular Writing in America*. Eds. Donald McQuade and Robert Atwan. New York: Oxford University Press. (Originally published in *Harper's*, January 1979, This was a shorter version of a draft published in *The Georgia Review*, Vol 32 1978.)

Stewart, Randall. 1975. "Tidewater and Frontier." *Voices from the Hills*. Eds. Robert J. Higgs and Ambrose N. Manning. New York: Frederick Ungar Publishing Co.

Stuart, Jesse. 1988. *Hie to the Hunters*. Ashland: The Jesse Stuart Foundation.

Herb Thompson is an Associate Professor of Education at Emory & Henry College, Emory, Virginia.

James Jones' Appalachian Soldier in His World War II Trilogy

Loyal Jones

James Jones is best known for his novel of the pre-World War II army, *From Here to Eternity*, but his other two novels which complete the trilogy, *The Thin Red Line*, about the Guadalcanal campaign, and *Whistle*, about the returning wounded, were also highly praised for their realism. Jones followed four soldiers through all three novels, although under different but similar names. They are the first sergeant, the company clerk, the mess sergeant, and a non-conformist, heroic rifleman from Appalachia. They are known in *From Here to Eternity* respectively as First/Sgt. Warden, Cpl. Mazzioli, Sgt. Stark and Pvt. Prewitt from Harlan County, Kentucky. Jones decided that Prewitt in *Eternity* must die as a result of his own non-conformity, pride and honor. Therefore, he had to re-create him in the other novels under different names—Witt (from Breathitt County, Kentucky) in *The Thin Red Line*, and Prell (from West Virginia) in *Whistle*. However, Jones made it clear that they were the same character.

Alice Cornett, a Kentucky writer, tracked down Robert Lee Stewart, the Letcher County Kentuckian on whom Jones based his Robert E. Lee Prewitt, Witt and Prell, and published an article on him in 1982. Stewart had served with Jones in "F" Company, 27th Infantry ("The Wolfhound") regiment, 25th Infantry "Tropical Lightning" Division, at Schofield Barracks in Hawaii before Pearl Harbor and later on Guadalcanal. Like the fictional Prewitt, Stewart was the son of a coal miner, was a guitar player, a bugler, a boxer and "above all, a hard-headed, independent mountain boy" (1982, 11-13). Stewart's life had not been as hard as Jones described Prewitt's, but his mother died when he was thirteen, and in 1936 at fifteen, lying about his age and signing his father's name, he joined the army. When he reenlisted in 1939, he was assigned to Hawaii (32-33).

James Jones, from Robinson, a small town in southern Illinois, came from an entirely different kind of family: his grandfather was a lawyer, his father a dentist. However, the Joneses' fortunes were diminished in the stock market crash of 1929, and when Jones graduated from high school, there was not enough money for him to go to college. He joined the army in 1939 and ended up in the infantry in Hawaii. Jones noted that Robinson was settled by people from Kentucky and Indiana, and thus he felt some kinship with Kentuckians. His own behavior in real life is similar to that he ascribed to Prewitt.

Jones proposed the idea for *Eternity* to Scribner's Maxwell Perkins in 1946, while he was trying to get Scribner's to accept an earlier manuscript. In a letter to Perkins, Jones proposed a novel on the peacetime army, and wrote that he would:

> draw Stewart's life in the army, his intense personal pride, his six months on stockade rockpile rather than admit he was wrong and accept company punishment when he felt he was right in his actions. The small man standing on the edge of the ocean shaking his fist, the magnificent gesture. . . . Almost a criminal, almost an artist, but not either . . . (1989, 55-59)

Perkins asked Jones to set aside the earlier novel and offered a $500 advance for the first 50,000 words of what he called "the Stewart novel" (60). Jones went to work at once on the new novel.

My purpose in this paper is to discern how Jones viewed and described the soldier based on Stewart and other Appalachians in his company and to reflect on the accuracy of his depiction of Appalachian characteristics.

In a letter to Ben W. Griffith, Jr., who after Perkins' death became his editor at Scribner's, Jones explained his main purpose in *From Here to Eternity*:

> The main theme I basically wanted to show in *Eternity* —one which I saw often and which never ceased to amaze me—was that the Army had an infallible way of destroying its own best advocates and adherents. The type of which Prewitt was one are almost always the best examples of real combat soldiers. I have seen such men do absolutely unbelievable things in combat. And

yet—what amazed me—was that these very characteristics and
ideas which made them the best possible soldiers in combat are
the same things which always threw them into conflict with
authority out of combat, or even in combat sometimes, for that
matter. There seemed to me to be here a very ironic paradox
which the smugness of the Army (i.e., society) does not allow
itself to see. (203-4)

Jones goes on to say something that shows his solidarity with Prewitt:

I guess you could say that philosophically—though not politically—I am an anarchist. I am not fanatical enough to believe
that such a way of life could be practicable. But I hate to see
everywhere today the encroachments of control over the individual. . . .It does tremedous good for the many and hamstrings
the superior few. (205)

Jones was profoundly affected by being an enlisted man in the prewar regular army. Even though he was reared in a middle-class family, he came to admire and to accept the values of his fellow soldiers, who at the time were mostly working-class or who had been down-and-out in the Great Depression. Society and his microcosm of society, "The Compny," had not dealt fairly with them. Yet, Jones saw in them a fanatical loyalty to the company. Prewitt, the Kentuckian, is the essence of an unbending pride and a sense of honor and integrity. And so, in the peacetime army, he is in trouble. He is the best bugler in Hawaii, but because someone else is made First Bugler for political reasons, he requests straight infantry duty. He is also a boxer and the company commander welcomes him with a promise of special favors and rank if he will box. He refuses because he once blinded a fighter in the ring. His life is made hell as the company tries to break him, but he will not give in. He winds up in the stockade after a fight with a sergeant. He is too proud to plead that he fought because the sergeant drew a knife on him.

Stewart himself went to the stockade because of a fight with the Charge of Quarters. He also refused to join the boxing squad (Cornett 1982, 11-13; 32-33). Bill Curran, a boxer in the company said, "Stewart didn't want to fight. The rumor was that he'd fought before and had hurt someone" (Curran 1990).

Jones wrote to Max Perkins about such men in 1946:

Having known a number of these men, I am convinced that the
great majority of real criminals—not petty thieves but criminals—are what they are because of a high personal integrity and

a high personal pride. . . (I have a strong feeling that most of the men in the recent Alcatraz riot were probably Prewitts; two of them were from Ky., two were Indians from the Cookson Hills in Okla.). (Jones 1989, 72)

These characteristics are exemplified in Prewitt when he vows to kill Fatso, the sadistic stockade sergeant (who incidentally is from Breathitt County, Kentucky,) for his brutal beating of Maggio and cruelty to others. Prewitt has plenty of time to reconsider his promise and the consequences of such an act, but he kills Fatso. In the fight he receives a knife wound making it impossible for him to return to the company. While he is AWOL, the Japanese bomb Pearl Harbor. He is shot as he tries to get back to his company and do what he knows he can do best—soldier.

Stewart was a guitar player, and thus so is Prewitt In *Eternity*. Jones writes:

Robert E. Lee Prewitt had learned to play a guitar long before he had learned to bugle or to box. He learned it as a boy, and with it he learned a lot of blues, songs and laments. In the Kentucky mountains along the West Virginia [sic] Line life led him swiftly to that kind of music . . .
In the Kentucky Mountains. . . guitar playing is not considered the accomplishment it is most places. Every wellbred boy learns to chord a guitar when he is still small enough to hold it like a string bass. The boy Prewitt loved the songs because they gave him something, and understanding, as first hint that pain might not be pointless if you could turn it into something. . . (Jones 1951, 13)

Another Kentuckian in Jones' "F" Company was George H. Wilkinson, of Hazard, "a wonderful guitar player," and he turns up as Sal Anderson who often plays with Prewitt in *Eternity*. Jones described their music as Prewitt's kind of music "—blues songs and hillbilly music—the kind of music these bums and field laborers and factory workers who had tried to escape their barren lives by enlisting in the Army understood and always played" (68). Emory Toms, from western Pennsylvania, another boxer, guitar picker and First Bugler of "F" Company told of his first meeting with Stewart:

I was working out in the ring one day. He came up and said, "Lefty, you ain't half bad." We got to drinking that night, and he found out that I played guitar. So we got to playing together.

> We'd sit out on the quadrangle with a bucket of beer and play
> and sing all night. I'd sing tenor and he'd sing straight. Stewart
> liked the Delmore Brothers. A few years ago he sent me a tape
> of 50 songs of the Delmore Brothers. (Toms 1990)

Yet another bugler and guitar picker was Frank Marshall, from Philadelphia, the Second Bugler of the company, whom Stewart nicknamed Friday. This name stuck on a character in *Eternity*, Friday Clark, who made music with Prewitt and Sal Anderson. Alice Cornett attributes "The Reenlistment Blues," sung by Merle Travis in the movie, to Stewart and Wilkinson (11-13, 32-33).

Accomplishment with music is one of the characterstics that Jones attributed to his mountain soldiers. Many good musicians have indeed come out of the mountains, although not every 'wellbred' boy learned to play the guitar and make up songs out of his travail.

Prewitt, like Stewart, was orphaned at thirteen when his mother died of consumption.

> There was a big strike on that winter and she died in the middle
> of it. . . . Her husband, who was a striker, was in the county jail
> with two stab wounds in his chest and a fractured skull. And her
> brother, Uncle John, was dead, having been shot by several
> deputies . . . They said blood actually ran like rainwater in the
> gutters of Harlan that day. . . . The boy Prewitt saw the battle. . .
> .(Jones 1951, 15)

And he hit the road, for his mother had told him, "from your father you got pride and endurance and I knowed that you would need it. But one of you would have kilt the other if it hatnt of been for me. And now I wont be standin atween you no more" (16). Before she died she extracted a promise from him, "Promise me you wont never hurt nobody unless its absolute a must, unless you jist have to do it." The gifts from his father and mother led him into trouble and kept him there in this novel.

Prewitt will not be a boxer for the regiment because he has hurt someone boxing, and he is true to his mother's promise. But beyond that he has an innate sense of basic rights. "Every man has certain rights," he said; "in life, I mean, not in ideals. And if he dont stand up for his own rights nobody else is going to stand up for them for him" (209). In talking with Sgt. Stark, the mess sergeant, he tells how there was a sign in Harlan that read, "DON'T LET THE SUN SET ON YOU IN HARLAN, Nigger!" (Actually, I believe such a sign was posted in Corbin. Harlan County had many blacks.) When the sergeant tries to rationalize this, Prewitt interrupts and says that isn't what he means and goes on to tell how as a kid on the bum he was threatened by a hobo and a black man protected him. "Out of that whole bunch of guys he was the only one who lifted a finger to keep me from gettin knifed. The rest of them just stood and watched" (194). Prell in *The Thin Red Line* is said to have hated Negroes, but he quits the company when Captain Stein, a Jew who has commanded well, is relieved of command by the battalion commander who dislikes Jews. Both Prewitt and Prell are called Bolsheviks, perhaps because of their mine union background. Prewitt is for the underdog and against the top dog.

> He had even made himself a philosophy of life out of it. So he had gone right on, unable to stop believing that if the Communists were the under dog in Spain then he believed in fighting for the Communists in Spain; but that if the Communists were the top dog back home in Russia and the (what would you call them in Russia? the traitors, I guess) traitors were the bottom dog, then he believed in fighting for the traitors and against the Communists. He believed in fighting for the Jews in Germany, and against the Jews in Wall Street and Hollywood. And if the Capitalists were top dog in America and the proletariat the under dog, then he believed in fighting for the proletariat against the Capitalists. This too-ingrained-to-be-forgotten philosophy of his has led him, a Southerner, to believe in fighting for the Negroes against the Whites everywhere, because the Negroes were nowhere the top dog, at least as yet. . . .
> It was, he realized, a very flighty philosophy, a chameleon philosophy always changing its color. You were a Communist one day and the next day you were an anti-Communist. . . .
> But where, you ask, does it put you politically? What are your politics?
> . . . I would say that politically you are a sort of super arch-revolutionary, the kind that made the Revolution in Russia and that the Communists are killing now, sort of a perfect criminal type, very dangerous, a mad dog that loves under dogs. . . .
> But you better not tell that to anybody unless you have to, Prewitt. They'll put you in the nut ward. Because here in America . . . everybody fights to *become* top dog, and then to *stay* top dog. (Jones 1951, 275-77)

First Sergeant Warden has harsh words for Prewitt and his kind,

> The only trouble with them guys is that they never learn. . . .
> They had rather let you kill them, than admit they're wrong. No

more sense than a goddam GI mule. . . . I seen too many of them mountain boys. They're a threat to the freedom of this whole country. (289)

Warden represents authority and order. Prewitt and his kind are always a threat to that order. Jones presents the rifle company as a microcosm of society, and his message is always that society has no use for the Prewitts of the world except in some sort of emergency. Prewitt has to deal with a peacetime army to which he is fanatically loyal, but which is inept at dealing with such as him.

Witt, in *The Thin Red Line* is in an entirely different setting— combat on Guadalcanal. He has been transferred out to a new company when the company has a chance to get rid of its misfits. Stewart himself stayed with the company through action on Guadalcanal, New Georgia, and after a rest in New Caledonia and training and reorganization in New Zealand, took part in the Philippines campaign and was wounded. However, Jones wishes to show Witt's devotion to C-for-Charlie. On Guadalcanal, he deserts his new company, which hasn't been issued weapons anyhow, and rejoins his old company out of loyalty and a sense of responsibility. He knows he is one of the best soldiers in the company.

When I think of old C-for-Charlie goin up there into them Japs without me, it like to breaks my heart. . . . You know how I feel about this compny. . . . Its my compny. It aint right, thats all. It aint. Why, who knows how many of the guys, how many of my old buddies, I might save if I was there. . . . I belong to the compny. (Jones 1962, 104)

When Witt rejoins C-for-Charlie, he volunteers to join an attack on a Japanese machine gun nest.

He had made his decision to volunteer himself back into the old outfit, and he had made his decision to volunteer for this thing, and he was a free individual human being as far as he was concerned. He was free, white and twenty-one and had never taken no shit off nobody and never would, and as the prospect of action got closer and closer he could feel himself tightening all up inside with excitement, exactly like he used to do in the coal strikes back in Bloody Breathitt. The chance to help, the chance to save all his friends that he could. . . . He had not shot squirrel all his life for nothing. He had not made High Expert on the range for the past six years for nothing, either. (266)

Witt leaves the company after the colonel relieves Captain Stein, the company commander, refusing to serve under an officer who would treat a good officer as he did. After rejoining C-for-Charlie, after the colonel is promoted, he volunteers to lead an ambush mission that he feels is foolish, and tells the new company commander so. However, he goes because he can protect his men better than anyone else. When the ambush goes wrong and only he and one other man survive, he cusses out the commander and once again leaves the company. When he learns that this commander is gone he returns, but the new company commander does not want him. One of his lieutenants argues for Witt:

> If you ever have to lead this outfit in combat, you'll wish to hell you had Witt with you. .
> I was around there on The Elephant's Head when Witt went in with that assault force. I tell you you're makin a serious mistake if you don't take him back. You're denying yourself one of the best potential platoon leaders you'll ever get a chance at. (471)

Whistle is the story of the returning wounded from Guadalcanal and New Georgia to a hospital in Luxor (Memphis, actually, where James Jones had been hospitalized after Guadalcanal). It is a story of the same four men whom I mentioned at the start, the First Sergeant (now named Winch), the Mess Sergeant (Strange), the Company Clerk (Landers) and the Appalachian soldier (Prell). Although they are not necessarily friends nor do they even like each other, they are bound to each other because they are from "The Compny."

> And the Company had been our family, our only home. Real parents, wives, fiancees did not really exist for us. Not before the fanatical devotion of that loyalty. Crippled, raging, enfeebled, unmanned in a very real sense and hating, hating both sides of our own coin and of every coin, we clung to each other no matter where or how far the hospital, and waited for the smallest morsel of news of the others to filter back to us, and faithfully wrote and mailed the messages that would carry it on to the other brothers. (Jones 1978, 4-5)

No one is more devoted to the Company than Prewitt-Witt-Prell. He is not only willing to die for it or with it, he feels a mission (since he knows he is a very good soldier) to look after his brothers. He is a born leader in his world. He has been promoted to corporal and sergeant more than once but is busted repeatedly to private because of his uncompromising nature. But, in the thick of battle on New Georgia he is there, and quickly becomes an acting sergeant again. He knows his business. Prell, in *Whistle*, is horribly wounded in both legs in the New Georgia campaign by a Japanese machine gun while leading a patrol. Even so he brings his men back safely. For his heroic actions he is nominated for the Congressional Medal of Honor, which he modestly thinks he does not deserve.

Stewart, a staff sergeant and platoon leader, was wounded in the Philippines campaign. Leading a patrol, he was shot in the legs by a machine gun, taking some 20 rounds, according to Emory Toms from "F" Company. Raymond Jordan, who was wounded on Guadalcanal and sent home, heard that Stewart was hit by "friendly fire." Doctors wanted to amputate his badly mangled leg, but he refused. The leg did heal, but he limped the rest of his life (Jordan and Toms 1990).

Prell's hardest battle is before him in the hospital. His legs are not healing and the doctors fear gangrene. They want to amputate one leg and possibly the other also. Prell will not give permission. His story in *Whistle* is about the fight for his legs:

> It was not that Prell was depressed, or defeated, or suicidal. That wasn't Prell's style. . . . Prell was just as mean and ornery as he's ever been. He'd always been a stubborn, proud West Virginia hardhead. . . .
>
> There had always been a streak of the heroics-lover in Prell. With his unbending West Virginia pride, Prell was not a gay, carefree laughing-boy type. He was dead responsible and steady, cool calculating. But he was vain to a fault. He took bigger risks than a motorcyle-jockey, wild-assed kind. He had done unbelievable things on the Canal. Like walking all night through the jungle, alone out beyond the lines, to get back to the company which was cut off somewhere a mile up ahead. And he never blinked an eye about it afterwards. (Jones 1978, 37;40)

Mess Sergeant Strange observed, "Prell was one of the people who should never be laid up like that. And yet Prell was one of the ones who would always get hurt the worst, and the most often, in his life" (40-49).

Landers, the Company Clerk, said, "Well, he's one of the best men our outfit ever had. I guess you know, he saved his whole patrol after he got shot up . . ." (129).

Prell's wounds are excruciating, but he never complains. "Only sheer stubbornness had kept him from crying out a dozen times. But he had made up his mind he was not going to let anybody see him blubbering" (52). Prell hangs on and saves his legs, and he is allowed to, partially because the Army doesn't want an amputee receiving the Medal of Honor. His legs begin to heal, his Medal is awarded, and he is chosen to speak at War Bond rallies. They intend to get him a commission. He meets a girl in the hospital and eventually marries her, but she is more in love with the Medal of Honor than with him. His life turns sour.

In fact, all four men are doomed. They never recover from the war. M/Sgt. Winch ends up in the psycho ward. Landers, the clerk, and Strange the mess sergeant, commit suicide, and perhaps so does Prell. He is killed by another soldier in a fight he starts in a dingy bar and poolroom. Prell, the soldier's soldier, does not adjust to ordinary society.

The character of Prewitt-Witt-Prell is strongly drawn. He comes from a deprived background, the coalfields of Appalachia with its labor strife that often was like a battlefield. He is a proud, stubborn person with his own set of values and principles. He is a person of aesthetics—a guitar player, a superb bugler who will not serve in an outfit that has elevated a lesser bugler to First Bugler, and he has a sense of social justice. He is willing to put up with extreme punishment rather than go back on a promise not to box again, and he is willing to go to the stockade rather than reveal the true reason for his fight with a sergeant. He vows to kill Fatso, the Stockade sergeant, and does, although as he fights Fatso he finds himself "wishing momentarily he had been born a different person . . ." (Jones 1951, 670)

How typical of Appalachians is Jones' soldier? There is no question but what Prewitt-Witt-Prell is based on one Appalachian soldier—Stewart—and perhaps to some degree on other mountain boys in the outfit. It is obvious also that he is shaped to a degree by Jones' own values and attitudes. Members of "F" Company attributed to Robert Lee Stewart some of the characteristics of the fictional soldier. Bill Curran, who won a commission on New Georgia, said, "Stewart was a damn good soldier" (1990). Frank Grzebinski, a New Yorker, thought that Prewitt in *Eternity* was about 80 per-cent true of Stewart. "Stewart was a good soldier, but he didn't volunteer any more than anyone else. It wasn't the thing to do. He was a tough little fellow. Prewitt didn't have nearly the character of Stewart" (1990). Frank Marshall, the model for Friday Clark, thought *Eternity* was about 80 or 90 percent true in regard to the company, although with the facts changed around. "Stewart was a good soldier. He was a tough guy and he could be mean," Marshall added (1990). "Stewart was a typical soldier of the Regular Army," said Raymond Jordan, now of Seminole, Florida. "The only thing he lacked was the normal build of an average man. He was a bantam weight. In his younger days he was a pistol! He had a gum band temper. It would snap, and he was ready to take you on. If he liked you, fine; if he didn't, stay away from him" (Jordan 1990).

Stewart's music was often mentioned by his company-mates. Jones made much of music-making in *Eternity*. Prewitt's ability with the bugle was an important aspect of the story, but also his guitar playing and singing. Emory Toms and Frank Marshall who played country-western music semi-professionally after the war, fondly remembered the music-making in the old company. "We played guitars and drank together," Toms recalled. "He [Stewart] could hold his own playing the guitar. We'd sit on the quadrangle with a bucket of beer and play and sing all night" (Toms, 1 February 1990). Bill Curran said, "Singing was a big deal. We'd get cofffee cans full of beer. We'd do this especially when someone was rotating back to the States. One of the kids wrote 'The Reenlistment Blues,' and we'd sing that" (Curran 1990). Alice Cornett thought Stewart and George Wilkinson had written the song, but Curran attributed it to one particular person. However, Raymond Jordan said,

> It came out of the guys sitting around at night. Toms and Stewart and Marshall would sit in the corner of the quadrangle and play and play and play. They played the old-fashioned hill music. One person would start a line, and another would add one. At our Atlanta reunion, Toms and Stewart were so happy. They brought their guitars, baloney, bread and condiments, and they'd just sit there in the hotel room and play. They made a tape which they sent to the rest of us. (Jordan 1990)

In real life and through the pages of James Jones' trilogy, Robert Stewart and the fictional Prewitt-Witt-Prell emerge as an Appalachian type. They were a product of a hard and sometimes dangerous life in the coalfields of Central Appalachia, of the Great Depression and of the Regular Army. No doubt Stewart, like Jones' hero, was a good soldier and a complex man. However, it is not true that Prewitt-Witt-Prell, or Appalachians, were sole possessors of the traits that Jones admired. There were other heroes, like Bill Curran of the company, who was awarded the Dinstinguished Service Cross for bravery on Guadalcanal. The two Pennsylvanians Marshall and Toms played the guitar and the bugle, perhaps as well as did Stewart. Jones himself had a lot of the characteristics of Stewart. He was in fights. He went AWOL and ended up in the stockade until he was discharged. The politics attributed to Prewitt-Prell-Witt appear to be as much those of Jones as of Stewart. However, Jones perceived accurately that the attributes of fair-mindedness, sympathy for the underdog, passion for social justice, and dogged independence were held to some degree by mountain people.

There is a strong perception that southern mountaineers make good soldiers and often heroes. Frank J. Wendsen, First Sergeant of "F"

Company from just after Pearl Harbor through the islands campaigns, said "Kentucky was my pride and joy. They were good soldiers. They'd do or die" (Wendsen 1990). Charles Earlywine, a West Virginian who was communications sergeant for "F" Company through the war, thought the southern mountaineers were exceptional soldiers. "I remember Ivy Jones, just an old hillbilly from North Carolina. He was there anytime you needed him. The Japanese used to cut our telephone lines, and when we went to find the break, they'd ambush us. When I called for volunteers, he say, 'I'll go with you, Earlybird.' He and a Sioux Indian named Russo saved my life many times" (Earlywine 1990).

Harry Caudill recently wrote about three Appalachian heroes from World War I, the most notable being East Tennessean Alvin York, who singlehandedly "killed 25 Germans with 25 shots and accepted the surrender of another 132 officers and men" who were in possession of 25 machine guns. Willie Sandlin, of Leslie County, Kentucky, like York, was awarded the Medal of Honor. He, by himself, "assaulted one after the other three entrenched German machine gun nests," with grenades and his rifle, killing all those inside and capturing a battalion headquarters, thus creating a hole in the German lines. Another Kentuckian, Peter McCoy of Pike County was nominated for the Medal of Honor, but was given instead the second highest award, the Distinguished Service Cross, for breaking into a German trench and killing seven of the enemy and capturing 17 more. "At the end of that foray his uniform and the pack on his back had been slashed by an unbelievable 177 bullet holes." Only he and seven others from his company survived. Caudill went on to report that a total of thirteen Kentucky mountaineers have received the Medal of Honor since it was established in 1861 (Caudill 1988).

Researchers at East Tennesse State University and the Veterans Administration have made a strong case for Appalachians being good soldiers. Steven Giles, chief psychologist at the Veterans Administration Medical Center at Mountain Home, Tennessee, said, "They chose to be in combat and they were chosen. . . . You can talk to Army officers and they'll tell you they chose Appalachians for point men and for patrols because they felt they were more motivated, more likely to be woods-wise and more familiar with the use of weapons." The result is that they are more likely to be killed in combat. "If you were from Appalachia, you were 50 percent more likely to have been killed in Vietnam," Giles reported. Pat Arnow, of the Center for Appalachian Studies and Services at ETSU, and Bert Allen, a professor of psychology at Milligan College, found that in the Korean War 18 percent of the Medals of Honor went to Appalachian soldiers although they made up only 8 percent of those who fought, and in the Vietnam War, Appalachian soldiers were awarded 13 percent of the Medals of Honor although only 7.3 percent of the soldiers were from Appalachia" (Waxman 1989).

These figures and public perception of Appalachians as good soldiers support James Jones' characterization of Prewitt-Witt-Prell as an ideal soldier. Rodger Cunningham, reviewing Grady McWhiney's *Cracker Culture: Celtic Ways in the Old South* (Cunningham 1990, 176-82) warns us, however, about applying romantic notions too liberally to Appalachians or other groups, even in admiration, lest we extend the stereotypes that we decry. For example, Jones' belief that Prewitt-Witt-Prell is a type of person who is unable to fit into ordinary society needs further examination. We know that Appalachian people have been able to do all sorts of jobs here and wherever they have migrated. They have adjusted, adapted, and they've done well as thirty-year men in military service, most of it in peacetime. Robert Stewart adjusted to civilian life very well from all accounts. After working briefly in Arizona, he moved to Seattle to be nearer his wife's family. There he worked for an automobile tire wholesaler until he retired. Mrs. Stewart, who is not happy with Jones' portrayal of her husband, is quick to point out that, while "Bob was a gutsy soldier who did not kowtow to anybody, he was highly respected and had no trouble getting along when he came home." She added, "He was the best husband in the world and the best father" (Stewart 1990). Robert Stewart, who died in 1989, and Mrs. Stewart, reared six children.

Yet, some Appalachian people have not chosen to become adjusted to mainstream society, but have lived life by their own set of values. Some religious groups, for example the Old Regular Baptist who are especially strong in Robert Stewart's native Letcher County, call themselves "a peculiar people," meaning they do not want to be like other people. Many Appalachians do possess the traits that Jones ascribed to his soldier, and society has not always been effective in dealing with such individualists. Jones saw such people as noble people, nevertheless. To him, organized society has many benefits, but those benefits do not justify the destruction of those with special qualities who do not choose to fit in.

Works Cited

Caudill, Harry M. 1988. "Hills Have Historically Produced Heroes." *The [Whitesburg, Kentucky] Mountain Eagle*, 21 September 1988, C3.

Cornett, Alice. 1982. "From Kentucky To Eternity." *The [Louisville] Courier Journal Sunday Magazine*, 18 April 1982, 11-13 and 32-33.

Cunningham, Rodger. 1990. "Eat Grits and Die: Or, Cracker, Your Breed Ain't Hermeneutical." *Appalachian Journal*, 17 (Winter 1990) : 176-82.

Curran, Bill. Telephone conversation with author. 5 February 1990.

Earlywine, Charles. Telephone conversation with author. 31 January 1990.

Grzebinski, Frank. Telephone conversation with author. 2 February 1990.

Jones, James. 1951. *From Here to Eternity*. New York: Charles Scribner's.

———. 1962. *The Thin Red Line*. New York: Charles Scribner's.

———. 1978. *Whistle*. New York: Delacorte Press.

———. 1989. *To Reach Eternity: The Letters of James Jones*. Ed. George Hendrick. New York: Random House.

Jordan, Raymond D. Telephone conversation with author. 6 February 1990.

Marshall, Frank. Telephone conversation with author. 1 February 1990.

Stewart, Mrs. Robert Lee. Telephone conversation with author. 2 February 1990.

Toms, Emory "Leo." Telephone conversations with author. 31 January 1990, 1 February 1990, and 6 February 1990.

Waxman, Leanne. 1989. "Vietnam's Cost Was High for Appalachian Soldiers." *The [Louisville] Courier-Journal*, 15 March 1989.

Wendsen, Frank J. Telephone conversation with author. 5 February 1990.

Loyal Jones is director of the Berea College Appalachian Center and is a frequent speaker on Appalachian topics. He has published numerous articles and books.

Southern Gothic and Appalachian Gothic: A Comparative Look at Flannery O'Connor and Cormac McCarthy

Louis H. Palmer III

> In these grotesque works, we find that the writer has made alive some experience which we are not accustomed to observe every day, or which the ordinary man may not experience in his ordinary life. We find that connections which we would expect in the customary kind of realism have been ignored, that there are strange skips and gaps which anyone trying to describe manners and customs would certainly not have left. Yet the characters have an inner coherence, if not always a coherence to their social framework. Their fictional qualities lean away from typical social patterns, toward mystery and the unexpected.
> —Flannery O'Connor,
> "Some Aspects of the Grotesque in
> Southern Fiction" (1979, 40)

"Southern Gothic" as a literary category is difficult to pin down. Most readers of southern literature recognize the term, and would be able to associate it with a canon of works of fiction, which would start with Poe's "The Fall of the House of Usher," continue through some of the more colorful of the local colorists, such as New Orleans' George Washington Cable, and result in modern works by William Faulkner, Carson McCullers, Flannery O'Connor, and others. We find a corresponding group of writers in Appalachian literature, from George Washington Harris' Sut Lovingood stories (which Faulkner acknowledged as an influence) to recent works by Breece D'J Pancake, Pinckney Benedict, Cormac McCarthy, and Lee Smith. In addition, the mountain region has been used as a setting for writers from the lowland South writing in the Gothic mode, a place to stage a journey into the irrational. Dickey's "Chautooga" is direct descendant of Conrad's "Congo."

I want to look at two novels, and at the question: Is there a difference? That is, is Appalachian Gothic a sub-group of Southern Gothic? The critic Irwin Malin considers the latter a sub-group of what he calls New American Gothic, which he "charts" in a book of the same name. William Van O'Connor, in an essay entitled "The Grotesque: An American Genre," extends the claim to modern literature in general. When he warns that "a frequent, and probably an essential, factor in this newer literature, especially in its more serious manifestations, is that one category tends to erupt inside another category (O'Connor 1962, 18)", he is using Grotesque as the larger category in which Gothic erupts, but the two could be reversed.

I want to use Malin's paradigm to deal with the relationship of Southern Gothic to Appalachian Gothic. He defines the Gothic mode in terms of the isolation and narcissism of its protagonists and their antagonistic relations with the primary social unit, the family. Then he explores three reoccurring images or symbols in Gothic literature: the mirror, the voyage, and the house, which reinforce the themes of self-love and rejection of family.

In this paper I want to focus these questions and criteria mainly on two novels: a classic of Southern Gothic, Flannery O'Connor's *Wise Blood*, and a recent novel by an Appalachian author, Cormac McCarthy's *Suttree*. I have chosen them because of their obvious similarities of setting—the "underside" of Southern urban life in the immediate postwar period—and because they provide some interesting contrasts. I will deal with Malin's themes and symbols as well as with the authors' views of the natural world, and will attempt to show that this treatment is where, in this and other cases, one can distinguish between the two Gothics.

In the history of fiction since the Romantic period, there are two distinct strands. Critics love to speak of highbrow, middlebrow, and lowbrow, as if to personify the novel or short story as a product to be aimed at a specific target audience. I find these distinctions to be euphemistic and inaccurate, a backhanded way to distinguish between the two strands of fiction. Hawthorne distinguished between them as the novel and the romance. On the one hand is the bourgeois tradition of Austen and her descendants, and on the other are Mary Shelley and the Brontes, the sort of literature that Mann had in mind when he called the grotesque "anti-bourgeois." History and the crossing of the Atlantic have led us from a predominance of the first tradition to a predominance of the second. The amusement that Austen lavished on the Gothic mode in *Northanger Abbey* has been replaced by Faulkner's parody of the bourgoise perspective in "A Rose For Miss Emily."

I would argue that both traditions are still alive, however, and that they can be distinguished from one another in basically social terms. The bourgoise tradition is concerned with the preservation of values within a community, with family and tradition, with the necessary sacrifices that the individual makes for the greater social good. Nature, *per se* and human, is a raw material that needs to be refined. The anti-bourgoise tradition concerns the individual's quest for value through freedom from and rejection of traditional structures. Nature is a force for change, both within and without the individual.

The Gothic, as a mode, can be used to reinforce either perspective, although it lends itself to the anti-bourgoise. Early Gothic fiction, such as Walpole's *The Castle of Otranto,* concerned the exotic and the supernatural, along with strange deformed characters and violent events. This continued through Poe, but was refined by Hawthorne and Melville and later in James, so that unusual events could be seen as psychological expressions of the protagonist's inner state. By the turn of the present century, the mechanisms of the Gothic could be manipulated to fit into the constraints of realistic or even naturalistic fiction.

Now let us take our historical survey to the South, a region divided in many ways, but most obviously into two geographic regions, Mountain and Lowland. These two areas have come to represent many of the same qualities as the two kinds of fiction. Jim Wayne Miller speaks of the mountains as a repository for our dreams and nightmares: fertile soil, obviously, for the Gothic. Mountaineers are supposed to represent a rebellious individuality coupled with bare-bones poverty.

The Lowland South is associated with the antebellum myth of the plantation, with its qualities of wealth and family and stability which, despite its dark underbelly, lends itself to a glorification of the traditional. Much of Southern literature comes from the tension between these two geographies, and the associative auras surrounding each. For the purpose of this paper, I will call them "redneck" and "genteel."

I do not mean to imply that these two poles of the Southern character actually are geographic. Quite the contrary. Like all contraries, to paraphrase Coleridge's expression, they coincide. They do this in any one town, in any one novel, in any one individual character. The fact that Hazel Motes is a poor, white-trash Tennessee redneck places him in this continuum as an outcast, gives him a recognizable location in social and mythic terms.

The Gothic apparatus requires the work to focus on one isolated character, whom we understand not only through the basic devices of characterization—what he does, thinks, says, and how others react—but also through mirror-image characters who work as reflections or foils. In Victorian Gothic, this character might be a ghost or supernatural creature, but we seem to require more realistic treatments. The doppelganger in *Wise Blood* is a contrived creature, but a crucially important one. The house, which someone has identified as the hero of the Gothic novel, has been likewise transformed: Suttree's is a houseboat, while Hazel's is a car. These mobile homes, if you will, also have their 'falls': again at crucial points in the plots. The third Gothic device is the voyage, and both of the protagonists take three of them, all somewhat unsucessful.

Much of O'Connor's early work, of which *Wise Blood* is a central example, takes place in the redneck fringe of the Lowland South. The novel describes Hazel's attempt to escape from his tradition, that of backwoods evangelism. He has no family left, and no desire to create one. He is a rebel against the genteel society of Talkinham. And he is such an individualist that he rejects every offer of love or assistance given to him.

Even though O'Connor claims that a character in her kind of fiction has "not always ... coherence to their social framework," at first Hazel does. He sees a car as a ready means of escape. He is quite consistent with street-preacher convention as he preaches his Holy Church Without Christ. He attracts equally dispossessed and redneck followers (although they have their own varied agendas). Despite his stubborn intransigence, he fits into the world of Talkinham's fringe. He is a quintessential redneck rebel, taken to and beyond the logical extreme—unlike the other characters, who are guided by self-interest, he rebels against himself, first symbolically, by murdering his alter ego, then completely, blinding himself and slowly torturing himself until he dies. His strength is in his fierce consistency, in his refusal to compromise.

Talkinham's street community is not anti-bourgeois. Each member accepts the values of the society that has disenfranchised him. Asa Hawks wants money, so he pretends to have blinded himself. Enoch Emery wants friends. Sabbath Lily Hawks wants a normal family life, savagely expressed in her maternal treatment of the mummy corpse. The landlady wants more money and a husband, even a strange and blind one. The false prophet has a family. Hazel is the only one who is so haunted (O'Connor's term) by Christ, or Christ's absence, that he will not compromise.

Although she presents it realistically, O'Connor's world is theologically oriented; it is the fallen world. Neither the genteel flocks of moviegoers nor the strange and grotesque fringe dwellers can escape from this fact, so they ignore it. Hazel is the only one with the courage or vision to see it. He tries, twice, to escape, but finds that he cannot. There is no redeeming factor in the bleak countryside. Here is Hazel leaving town:

> The highway was ragged with filling stations and trailer camps and roadhouses. After a while there were stretches where red gulleys dropped off on either side of the road and behind them were patches of field buttoned together with 666 posts. The sky leaked over all of it and then it began to leak into the car. The head of a string of pigs appeared snout-up over the ditch and he had to screech to a stop and watch the rear of the last pig disappear shaking into the ditch on the other side. He started the car again and went on. He had the feeling that everything he saw was a broken-off piece of some giant blank thing that he had forgotten had happened to him. (O'Connor 1949, 74)

These are images of enclosure and limitation. The world is still enclosed within what Blake called "the mundane egg" of the sky. O'Connor presents us with a world, like Blake's, that can be transcended only through the vision that Hazel obtains, paradoxically, through blindness: Hazel's act of self-blinding allows him to escape from the self-blindness the others are trapped in.

Unlike the traditional Gothic hero, obsessed with himself and/or a lover and isolated from the world, we see this protagonist's antagonistic relationship to self and to the world, which is just a larger version of the self, as an enclosure to break through to freedom. Hazel is "mirrored" by a series of other characters, genteel and redneck, from Mrs. Wally Bee Hitchcock to the brutal and insensitive policemen who pick him up, dying. The Gothic mansion is one "high, rat-colored car" which is a pulpit, an illusion of freedom, and finally a murder weapon. And the journey begins with Hazel trying to go home, goes through three thwarted escape attempts, and resolves in a true journey 'home', through redemption and death. The family that Hazel rejects is the company of other fallen souls, rejected because of their blindness. O'Connor uses the Gothic apparatus to give us a Christian vision that might be thought to be genteel, insofar as it is Christian, but one that is so demanding it rejects gentility. At their weakest and most depraved, her redneck characters are interesting.

I will not claim that O'Connor is typical of Southern Gothic. Her vision is too idiosyncratic, her agenda too divergent. In this, she may have more in common with Blake, another visionary oddball, than with Faulkner. Her later work transfers her themes to the more familiar (to her) world of the genteel South, partly, I think, because her depiction of anarchic and rebellious characters led her readers to assume she espoused their views. In later work she looks for the "mystery and the unexpected" (O'Connor 1979, 40) that defined her fiction closer to home.

McCarthy's underrated novel, *Suttree*, shares much with *Wise Blood*. It takes place during the 1950s in Knoxville—like Talkinham a large industrial Southern town. The hero, Cornelius Suttree, like Hazel, has chosen a life without family. He lives in a shanty houseboat, and makes a meagre living as a fisherman on the Tennessee River. Unlike Motes, he is a college-educated scion of a prominent Knoxville family. Again the book contains a ragged but fascinating band of secondary characters—whores, drunks, ragpickers, 'inverts',—even a young watermelon molester. But McCarthy's language differs radically from O'Connor's. The book is described by Jerome Charyn in a review as a "horrifying flood . . . a poetic, troubled rush of debris" (1979, 15). Long descriptive passages use archaic and Latinate terms that contrast sharply with O'Connor's disciplined prose—except in conversation, where both authors have a definitive control of the colloquial and idiomatic speech. McCarthy has also been accused of disorganization. Again, Jerome Charyn: "[It is] ... without that boring neatness and desire for resolution that you can get in any well-made novel" (Charyn, 15), but I would argue that it is as consistent with narrative integrity of *Suttree* as O'Connor's economy is within *Wise Blood*. *Suttree* centers around the river, described here during the flood season:

> Bearing along garbage and rafted trash, bottles of suncured [sic] glass wherein corollas mauve and gold lie exploded, orangepeels ambered with age. A dead sow pink and bloated and jars and crates and shapes of wood washed into rigid homologues of viscera and empty oilcans locked in eyes of dishing slime where the spectra wink guiltily.
> One day a dead baby. Bloated, pulpy rotted eyes in a bulbous skull and little rags of flesh like tissuepaper. (McCarthy 1979, 306)

McCarthy's narrative organization alternates between floods of description and trickles of conversation, giving a concrete picture of his world and its inhabitants in a picturesque spread. The episodes, like *Wise Blood*'s center around the main character Suttree, with occasional sidetrips to follow his comic sidekick, the 'melonmounter' Gene

Harrowgate.

Cornelius Suttree is unlike Hazel Motes in the ability to reflect. In comparison he seems almost passive, falling into situations and relationships as if by accident. Like Motes, he rebels against his past—rejecting and deserting his parents as well as his own wife and child to live an outcast life. But his isolation is never really complete—he becomes responsible, in spite of himself, for helping a series of characters, including Harrowgate. As Anatole Broyard puts it, "People trust Suttree because he does not want anything they've got, he does not compete. He is interested, but he does not judge" (1979). His major motivation seems to be guilt: first, for living when his stillborn twin brother died, then for becoming less than he was expected to be. He visits the scenes of his past, filled with regret—the old decaying mansion, the school, the church. He travels to his son's funeral and fills in the grave by hand while the cemetery staff stand by with a bulldozer. He can be brutally honest with his mother's brother, whom the family have rejected as a drunk, but when his mother visits him in jail, he breaks down: " 'Hopes wrecked, love sundered. See the mother sorrowing. How everything that I was warned of's come to pass. . . . I can't', he said. Hot salt strangled him" (McCarthy 1979, 61). He has rejected his father's advice, "the world is run by those who are willing to take the responsibility for the running of it" (McCarthy, 13), but has internalized his father's image of him: "My case was always doubtful. I was expected to turn out badly" (McCarthy, 19). He is on the river doing a nameless penance, participating in what his father calls: "a dumbshow composed of the helpless and the impotent" (McCarthy, 14). Self-love is not his problem.

Suttree's character is mirrored by the many strange denizens of McAnally Flats—a sorceress, a transvestite called Trippin' Through The Dew, Billy Callahan—a shameless, goodnatured bully who takes several hours to die with a bullet between his eyes, and Ab Jones, a black bootlegger, "like a tree" (McCarthy, 202) covered with scars, whose refusal to bow down to authority results in frequent violent fights with the police and his status as a neighborhood hero. Suttree is accepted, but different. Indeed, the toleration of difference is what makes the characters of McAnally Flats different from their genteel counterparts. They may be foul and unhealthy, drunk and profane, but they are rarely deliberately cruel. The police always are.

The Gothic elements in the story are profuse. There are many deaths, even though Suttree is allowed to escape. There is a decaying mansion, Suttree's childhood home, but his castle is the houseboat, which, although it does not have the symbolic significance of Hazel's car, seems, like his friends, to suffer when he is gone—one time it almost sinks, another it gains a corpse. The doppelganger theme recurs again and again, from Suttree's vision of his dead twin: "He saw his brother in swaddling, hands outheld, a scent of myrrh and lilies" (McCarthy, 113), to two mirror-image possumhunters who appear out of the woods. Suttree's social position between the two worlds brings into being by implication the "Antisuttree" (McCarthy, 28) he glimpses in a glass door—the genteel person he might have been (just as an Antihazel would have been the preacher his grandfather wanted him to be).

It is the element of the voyage or journey that is especially significant in this novel. Hazel's three escape attempts, thwarted by the Bible verse on the rock, Sabbath Lily Hawks and the state trooper, offer him nothing apart from what he might have experienced in the city. Suttree's forays are otherwise. They are attempts to come to terms with his life. The first is to his son's funeral, where he fills the grave, gets attacked by his wife's family, and is escorted out of town by the local sheriff. This is an ineffective attempt to deal with his past. The next trip is to the Great Smoky Mountains, where he starts off hiking and ends up "..run[ning] crazy in the woods" (McCarthy, 290), having visions of "some doublegoer, some othersuttree" (McCarthy, 287) and "old spectral revenants armed with rusted tools of war colliding paralactically upon each other" (McCarthy, 287). He is surprised out of this bemusement by a seeming divine intervention:

> Clouds lay remote and motionless across the evening sky like milk awash in some backwater of the planet's seas and a white woodcock rose from the ferns before him and dissolved in smoke.
> A curling bit of down cradled in this green light for the sake of my soul's sanity. Unreal and silent bird albified between the sun and my broken mind godspeed. (McCarthy, 291)

This death-and-rebirth ordeal left him ready for his third trip, up the river with a family of mussel gatherers. He becomes involved with the daughter, but when she is killed by a rockslide he returns to the city. The mountain trip is transformative. He is no longer obsessed with his twin or his former family, and so the attempt to become a family member, although it is a redneck family. After this he falls in with a whore, and lives well on her earnings. But the essential instability of this relationship finally throws it off balance, and at the end we see a corpse in Suttree's houseboat—the old Suttree? the past? the twin?—and Suttree leaves his town of ghosts and dependents for parts unknown. He has done his time in hell.

The world of nature, as McCarthy presents it, is different in kind from the world of men. Represented by the river and by the mountains, it is a powerful and transformative force, which can be deadly, but which can have a positive effect on those who come into contact with it. This is the major difference between the worlds of these two novels. *Suttree* depicts a fallen world, but it is the human world, human structures, human relationships, that are flawed, and human effort can find "...vengeances for the wrongs of the world" (McCarthy, 290). Suttree's vocation, fishing, is in concert with that world, and being alone with nature gives him strength. This seems to be characteristic of Appalachian Gothic literature in general—the Romantic belief in the essential innocence and purity of nature, contrasted with the depravity of humans.

Finally, I can't resist pointing out the similarity of the two humorous 'sidekick' characters, Enoch Emery and Gene Harrowgate. Who says the novel hasn't learned from the movies? O'Connor dismisses her secondary character as "a moron and chiefly a comic character" (O'Connor 1979, 116), but he functions dramatically as a foil to Hazel, compelled by a need to belong that is so strong he finally puts on a gorilla suit. He becomes less than human just as Hazel attempts to become more than human. Harrowgate has a similar function in *Suttree,* providing both comic relief and a character who—in contrast to Suttree—does not reflect on his lot, just on schemes by which he can better it. He exists on a level of basic gratifications. Both secondary characters are endearing in their depravities, for example, when Harrowgate quizzes Suttree on the niceties of seduction:

> "How do you get em to take off their clothes? That's what I'd by god like to know."
> "You take them off."
> "Yeah? Well what does she do when you're doin that? I mean hell, does she look out the winder or somethin? I don't understand it at all Sut. The whole thing seems uneasy to me."
> (McCarthy, 316)

Much of the humor comes from the reaction of other characters to these two, such as when a bartender compliments Harrowgate on his shirt, which is an inverted pair of shorts with the seam ripped out, or when Enoch observes that he: "...was not very fond of children but children always seemed to like to look at him" (O'Connor 1949, 177). Both characters distort the genteel idea of enlightened self-interest. I read Enoch's gorilla suit as a parody of the naturalistic novel's social Darwinism.

The defining characteristic of the Gothic hero, according to Malin, is self-love or narcissism. Neither Suttree nor Hazel fit this definition. They are defined by contrast to a series of characters blinded by self-love. Both are self-willed and stubborn, and both choose exile from and confrontation with the representatives of genteel society. Perhaps this is an inversion of values from the traditional Gothic novel, or perhaps it is historic—do we not now generally identify the genteel with the narcissistic? These novels do.

Both novels can be interpreted in Christian terms, or at least as chronicles of spiritual growth. The operation of grace is, as O'Connor claims, a mystery, and each protagonist comes into contact with that mystery in the course of the novel. Both go through trials and penance, time done to justify a purpose higher than the individual self. The primary differences between the two concern the geography of the imagined world—its open or closed quality, and they differ in their interpretation of the state of nature rather than that of man. O'Connor writes: "The novelist is required to create the illusion of a whole world with believable people in it, and the chief difference between the novelist who is an orthodox Christian and the novelist who is merely a naturalist is that the Christian novelist lives in a larger universe" (O'Connor 1979, 175). I have no idea whether McCarthy considers himself to be an orthodox Christian—but I think it is obvious that *Suttree* inhabits the larger universe. Here Suttree speaks to "any soul to listen":

> No final word?
> Last words are only words.
> You can tell me, paradigm of your own sinister genesis
>   construed by a flame in a glass bell.
> I'd say I was not unhappy.
> You have nothing.
> It may be that the last shall be first.
> Do you believe that?
> No.
> What do you believe?
> I believe that the last and the first suffer equally. Pari passu.
> Equally?
> It is not alone in the dark of death that all souls are one soul.
> (McCarthy, 414)

Works Cited

Broyard, Anatole. 1979. "Where All Tales Are Tall." *New York Times*. 20 January 1979.

Charyn, Jerome. 1979. "Doomed Huck." *New York Times Book Review*. 18 February 1979, 14-15.

Malin, Irving. 1962. *New American Gothic*. Carbondale: Southern Illinois University Press.

McCarthy, Cormac. 1979. *Suttree*. New York: Random House.

O'Connor, William Van. 1962. *The Grotesque: An American Genre*. Carbondale: Southern Illinois University Press.

O'Connor, Flannery. 1949. *Wise Blood*. New York: Farrar, Strauss, and Giroux.

———. 1979. *Mystery and Manners*. Eds. Robert and Sally Fitzgerald. New York: Farrar, Strauss, and Giroux.

Tersh Palmer is completing a master's degree in English at Appalachian State University. His thesis is on Cormac McCarthy. He taught in public schools for thirteen years.

The Roots of Appalachian English: Scotch-Irish or British Southern?

Michael Montgomery

In the popular television series *The Story of English* and the resulting best-selling book (McCrum et al. 1986), the idea of tracing varieties of American English back to the British Isles has recently renewed attention. One episode of the series, *A Muse of Fire*, featured a New Englander dropping in on an East Anglian pub, purportedly in search of the speech patterns of his Puritan ancestors. A later show, *The Guid Scots Tongue*, examined the English of Scotland, exemplified by a Scotsman reading from William Lorimer's 1983 translation of the New Testament into Scottish English. In the course of an hour this program made the case for how the language of Lowland Scotland and Northern Ireland evolved into the English used today by North Carolina's denizen mountaineers, those latter-day descendants of hardy "Scotch-Irish" frontiersmen, and even into the Citizens Band Radio slang of long-distance truck drivers.[1]

American linguistic scholars have long been interested in exploring the roots of American English in the British Isles, notably in the early days of the well-known *Linguistic Atlas of the United States and Canada* project in the 1930s and 40s (Kurath 1929, 1949).[2] But for a variety of reasons the progress of the *Linguistic Atlas* has been slow, and in recent decades linguists working on the project have had little to say about tracing these connections, as it has become clear that more than was originally foreseen is required to pin them down.[3]

Determining whether, and to what extent, Appalachian speech may be linked to the British Isles has been part of larger questions of drawing specific trans-Atlantic connections ever since the late nineteenth century, with commentators variously labeling the region's language as "Scotch-Irish," "British," "Elizabethan English," or the like. Yet, while folklorists and historians have made significant progress in describing the diffusion of cultural patterns into Appalachia, for language patterns this has hardly been the case for either the *Linguistic Atlas* or any other effort to date. For decades, hosts of researchers and collectors have prowled the hills of southern Appalachia to study the spread of Scottish, Irish, and English traits and to capture the echoes of early American immigrants in song, in story, and in voice. One early example was the Englishman Cecil Sharp, who sought child ballads in Eastern Kentucky in 1916 and 1917 with his assistant Maud Karpeles (Sharp 1932). Many others could easily be cited.

One of the most recent efforts is that of Civil War historian Grady McWhiney, who, in *Cracker Culture: Celtic Ways of the Old South* (1988), has claimed that such personality traits as hospitableness, love of leisure, propensity for violent behavior, and aversion to work were carried over from Ireland, Scotland, and the "Celtic Fringe" areas of the British Isles to the American South as a whole and were significantly reinforced to steer the "Celtic" South onto a collision course with the "English" North, most of whose early immigrants came from the south and east of Britain, in that fateful year of 1861.

Closer to home, many authorities within Appalachia, such as John C. Campbell (1921), Josiah Combs (1943), and Cratis Williams (1961), the latter two native to the region, have devoted a good deal of energy to untying the early settlement patterns in an effort to determine the collective genealogy of the region's inhabitants, and to assess the relative proportions of Scotch-Irish, English, and German population groups in the region. To do this, Campbell and Combs examined patterns of surnames, Campbell of 1,200 old families from the Kentucky, Tennessee, and North Carolina mountain areas and Combs of his Eastern Kentucky schoolchildren from local families. Campbell (65) found equal portions of English and Scotch-Irish, while Combs' smaller sample included predominantly English names.[4] One explicit purpose of such efforts was, in addition to the straightforward calculation of national stocks in Appalachia, to temper the extravagant statements about how the Scotch-Irish almost single-handedly settled and subdued the frontier, statements being made around the turn of the twentieth century by such writers as Theodore Roosevelt in *The Winning of the West*. But an implicit goal, for Campbell and Williams, was to provide, by exploring the history of the region, a cultural identity for the people of Appalachia—an identity connected directly to Old World forebears—in the face of a prevailing national view that saw the region in negative terms, having little culture and an unflattering history. Of course, this goal of cultural affirmation also has been held by many of the ballad-collectors and other researchers who have written about the region.

The Lack of Research

However, despite much work by folklorists and cultural historians to identify the formative immigrant groups of Appalachia and to itemize their contributions, and despite the assumption that the same should be possible for language, it is a fact that there has yet to be a systematic effort to make the language connection to regional varieties of British English. The *Linguistic Atlas* has, for better or worse, spent its energy largely on mapping individual words and has never developed a framework for making a comparison. As a result, only impressionistic, cursory statements have been made, and we are hardly any closer than a half century ago to an objective determination of the extent to which the distinctive features of Appalachian speech are from Scotch-Irish settlers or from English settlers coming from southern Britain—the basic research question of this paper. Cratis Williams often claimed that they were the former, but others have more often claimed the latter, producing the familiar statement that Appalachian English is "Elizabethan." Neither Williams nor anyone else, including linguistic scholars, has yet attempted the careful sorting out of the major strands woven together into Appalachian English and to calculate more precisely the significance of each one.[5]

The present paper, an initial report of a much larger effort to explore the history of Appalachian English, examines a range of grammatical features that have been noted in the literature as characteristic of Appalachian speech. This is an attempt to identify which are most likely Scotch-Irish and which are English (very little, if any, German influence on Appalachian grammar turns out to be detectable), and to compare the relative significance of these two linguistic ancestries.

The Scope of the Challenge

Before continuing, it is necessary to say a few things about the scope and significance of such a project. Why, despite frequent comments in the literature, has a concerted assessment of the relative linguistic contributions of the aforementioned groups not been undertaken, especially given the keen interest over the past century in determining the ancestry of Appalachian people? There are basically two reasons for this.

First is a problem of knowledge and sources. American researchers tend to know quite little about the earlier stages of English spoken in Scotland and Northern Ireland (the general familiarity with the writings of Shakespeare and his contemporaries has no doubt led many writers to believe that Appalachian English is more "Elizabethan" than it actually is). Very few, if any, of those who have written on Appalachian speech are acquainted with the fact that there is not one, but two multi-volume historical dictionaries of Scottish English, the *Scottish National Dictionary* (Grant and Murison 1931-84) and the *Dictionary of the Older Scottish Tongue* (Craigie and Aitken 1933-). The question at hand cannot be addressed by using the *Oxford English Dictionary*, the best-known and most comprehensive historical dictionary of the language, because its coverage of non-literary and regional varieties of English is quite limited. All historical dictionaries, moreover, have built-in handicaps; they are only as good as their written citation files, and they are heavily biased toward literary language, offering little direct evidence on the speech patterns of the common people. Also, they suffer from the problem of negative evidence; that is, while we may discover from the entry of a word in a dictionary when and where that word was used, we cannot necessarily conclude from the absence of a word that it did not exist, or from the absence of a citation that a word was not used at a certain time and place.

Thus, it is necessary to go beyond dictionaries and to consult other types of material—linguistic studies and the original sources themselves. An extensive literature on Scottish English does exist, although it is largely tucked away in the nooks of major British libraries and no good bibliography yet exists. The problem for the English language of Northern Ireland is compounded by the problem that most of the few studies that have been done are unpublished.[6]

The second reason why such an assessment has not been achieved is that previous claims that Appalachian English was basically "Scotch-Irish" or basically "Elizabethan" lacked a methodology for making a determination.

The present paper draws on an extended research effort to identify the roots of Appalachian English, an effort that uses, as well as a wide range of reference works on American and British English[7], primary sources (local dictionaries and archival material from the 17th and 18th centuries, and consultations with local authorities in both Northern Ireland and Scotland). It bases the comparison of Appalachian English and Scotch-Irish English on a variety of sources not used heretofore by American linguists.

As far as the Appalachian material is concerned, the published resources have recently been marshaled in an annotated bibliography

(McMillan and Montgomery 1989), and unparalleled unpublished resources (e.g. Joseph Hall's recordings of Smoky Mountain speech from the 1930s) are now being used to fill in the gaps between present-day Appalachian English and the language of the immigrant period (Montgomery and Hall, in progress). In short, for the first time the research tools and materials are available to address the question of the ancestry of distinctive Appalachian speech patterns in a valid way.

This project uses principles of historical linguistics that establish linguistic and sociolinguistic standards by which individual features may be judged as deriving from one part of the British Isles or another (Montgomery 1989a). Thus, it offers a principled basis for saying whether a feature like *a*-prefixing (in "that bear come *a-runnin* at me") is Scotch-Irish, Southern British, German, or none of these. From the comparison undertaken in this paper, we can state much more precisely how "Elizabethan" and how "Scotch-Irish" Appalachian English is than has been the case before now.

This paper focuses on grammatical features rather than on vocabulary or pronunciation. Grammar has been shown by linguists to be "deeper" in a language and more resistant to change, at least rapid change, than the vocabulary and pronunciation of a language. Because grammatical features and forms usually exist in relation to one another and participate in certain systems like the expression of verb tense or noun plurality, this makes them more likely to preserve traceable elements. By comparison, vocabulary is much more easily and quickly borrowed across languages and dialects. Pronunciation is also less stable, as linguists have shown; even in isolated communities it continually evolves according to the social dynamics of the speakers. Grammatical features have two further advantages: they can be clearly determined from old written documents, and they are quantifiable.

Beyond the motivation for undertaking this study—to pin down the ancestry of Appalachian language patterns—lies an important and more general linguistic question of whether an assessment can be made. The most common view in American dialect studies is that features distinctive to one British dialect or another were probably brought to the American colonies, but they were more or less leveled out and lost in the colonial period. Thus a few items, it is thought, may have lingered on as "colonial lags" but most distinctive grammatical patterns in American English represent general patterns of rural and old-fashioned speech that have been inherited from the folk speech of Britain and were to be found throughout much of the U.S. in the eighteenth and nineteenth centuries, at least for the white population. In other words, historians of American English are generally skeptical about how many older elements of specific British dialects have been preserved in the U.S., and especially about how many of these elements have been confined to a specific region of North America such as Appalachia.

Thus, to linguists, undertaking the comparison discussed here and as a result answering the questions about the roots of Appalachian English will do at least three things: a) tell us about processes of dialect migration, contact, and change; b) show us how individual features of American English have evolved from their Old World progenitors; and c) fill in the gaps in the evolution of American English, particularly in the colonial period.

Methodology

We turn now to the grammatical data, which are assembled (with examples) in a list in the appendix to give the broadest view of characteristic Appalachian grammatical features. These forty features, listed by part of speech, are the primary items examined in this project so far. A "characteristic Appalachian grammatical feature" is a grammatical structure or category whose occurrence is more or less limited to the Appalachian or to the Midland territory (as defined by Kurath 1949, 27) or which occurs to a significantly higher degree in these regions than anywhere else in the U.S. Not every feature in this list is unique to the region (in fact, a number of features discussed in studies of Appalachian English are also characteristic of older-fashioned American English in general, such as *blowed* and *growed* as past-tense forms). It is also not argued that all forty features are used by all Appalachian speakers or are found throughout Appalachia. Many of them are quite rare, many others definitely recessive, but all have been identified in the literature by several sources as occurring in the southern mountain region.[8]

Using the published and unpublished resources cited earlier, a determination has been made, for each feature, as to whether its historical currency in Britain was general or limited to a region of the British Isles. The designation "Scotch-Irish" is applied to features either unique to Ulter or traceable to Scotland but not attested in England. "Southern British" refers to a feature attested in England but not in Scotland or Ulter.

Space limitations prevent the explication of more than three individual features. Feature A1, the suffix -S, which is common in Appalachian English on present-tense verbs after plural nouns (*people knows*) but does not occur on present-tense verbs after plural personal pronouns (*they know*), has historically been limited to Scottish and northern British speech, and by extension to the English of Northern Ireland. In the present day, so far as an exhaustive search of the literature shows (Montgomery 1989a), it occurs with frequency only in Appalachian speech. Much the same can be said for feature A4, multiple modal verbs (Montgomery 1989b) such as *might would, might can, may would*, and *might should ought to*; although these are not documented in Scottish English until the mid-18th century and in American English not until the mid-19th century, they are or have been attested only in Scotland and Northumbria in Britain, in Northern Ireland, and in mid-Atlantic and southeastern regions of the United States. Like the plural -*s* suffix for verbs, multiple modals are indisputably a Scotch-Irish feature. Feature A6, *a*-prefixing, is historically almost unknown in Scottish English outside ballad style, while in southern Britain it was a feature of folk speech for centuries; in the U.S., its use is now largely confined to Appalachia and to the Ozarks, the latter a cultural area largely derived from Appalachia. This is thus classified as a southern British feature.

The detailed investigation of the origin and history of each of the forty features shows the following results:

1) Seventeen are Scotch-Irish: A1, A4, A7, A9, A10, B1-B4, B8, D3-5, E2, E4, F1, F5.
2) Four are southern British: A2, A6, B5, C2.
3) Thirteen are general British: A5, B6, B7, B9-B11, C1, D2, D6, E1, E5, F3, F4.
4) Six are of uncertain origin (i.e., dictionaries and other reference works provide no information): A3, A8, B12, D1, E3, F2.

From this, perhaps the broadest, point of view, two things are clear: 1) the Scotch-Irish contribution to the grammar of Appalachian English significantly outweighs the southern British contribution and appears to be much more responsible for the grammatical features distinguishing Appalachian English today; 2) many grammatical features were shared by both major immigrant groups that settled in Appalachia.

This compilation views each of the forty grammatical features as equal in significance and level of structure. Another way to classify these forty features is according to five types of grammatical structures:

1) inflectional forms (word endings): A1, A2, B5, C1, C2, one of Scotch-Irish, three of southern British, and one of general British origin.
2) word order patterns (the combination of two or more words in a distinct way): A4, A8, A9, A10, B4, B10, D1, E4, F1, F2, six of Scotch-Irish, none of southern British, one of general British, and three of questionable origin.
3) categorical differences (involving a grammatical category not found in other dialects; often a familiar form such as *done* is employed in a way unfamiliar to other dialects): A3, A5, A6, A7,

B1, B2, B7: three of Scotch-Irish, one of southern British, two of general British, and one of questionable origin.

4) morphological forms varying from other dialects: B3, B6, B8, B11, B12, two of Scotch-Irish, none of southern British, two of general British, and one of questionable origin.

5) function words (preposition, adverbs, and conjunctions whose function is to relate other words or elements in a clause to one another): B9, D2, D3, D4, D5, D6, E1, E2, E3, E5, F3, F4, F5, five of Scotch-Irish, none of southern British, seven of general British, and one of questionable origin.

Discussion and Conclusions

Scotch-Irish English has contributed to Appalachian English in all categories of grammatical features. This is particularly true for word order patterns (like A4, "We *might should* go on," and A10, "That boy *needs taught* a lesson") and function words (like D4, *till*, and D, "wait *on*"). Only four items (A6, *a*-prefixing, and three inflectional features—the long plural in nouns like *postes* (C2), pronouns in-*n* like *hern* (B5), and regularized past-tense forms like *blowed* (A2) can be traced back specifically to southern Britain and have been current in neither Scotland nor northern Britain. Although this might suggest a minimal contribution from southern British English, we must remember that southern Britain and Scotland shared seven grammatical features that are now identified as Appalachian, including *liked to* (A5) and the ethical dative (B8). Moreover, the majority of grammatical features—the hundreds not in our tables—are also shared.

Of particular note is that many of the Scotch-Irish features are now general Southern, indicating they spread throughout the South: multiple modals such as *might could*, perfective helping verb *done*, pronoun *y'all*, and preposition *till*, among others. Doubtless this is because they were carried into the lower South by Scotch-Irish who came directly to Charleston and Savannah, as well as by descendents of the earlier backcountry and piedmont Scotch-Irish. Settlers were constantly on the move, looking for their "main chance," often crisscrossing each other's paths as they sought a better situation. Not only do dialect forms often not confine themselves to one area for very long; more importantly, they take lives of their own, migrating according to such social factors as prestige, status, and so on.

While it is not very often that we can document the migration of speech forms before the modern age of audio recordings, an unusual emigration of southerners in the postbellum period allows us to verify the spread of such grammatical patterns as the combination of modal verbs like *might could*, and pronunciation tendencies as the identical sounding of *pen* and *pin*. Specifically, in the decade following the Civil War, around twenty thousand ex-Confederate Americans from the lower South (mainly from Texas, Georgia, and Alabama) who decided they could not tolerate living in the reunited United States moved to Brazil. Their descendents today, while bilingual, continue to speak English with a distinct southern accent; they have no recognition of *might could*, nor do they ever pronounce *ten* as *tin* (Montgomery and Melo 1989; Bailey and Smith 1989). These upper South/Appalachian linguistic features must have spread into the lower South after the ex-Confederates left, later in the 19th or early in the t20th centuries. Thus for speech patterns Appalachia is demonstrably a part of the South—a region within a region.

Our analysis and discussion have focused on tracing connections in grammatical patterns between Appalachian English and varieties of British English. Such an effort even at a relatively shallow time depth of less than three hundred years obviously faces a number of analytical and documentary challenges that the current investigation has tried to meet through consulting an exhaustive range of published and unpublished sources. By comparison, previous attempts to make the connection have been small-scale, unsystematic, and tentative. If we assume the relative homogeneity of what we have been calling Scotch-Irish English and Appalachian English and if we assume the correct identification and comparison of grammatical forms in context from our work with dictionaries and grammars, local linguistic literature, original documents, and consultation with local observers, we can posit a strong link in the grammatical systems of Scotch-Irish English and Appalachian English, a link that extends across a range of types of grammatical features. Moreover, we can see some of the outlines of how Scotch-Irish English extended into the lower South.

It is hoped that these results will be relevant not only to linguists, but also to cultural geographers, historians, folklorists, and other scholars concerned with the diffusion of Old World patterns into the New World. It may just be possible, as a result of the type of research outlined and begun here, that we will finally be able to say how "Elizabethan" or "Scotch-Irish" Appalachian English in fact is.

Appendix:
Appalachian Grammatical Features

A. Verbs

1. Third Plural -S (including IS) with Noun Subjects but not with Pronoun Subjects: People *knows* vs. They *know*; People *is* vs. They *are*.

2. Regularized Past - ED in BLOWED, THROWED, etc.: Who *blowed* up the churchhouse?

3. GET TO/GO TO (= BEGIN TO): Just after he left, the roof *went to* leaking again; We *got to* laughing and giggling.

4. Multiple Modal Verbs: We *might should* break the bad news to him.

5. LIKED TO (= ALMOST): I got lost and *liked to* never found my way out.

6. A-prefixing: All of a sudden that bear come *a-runnin'* at me.

7. Perfective DONE: They have *done* landed in jail again.

8. Preposed USED TO: *Used to* Pa wouldn't have done a thing like that.

9. USED TO + WOULD, COULD: I can't do it now but I *used to could*.

10. NEED + Past Participle: That boy *needs taught* a lesson.

B. Pronouns

1. Y'ALL/YOU ALL: Can *y'all/you all* give me a hand with this load?

2. YOU'UNS/WE'UNS, etc.: *You'uns* come down with me.

3. YOU/YE variation: I told *ye* to keep away from there.

4. Combinations with ALL: *You-all, we-all, us-all, they-all, who-all, what-all, where-all, why-all, ye-all, you-all's, your-all's.*

5. HISN/HERN/THEIRN/OURN/YOURN: I didn't like that look of *hern*.

6. HISSELF/THEIRSELVES: You can meet Mister Jones *hisself*.

7. Ethical Dative: I bought *me* a dog.

8. THEY existential (= There): *They*'s about five people in that house.

9. IT existential: *It*'s many people that think so.

10. Deletion of Subject Relative Pronoun: They's about five people *'o* could have done it.

11. HIT (= IT): *Hit*'s a long time since I tasted it.

12. EVERWHAT/EVERWHICH/EVERWHO: *Ever who* was here sure left in a hurry.

C. Nouns

1. Zero Plural after Quantifier: five *bushel*, many *mile* away.

2. Syllabic Plural after SP, ST, SK: post*es*, nest*es*, wasp*es*, desk*es*.

D. Prepositions

1. Compounding: Come *out from up under* the table; Cal, ain't you a-going *across down over to* Rose's?

2. ANENT (= OPPOSITE, NEARBY): He was layin' the road *anent* the springhouse.

3. FORNENT/FERNENT (= AGAINST, NEXT TO): It's over *fernent* the wall.

4. TILL (= TO): It's quarter *till* five.

5. WAIT ON (= WAIT FOR): Would you mind *waiting on* me?

6. AGAIN/AGAINST (= BEFORE, BY THE TIME THAT): She'll be back *again* five o'clock.

E. Conjunctions:

1. AGAIN/AGAINST (= BEFORE, BY THE TIME THAT): I'll be ready *again* you are.

2. WHENEVER (= AT THE TIME THAT OR AS SOON AS): *Whenever* I was young, people didn't do that; *Whenever* I heard about them, I bought one right away.

3. TILL (= SO THAT): They ... got 'em in a good jail there *till* the mob can't get 'em (Jesse Stuart).

4. AND in Absolute Phrases: They all wore mother hubbard dresses, *and* them loose.

5. NOR (= THAN): He's better *nor* you.

F. Adverbs

1. Positive ANYMORE: It's a pretty skilled job *anymore*.

2. ALL THE FAR (= AS FAR AS): That's *all the far* I want to go.

3. RIGHT (intensifier): It's *right* airish this morning.

4. YONDER: That's my field down *yonder*.

5. YAN: Snakes was everywhere going here and *yan*.

Notes

[1] The research on which this paper is based was supported in part by travel grants from the National Endowment for the Humanities and the Southern Regional Education Board and by a Research and Productive Scholarship grant from the University of South Carolina. The author would especially like to thank A. J. Aitken, John Kirk, Caroline Macafee, and Philip Robinson for their advice and observations on Scottish and northern Irish English. Any errors of interpretation, however, are strictly those of the author of this paper.

[2] Three branches of the atlas cover states within Appalachia: the *Linguistic Atlas of the Middle and South Atlantic States* (North Carolina, Virginia, and West Virginia), the *Linguistic Atlas of the Gulf States* (Georgia, Tennessee, and Alabama), and the *Linguistic Atlas of the North Central States* (Kentucky).

[3] One might compare Kurath (1949), whose first chapter, "The English of the Eastern States: a Perspective" (1-10), focuses in detail on British and Continental European sources of American vocabulary with Carver (1987), a work comparable in scope written a generation later. Carver has almost nothing to say about such sources.

[4] These calculations have questionable reliability. Surnames often reveal nothing about ancestry. Among other problems, as Campbell states, is the fact

that many English names have been used by the Irish or the Scottish for centuries.

⁵The only exceptions to this are two brief studies by Wylene Dial (1969) in West Virginia and Alan Crozier (1984) in Western Pennsylvania.

⁶A trove of these is on deposit at the Ulster Folk and Transport Museum at Cultra Manor, Holywood, County Down, Northern Ireland.

⁷Carver (1987), Cassidy (1985), Craigie and Aitken (1933-), Feagin (1979), Grant and Murison (1931-84), Hall (n.d.), Hunter (1925), Jesperson (1954), McDavid (1958), Visser (1970), Wentworth (1944), Wilson (1952), Wolfram and Christian (1976).

⁸It must be emphasized that these assessments reflect information from reference works (dictionaries, historical grammars, etc.) and original documents. They are only as reliable as the sources on which they are based and cannot be claimed to be definitive. As stated earlier in this paper, reference works do not give negative information on whether a certain form does *not* occur at a particular time and place. While the number and range of sources from which information is drawn enhances the reliability of assignment of features to categories according to origin, for some forms (such as *get to* and *go to* meaning "begin to") no information has been found on the regional demarcations either in Britain or in America. They are included in this assessment because they are quite common in Appalachian speech, are discussed in studies of Appalachian speech, and are apparently not widely found in rural and old-fashioned speech elsewhere in the U.S. In some cases the classification of grammatical features has a degree of subjectivity, but grammatical forms widely used throughout the U.S. are excluded even if common in Appalachia. These include *ain't*, the combination of objective pronouns (e.g., *me and him*) used as a subject, the use of *was* with plural subjects (*they was*, etc.), and a number of others.

Works Cited

Bailey, Guy, and Clyde Smith. 1989. *Southern English in Brazil*.

Campbell, John C. 1921. *The Southern Highlander and his Homeland*. Reprinted in 1969. Lexington: University of Kentucky Press.

Carver, Craig M. 1987. *American Regional Dialects: A Word Geography*. Ann Arbor: University of Michigan Press.

Cassidy, Frederic, ed. 1985. *Dictionary of American Regional English*. Volume 1, A-C. Cambridge: Harvard University Press.

Combs, Josiah. 1943. *The Kentucky Highlands from a Native Mountaineer's Viewpoint*. Lexington, Kentucky: J. L. Richardson.

Craigie, William and A. J. Aitken, eds. 1933- . *A Dictionary of the Older Scottish Tongue: From the Twelfth Century to the End of the Seventeenth*. Chicago: University of Chicago Press.

Crozier, Alan. 1984. "The Scotch-Irish Influence on American English." *American Speech* 59: 310-331.

Dial, Wylene. 1969. "The Dialect of the Appalachian People," *West Virginia History* 30: 463-471.

Feagin, Crawford. 1979. *Variation and Change in Alabama English: A Sociolinguistic Study of the White Community*. Washington: Georgetown University Press.

Grant, William and David Murison, eds. 1931-84. *The Scottish National Dictionary*. Edinburgh: Scottish National Dictionary Association.

Hall, Joan B. n.d. [DARE items labeled "Appalachian," "Scottish," or "Irish"].

Hall, Joseph S. 1942. "The Phonetics of Great Smoky Mountains Speech," *American Speech* 17: part 2.

Hunter, Edwin R. 1925. *The American Colloquial Idiom, 1830-1860*. Chicago: University of Chicago dissertation.

Jesperson, Otto. 1954. *A Modern Grammar on Historical Principles*. 7 vols. London: Allen and Unwin.

Kurath, Hans. 1929. "The Conference on a Linguistic Atlas of the United States and Canada," *Bulletin of the Linguistic Society of America* 4: 20-47.

———. 1949. *A Word Geography of the Eastern United States*. Ann Arbor: University of Michigan Press.

Lorimer, William L., translator. 1983. *The New Testament in Scots*. Harmondsworth: Penguin.

McCrum, Robert, et al. 1986. *The Story of English*. New York: Viking.

McDavid, Raven I. 1958. The Dialects of American English. The Structure of American English, by W. Nelson Francis: 480-543. New York: Ronald Press.

McMillan, James B. and Michael Montgomery, eds. 1989. *Annotated Bibliography of Southern American English*. Tuscaloosa: University of Alabama Press.

McWhiney, Grady. 1988. *Cracker Culture: Celtic Ways of the Old South.* Tuscaloosa: University of Alabama Press.

Montgomery, Michael. 1989a. "Exploring the Roots of Appalachian English," *English World-Wide* 10: 227-78.

———. 1989b. "Multiple Modals and the Linguistic Atlas of the Gulf States." Paper read at the Forty-first meeting of the Southeastern Conference on Linguistics, Atlanta.

Montgomery, Michael, and Cecil Melo. 1989. "The Phonology of the Lost Cause."

Montgomery, Michael and Joseph S. Hall. In progress. "The Grammar of Smoky Mountain English."

Sharp, Cecil J. 1932. *English Folk Songs from the Southern Appalachians.* Ed. Maud Karpeles. Oxford: Oxford University Press.

Visser, F. Th. 1970. *An Historical Syntax of the English Language.* Leiden: E. J. Brill.

Wentworth, Harold, ed. 1944. *American Dialect Dictionary.* New York: Crowell.

Williams, Cratis. 1961. *The Southern Mountaineer in Fact and Fiction.* New York: New York University dissertation.

Wilson, George P., ed. 1952. Folk speech. The Frank C. Brown collection of North Carolina folklore. Durham: Duke University Press.

Wolfram, Walt and Donna Christian. 1976. *Appalachian Speech.* Arlington, Va.: Center for Applied Linguistics.

Michael Montgomery is Associate Professor of English and Linguistics at the University of South Carolina in Columbia. He was Contributing Editor for the "Language" section of the Encyclopedia of Southern Culture. He is working on two books on Smoky Mountain English and plans a book examining the linguistic connections between Scotland, Ireland, and Appalachia.

"Shall We Teach 'Em or Learn 'Em?" Attitudes Toward Language in Appalachian Children's Literature

Roberta T. Herrin

In Kenneth Grahame's British children's classic *The Wind in the Willows*, a scene develops where Badger, Rat, Mole, and Mr. Toad plan to oust the stoats and weasels from Toad Hall. Mr. Toad "picked up a stout stick and swung it vigorously, belabouring imaginary animals. 'I'll learn 'em to steal my house!' he cried. 'I'll learn 'em, I'll learn 'em!'" He is immediately chastised by Rat: "Don't say 'learn 'em,' Toad.... It's not good English." Badger counters with, "But we don't *want* to teach 'em.... We want to *learn* 'em—learn 'em, learn 'em!" (Grahame 1969, 197). Such discussions are common among characters in classic children's books — *Peter Pan, Little Women, Anne of Green Gables, Alice's Adventures in Wonderland*. If concern for language propriety is so common in *classic* children's books, what about Appalachian children's literature where dialect and "nonstandard" features are so prominent?

My reading of dozens of Appalachian children's books—only eight of which are treated here—has produced three major observations: The first is that false representations of Appalachian speech abound in children's books. The second is that, in spite of these misrepresentations, two cultural phenomena are accurately demonstrated—assimilation and isolation. The third observation is that the language features most often singled out—*might could*, for example—are the common ones which purists and schoolmarms have sought to stamp out for decades with no success.

Of all the phony depictions of Appalachians and their speech, the most ridiculous is Beverly Courtney Crook's 1978 novel, *Fair Annie of Ole Mule Hollow*, set in 1965 on the West Virginia-Kentucky border. Fair Annie has never been out of the hollow, has never ridden in a car or seen a building taller than one story, doesn't know what a traffic light or an elevator is. Yet, she is a bright girl with an eighth-grade education, and she aspires to be a lawyer. Immediately, in the first few pages of the novel, the reader is assaulted by the difference between her speech and her brother's: Sweet William teases her, "Yore spendin' so much time with them pigs, yore beginnin' to look like 'em." Her prim retort is astounding: "They're still prettier than any of your girlfriends! You could kiss one of my pigs and not know the difference" (Crook 1978, 3).

Fair Annie has been singled out by her father as the only child to get some "learnin." According to Pa, "Somebody in this family's got to keep ahead of the govermint and all them papers they're a-wantin' you to sign.... Might sign the wrong ones if you cain't rightly read. And somebody's got to talk good, too. That lights a fire under them govermint people..." (Crook,5). Pa is adamant about Fair Annie's education: "Nary bug-brained boy's goin' to bust up your schoolin'" (4).

Beverly Crook never addresses the issue of *how* Fair Annie learns to talk "proper" or where she gets her instruction. It is a simple, accepted fact that her language is grammatically correct, free of dialect features, and good enough to deal with the "govermint." And the father's generous attitude toward standard English is absurd. Every English teacher knows that the use of "proper" English in a home such as Fair Annie's would prompt ridicule, not praise. But I am intrigued with the notion that good English helps Appalachians deal with "govermint" people.

A slightly more realistic, but still romanticized, depiction of Appalachian language is found in *Blue Ridge Billy*. Written in 1946 by Lois Lenski, it is a typical portrayal of Appalachian dialect. Lenski collected material for this book in Ashe County, North Carolina, and in the foreword she says, "When I remember ... the mountain people with fine old forgotten Elizabethan phrases on their lips, it seems to me sacrilege to transfer their speech to correct grammatical, School-Reader English.... To me, this would be a travesty on all the beauty and character in the lives of these people" (Lenski 1946, xv). Her belief that Ashe Countians speak the "fine old forgotten Elizabethan" English of Shakespeare is a common attitude, but one which linguists have rejected for decades.

The following is a typical conversation from *Blue Ridge Billy*:

> "Been yarbin' lately?" asked Billy, using the usual mountain expression for 'gathering herbs.'
> "Law, yes, we been out all evenin'," said Sarey Sue. . . .
> "Where'd you go? Back up on Laurel Mountain?"
> "Law, no" said Granny, "over to the Peak. There was some certain roots there I'd a mind to get."
> "Why that's a fur piece?" exclaimed the boy. "Must be nigh five miles, ain't hit? You-all must be tired in your bones." (Lenski, 7)

Among the characters themselves, there is no self-consciousness regarding speech. The reader, however, is always aware that Lenski labors to render the "fine old forgotten Elizabethan" language.

Another book which romanticizes the mountain dialect is Mildred Lee's *The People Therein*, published in 1980. It opens in 1910 in Dewfall Gap, Brightwater County, North Carolina, fifty miles south of Bryson City. This is the story of eighteen-year-old Ailanthus "Lanthy" Farr—who is lame, but beautiful and scholarly—and Andrew "Drew" Thorndike, a botanist from Boston.

In a letter to his sister, Thorndike comments on the language of the mountain people:

> I have grown accustomed to the speech of the people, which at first was like a new language to me; actually it is in some instances an ancient one become corrupted, confusing to an outlander like myself. The word "ill" does not mean sick but cross or irritable (possibly a shortening of "ill-tempered"?), and one with an unpleasant disposition is often called "feisty"—a feist being a yappy little mongrel dog. The past tense of "help" is frequently "holp" (one of Chaucer's, I believe). (Lee 1980, 45)

Just as Drew is attracted to the speech of North Carolinians, Lanthy Farr is attracted to the speech of outsiders. She "had set great store by the way Mr. Colver [the schoolteacher] talked; sometimes, after she quit going to Peavine School, she had walked over there just to have a little conversation with him. They laughed at home about it, but she hadn't cared" (Lee, 12).

This passage prompts two observations. Unlike Fair Annie, Lanthy is ridiculed at home for her interest in "proper" English, and unlike Blue Ridge Billy, she perceives that Mr. Colver's language is superior to her own, an attitude which linguists such as Marckwardt, Leonard, and Joos have documented. In American culture in general—not just in Appalachia—when an individual or group accepts its social position, there is indifference toward language and no concern for correctness. But when an individual becomes conscious of his place in society, or aspires to a higher social level, correctness in language becomes paramount. In Fair Annie's family, for example, only Annie is expected to "better herself"; thus, language propriety is a must for her. Blue Ridge Billy never expects to live anywhere but Ashe County, so he has absolutely no concern for language. Lanthy Farr, though she accepts her place, had once desired to go to the high school "in town" and eventually marries Drew Thorndike.

All three of these characters—Lanthy Farr, Drew Thorndike, and Fair Annie—are engaged in the social processes of assimilation and its ironic opposite, isolation. A book which illustrates both of these conditions is the 1963 novel *The Rock and the Willow*, also written by Mildred Lee. Thirteen-year-old Earline "Enie" Singleton, who lives in Tired Creek, Alabama, in the 1930s, is the central character. Enie makes straight A's and wants to go to college, but her father is suspicious of education. It fills "younguns ... full of notions, making 'em dissatisfied with what they've got" (Lee 1963, 13). Enie studies words: " 'Restraint. Crystallize. Fascination. Epitomize. Manifestation. Delectable. Inimitable.' Someday she would speak words like these with ease. She practiced a lot, already, when no one was around to mock her" (17-18).

> She thought she could feel her mind growing. . . . She knew she had improved herself; she no longer had to think before she spoke grammatically, or stop to correct in embarrassment a word too hastily used. . . .(90)

Enie expects correct grammar and a good vocabulary to be her tools in the outside world. Unlike Fair Annie, however, she struggles to learn "proper" English and she is mocked at home. Her desire for assimilation produces isolation and ridicule. Ironically, she expressly wants to avoid such embarrassment—embarrassment at home when she uses good English and embarrassment abroad when she does not.

John Henry McCoy is a 1971 Appalachian children's book that focuses on a ten-year-old boy's struggles with assimilation and isolation. John Henry has been thoroughly assimilated. He has moved around so much that he doesn't know what grade he belongs in. He has moved "from the head of a hollow . . . right smack-dab to one or two rooms in the middle of a big city"—Cleveland, Columbus, Detroit, Chicago—"Then back to another hollow, where it was too lonesome for even a hoot owl. . . . Then to another town when Henry McCoy had found another job" (Chaffin 1971, 1-2).

John Henry is ridiculed because his language has been affected by living "in town." The children of Hatfield Branch tease him about "being stuck-up" (Chaffin, 77). But John Henry has learned how to avoid embarrassment: "He would say a flat *I*, if he said it, not roll it around and make two syllables, the way people said it in Cleveland" (78). Unlike Enie, who wants to leave Tired Creek, Alabama, John Henry wants a home in Hatfield Branch, Kentucky. He has no interest in assimilation. Unfortunately, he is just as isolated as Enie Singleton.

Most Appalachian children's books make it clear that attitudes toward grammar and usage are controlled by parents and teachers. Typically, children are urged to use verbs and pronouns correctly, and not to end sentences with prepositions. A good example is Juliette Ann Holley's 1975 book, *Jamie Lemme See*, the story of James Edward Riley Pettigrew, a six-year-old black boy living on Peel Chestnut Mountain, West Virginia. Jamie has the habit of asking, "Where is it at?" His mother's response is amazing: "You're using bad grammer [sic]. You should say, if you must, 'Take me where it is' " (Holley 1975, 9).

On first thought, Jamie's mother's correction seems absurd. On second thought, it seems entirely realistic. My own mother who routinely says "hit" corrected me as a child on the different pronunciations of *pin* and *pen*, *Joy* and *Joey*, and where to put the accent in *Eli* and *Elijah*, none of which have anything to do with Appalachian dialect. She simply felt it her duty to make corrections.

Appalachian children's books routinely show teachers performing the same function. John Henry McCoy's teacher, Miss Day, runs a fairly universal English class: "Sometimes we hear people use the wrong word for burst. Who can give the right forms for burst and rise?" She gets a typical answer. A student uses the verb *burst* in this sentence: "When it's time for breakfast, Mommy lets me bust the biscuits," meaning that her mother lets her open the canned biscuits (Chaffin 1971, 100). Then another child conjugates the verb *rise*: rise, rose, riz. Miss Day makes all the usual corrections. She tells John Henry, "The word is ghosts, not ghostes" (Chaffin, 101). And she has the typical problem with I: When John Henry and Silas are caught fighting, Miss Day asks them to explain. Si begins, "Me and John Henry" and is quickly interrupted by Miss Day with, "'John Henry and I. . . .it was John Henry and I."

> Si rolled his eyes at John Henry. "You was in the house, Miss Day. It was me and John Henry a-wrestling, and he's a pretty good hand at it."
> "All right, I'll take your word for it." (Chaffin, 122)

Miss Day will not get much help from John Henry's mother. When his sister Sara uses the double auxiliary *might could*, John Henry responds, "You know Miss Clay told us not to say might could." Sara

Mrs. McCoy answers, "Not that I know of. So's people understand what you're saying's all that matters to me" (Chaffin, 42).

Though the attitudes toward language in this book provide much of its humor, they strike the reader as realistic. A novel which takes a similar attitude is *Queenie Peavy*, by Robert Burch, published in 1966. Set in the 1930s in rural Georgia, this novel is the story of thirteen-year-old Queenie and an entourage of other school children.

One of the most unusual characters is Martha Mullins, called Little Mother because she tries to "promote good will and understanding for the whole world" (Burch 1966, 36). When Cravey Mason ridicules Queenie's lunch which consists of "biscuit and sowbelly," Little Mother instructs him to say "home-grown bacon," not "sowbelly." "Call it anything you please," said Cravey. "—sidemeat, fatback, city chicken, streak-'o-lean, 'streak-o'-fat," it's still "lousy stuff" (34). Later on Little Mother announces that she lives in "a remote rural area." Cravey replies, "Remote rural Area! . . . Is that a new term for 'the sticks'? . . . How come you to put on airs?". Little Mother insists that she doesn't mean to sound "affected," but that "it seems almost disrespectful of nature not to use a dignified term for countryside that's so beautiful". Cravey yells, "Hey, everybody! Guess where Little Mother Martha Mullins lives. She lives in a *remote rural area*" (55-56).

The effect of this interchange is obviously to ridicule the Little Mothers of the world who expect euphemisms to improve life. But it also makes an important point about the children. They soundly reject—isolate—those who are concerned with language propriety, be it a peer, parent, or teacher.

From the ridiculous *Fair Annie of Old Mule Hollow* to the realistic *Queenie Peavy*, Appalachian children's books promote standard English and condescend toward Appalachian speech—even when such books praise the common language of the region. It is true that many of these books address the emotional effects of assimilation and isolation; that in itself is of great value to the child reader who has endured ridicule from within and from without his own culture. But what is absent from all these books is any understanding of the language these children actually speak.

I began with the 1908 British classic *The Wind in the Willows*. I will end with another turn-of-the-century masterpiece, *Peter Pan*, by J. M. Barrie. The narrator opens chapter five with this comment:

> Feeling that Peter was on his way back, the Neverland had again woke into life. We ought to use the pluperfect and say wakened, but woke is better and was always used by Peter. (Barrie, 47)

Did Barrie and Kenneth Grahame know something that we in Appalachia do not? If Mr. Toad, Badger, and Peter can misuse verbs, who is to criticize?

Works Cited

Barrie, J. M. 1984. *Peter Pan*. New York: Bantam.

Burch, Robert. 1966. *Queenie Peavy*. New York: Viking.

Chaffin, Lillie D. 1971. *John Henry McCoy*. New York: Macmillan.

Crook, Beverly Courtney. 1978. *Fair Annie of Old Mule Hollow*. New York: McGraw-Hill.

Grahame, Kenneth. 1969. *The Wind in the Willows*. New York: Signet.

Holley, Juliette Ann. 1975. *Jamie Lemme See*. Radford, Va.: Commonwealth.

Joos, Martin. 1961. *The Five Clocks*. New York: Harcourt, Brace & World.

Lee, Mildred. *1980. The People Therein*. New York: Houghton Mifflin.

———. 1963. *The Rock and the Willow*. New York: Lothrop, Lee and Shepard.

Lenski, Lois. 1946. *Blue Ridge Billy*. New York: Lippincott.

Leonard, Sterling A. 1938. "Current English Usage." In *Facts About Current English Usage*. Eds. Albert H. Marcwardt and Fred G. Walcott. New York: Appleton-Century-Crofts.

Roberta T. Herrin is Assistant Professor of English at East Tennessee State University where she teaches children's literature and Appalachian children's literature. She also directs the National Endowment for the Humanities-sponsored institute in children's fantasy literature—Journey Through Fantasy Literature.

Journal of the Appalachian Studies Association
Subscriptions and Order Form

Detach, fold, and staple this form and mail to:
Appalachian Consortium
University Hall
Boone, NC 28606

Please make checks payable to the Appalachian Consortium.

No. of Copies	Issue	Price	Total
	Journal of the Association Studies Association		
	Volume 3, 1991 "Southern Appalachia and the South: A Region Within a Region"	$10.95	$____
____	Volume 2, 1990 "Transformation of Life and Labor in Appalachia"	$10.95	____
____	Volume 1, 1989 "Mountains of Experience"	$10.95	____
	Proceedings of the Appalachian Studies Conference		
____	(10) "Rememberance, Reunion, Revival"	$10.95	____
____	(9) "Contemporary Appalachia"	$10.95	____
____	(8) "The Impact of Institutions in Appalachia"	$10.95	____
____	(7) "The Many Faces of Appalachia"	$10.95	____
____	(6) "The Appalachian Experience"	$10.95	____
____	(5) "The Critical Essays"	$10.95	____

Subtotal $____
5% North Carolina sales tax
(NC residents only)
handling $ 2.00
shipping ($1.00 per copy)
Total Enclosed $____

Name _____
Address _____
_____
Phone _____

Please enter my name on the subscriber's list. I understand that subscriptions for the *Journal of the Appalachian Studies Association* are available through the Appalachian Consortium. The cost is $13.95 per copy, which includes shipping and handling. I understand that orders will be kept on file and automatically shipped and billed once each year unless cancelled by written correspondence.

Return Address

Stamp

Appalachian Studies Association Journal
Appalachian Consortium Press
University Hall
Boone, NC 28608

Journal of the Appalachian Studies Association
Subscriptions and Order Form

Detach, fold, and staple this form and mail to:
Appalachian Consortium
University Hall
Boone, NC 28606

Please make checks payable to the Appalachian Consortium.

No. of Copies	Issue	Price	Total
	Journal of the Association Studies Association		
	Volume 3, 1991 "Southern Appalachia and the South: A Region Within a Region"	$10.95	$____
	Volume 2, 1990 "Transformation of Life and Labor in Appalachia"	$10.95	____
	Volume 1, 1989 "Mountains of Experience"	$10.95	____
	Proceedings of the Appalachian Studies Conference		
	(10) "Rememberance, Reunion, Revival"	$10.95	____
	(9) "Contemporary Appalachia"	$10.95	____
	(8) "The Impact of Institutions in Appalachia"	$10.95	____
	(7) "The Many Faces of Appalachia"	$10.95	____
	(6) "The Appalachian Experience"	$10.95	____
	(5) "The Critical Essays"	$10.95	____

```
            Subtotal                                $____
            5% North Carolina sales tax
            (NC residents only)
            handling                                $ 2.00
            shipping ($1.00 per copy)
            Total Enclosed                          $____
```

Name _____
Address _____
_____
Phone _____

☐ Please enter my name on the subscriber's list. I understand that subscriptions for the *Journal of the Appalachian Studies Association* are available through the Appalachian Consortium. The cost is $13.95 per copy, which includes shipping and handling. I understand that orders will be kept on file and automatically shipped and billed once each year unless cancelled by written correspondence.

Return Address

Stamp

Appalachian Studies Association Journal
Appalachian Consortium Press
University Hall
Boone, NC 28608

www.ingramcontent.com/pod-product-compliance
Lightning Source LLC
Chambersburg PA
CBHW051052160426
43193CB00010B/1159